Staatsverständnisse | Understanding the State

edited by
Rüdiger Voigt

Volume 182

Stefan Machura [Ed.]

Law and War
in Popular Culture

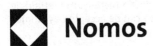 **Nomos**

The Deutsche Nationalbibliothek lists this publication in the
Deutsche Nationalbibliografie; detailed bibliographic data
are available on the Internet at http://dnb.d-nb.de

ISBN 978-3-7560-0735-6 (Print)
 978-3-7489-1829-5 (ePDF)

Online Version
Nomos eLibrary

1st Edition 2024
© Nomos Verlagsgesellschaft, Baden-Baden, Germany 2024. Overall responsibility
for manufacturing (printing and production) lies with Nomos Verlagsgesellschaft mbH
& Co. KG.

Editorial

Das Staatsverständnis hat sich im Laufe der Jahrhunderte immer wieder grundlegend gewandelt. Wir sind Zeugen einer Entwicklung, an deren Ende die Auflösung der uns bekannten Form des territorial definierten Nationalstaates zu stehen scheint. Denn die Globalisierung führt nicht nur zu ökonomischen und technischen Veränderungen, sondern sie hat vor allem auch Auswirkungen auf die Staatlichkeit. Ob die „Entgrenzung der Staatenwelt" jemals zu einem Weltstaat führen wird, ist allerdings zweifelhaft. Umso interessanter sind die Theorien früherer und heutiger Staatsdenker, deren Modelle und Theorien, aber auch Utopien, uns Einblick in den Prozess der Entstehung und des Wandels von Staatsverständnissen geben.

Auf die Staatsideen von Platon und Aristoteles, auf denen alle Überlegungen über den Staat basieren, wird unter dem Leitthema „Wiederaneignung der Klassiker" immer wieder zurückzukommen sein. Der Schwerpunkt der in der Reihe *Staatsverständnisse* veröffentlichten Arbeiten liegt allerdings auf den neuzeitlichen Ideen vom Staat. Dieses Spektrum reicht von dem Altmeister *Niccolò Machiavelli*, der wie kein Anderer den engen Zusammenhang zwischen Staatstheorie und Staatspraxis verkörpert, über *Thomas Hobbes*, den Vater des Leviathan, bis hin zu *Karl Marx*, den sicher einflussreichsten Staatsdenker der Neuzeit, und schließlich zu den zeitgenössischen Staatstheoretikern.

Nicht nur die Verfälschung der Marxschen Ideen zu einer marxistischen Ideologie, die einen repressiven Staatsapparat rechtfertigen sollte, macht deutlich, dass Theorie und Praxis des Staates nicht auf Dauer voneinander zu trennen sind. Auch die Verstrickung Carl Schmitts in die nationalsozialistischen Machenschaften, die heute sein Bild als führender Staatsdenker seiner Epoche trüben, weisen in diese Richtung. Auf eine Analyse moderner Staatspraxis kann daher in diesem Zusammenhang nicht verzichtet werden.

Was ergibt sich daraus für ein zeitgemäßes Verständnis des Staates im Sinne einer modernen Staatswissenschaft? Die Reihe *Staatsverständnisse* richtet sich mit dieser Fragestellung nicht nur an (politische) Philosophen und Philosophinnen, sondern auch an Geistes- und Sozialwissenschaftler bzw. -wissenschaftlerinnen. In den Beiträgen wird daher zum einen der Anschluss an den allgemeinen Diskurs hergestellt, zum anderen werden die wissenschaftlichen Erkenntnisse in klarer und aussagekräftiger Sprache – mit dem Mut zur Pointierung – vorgetragen. Auf diese Weise wird der Leser/die Leserin direkt mit dem Problem konfrontiert, den Staat zu verstehen.

Prof. Dr. Rüdiger Voigt

Editorial – Understanding the State

Throughout the course of history, our understanding of the state has fundamentally changed time and again. It appears as though we are witnessing a development which will culminate in the dissolution of the territorially defined nation state as we know it, for globalisation is not only leading to changes in the economy and technology, but also, and above all, affects statehood. It is doubtful, however, whether the erosion of borders worldwide will lead to a global state, but what is perhaps of greater interest are the ideas of state theorists, whose models, theories and utopias offer us an insight into how different understandings of the state have emerged and changed, processes which neither began with globalisation, nor will end with it.

When researchers concentrate on reappropriating traditional ideas about the state, it is inevitable that they will continuously return to those of Plato and Aristotle, upon which all reflections on the state are based. However, the works published in this series focus on more contemporary ideas about the state, whose spectrum ranges from those of the doyen *Niccolò Machiavelli*, who embodies the close connection between the theory and practice of the state more than any other thinker, to those of *Thomas Hobbes*, the creator of Leviathan, those of *Karl Marx*, who is without doubt the most influential modern state theorist, those of the Weimar state theorists *Carl Schmitt, Hans Kelsen* and *Hermann Heller*, and finally to those of contemporary theorists.

Not only does the corruption of Marx's ideas into a Marxist ideology intended to justify a repressive state underline the fact that state theory and practice cannot be permanently regarded as two separate entities, but so does Carl Schmitt's involvement in the manipulation conducted by the National Socialists, which today tarnishes his image as the leading state theorist of his era. Therefore, we cannot forego analysing modern state practice.

How does all this enable modern political science to develop a contemporary understanding of the state? This series of publications does not only address this question to (political) philosophers, but also, and above all, students of humanities and social sciences. The works it contains therefore acquaint the reader with the general debate, on the one hand, and present their research findings clearly and informatively, not to mention incisively and bluntly, on the other. In this way, the reader is ushered directly into the problem of understanding the state.

Prof. Dr. Rüdiger Voigt

Table of Contents

Stefan Machura

Introduction: Law and War in Popular Culture

As Eugen Ehrlich wrote, law is about the organisation of society.[1] "Living law" to Ehrlich is the law that's actually practiced and can be different from the written state law. Others noted that law is "ubiquitous"[2], and "everybody does law all the time"[3]. Law does not stop in times of war. Rather, it often goes into overdrive, with new conflicts to be regulated and decided, and special provisions brought in as part of the war effort. Yet, as war results in existential threats, all sorts of actors, the state, the military, other organisations, and individuals, may deviate from the normal paths of law. Transgressions can take particularly gruesome forms. Ann Ching in her contribution to this volume states that wars come with war crimes. The horrors of war may wash away legal scruples, compassion with strangers and basic humanity. The enormity of war's consequences has since ancient times found expression in popular culture.

Popular culture forms a major source of information for people on all sorts of areas: including on the law. Fictional media such as films, television shows and novels tell people about war and law, like news media, documentaries, education in school and university. Within socio–legal studies, popular legal culture, covering law and film and related areas, is by now an established research field. Scholars of popular legal culture study what people think about the law, mainly the (wo)man on the street,[4] and only occasionally the views of officers of the law. Other sources of information are direct personal experience with the law, as well as the information trusted others provide about their experience. Family members, friends and colleagues typically share stories in which something went wrong, when the law's application led to results seen as unjust and dissatisfying.[5] Similarly, news media outlets apply a range of "news values"[6] which systematically pick up when law, legal personnel, and legal institutions act in ways likely to meet public disapproval. Though, media may also report on the successful utilisation of law, such as a milestone judicial ruling in favour of a "progressive" cause, or when law supported

---

1 *Ehrlich* 1967, p. 73.
2 *Parsons* 1971, pp. 121-122.
3 *Holzleithner* 2015, p. 288.
4 *Friedman* 1981, p. 191.
5 E.g. *Machura* et al. 2014, p. 297: effect on trust in courts and in police.
6 *Luhmann* 2000, pp. 27-35.

a weaker party against a powerful adversary, or when a serious offender was brought to justice.

The depiction of law and war in popular legal culture forms the focus of this book. The authors are from a variety of academic fields of expertise, such as film studies, musicology, law, sociology of law and criminology. They analyse works of popular culture, place them into their context at the time of origin and discuss their meaning for today's audiences. Special emphasis lies on the role of the state in the context of law and war. Modern warfare tends to take place either between states or within states with the latter as one of the parties or as a third party in armed internal conflict.

Like with law, people's views on war are based on a range of sources. They include media of popular culture. Countless works of music, books, films and television shows have covered war in all its manifestations. In the 1970's West Germany, for example, a party was incomplete without youths dancing to the tunes of *Hiroshima* (Wishful Thinking, 1972). Talk of WWII was omnipresent and newspapers and television were full of war stories. In Britain, postwar cinema excelled in the genre of war films many of which portrayed the darkest side of living through military conflict. In the countries that were part of the Soviet Union, the memory of war was expressed by large sculptures, often huge memorials with heavy weapons on display, as well as in printed products and as part of education. For the U.S., there was a notable change in the content of war films as the country became weary and troubled by the Vietnam War. They became more critical of the government and the military, even if the story was placed in an earlier war. The topic of law and war in popular culture is varied and impossible to cover exhaustively on the pages of one book. However, the authors assembled here are making a start by discussing important aspects.

1. Law and War – The Broader View

When reflecting on the relation between law and war, one may initially think of special regulations for the conduct of war. Such as the Geneva Conventions or law developed by international courts. Ann Ching in her chapter provides an overview of how international humanitarian law (IHL) protecting civilians is depicted in U.S. films. She concludes that the films demonstrate "a shallow, nationalistic understanding of the protections that IHL affords civilians in wartime" and that "U.S. policymakers should be sensitive to their large–scale influence on public perceptions of warfare and the military."

On a more fundamental level, law is an aspect of daily life and continues to do so in times of war. Even in these, the law facilitates and restricts a huge variety of actions people and organisations take. Law is purposefully created to further a plethora of objectives and interests. As Eugen Ehrlich famously highlighted: the main place where law is developed is outside of the state.[7] Contracts are a major way by which law is set. The state also continues its legal actions in war, some of which are now a specific response to the challenges of the conflict situation. Laws are created and administered including to organise the recruitment of soldiers, to ration food and other supplies, or to impose media censorship. At any time, there will be law–breaking, some of it constituting crime, and so during wars. "Useful illegality"[8] appears: deviations from rules deemed necessary by state officials, here for the war effort. Popular culture has depicted the everyday use and abuse of law in war in countless stories.

Long–running TV series covering times of war therefore confront the audience with different aspects. The fiction series *Foyles' War* (U.K., 2002–2015) follows the life of and the cases covered by Detective Chief Superintendent Christopher Foyle during World War II and beyond during the Cold War. In 22 episodes, a range of legal conflicts and crimes is experienced. As can be expected for a TV detective show, much is about the crime of murder in its various manifestations and not all of them are unique to a war situation. However, the series also has crimes which are a consequence of war. Rationing causes some enterprising perpetrators to come up with schemes satisfying the demand of goods which are in limited supply. The state is in danger of overreach as people start to disregard rigid commands. The necessities of war skew justice. In the episode *Fifty Ships*, an influential American industrialist who is key in securing U.S. support in the early years of war, while the U.S. was still influenced by isolationist policies, murders a former business partner to protect his wealth. Just as Foyle is about to arrest the perpetrator, he is stopped for the reason of superior political interest: the delivery of 50 ships depends on this man's influence. Powerless, Foyle is reduced to promising that this will not be the last word. Only after the war, the detective is free to follow up on the case. While this story is already beyond a standard treatment of law, crime, and state power in war, the first episode covers a different aspect of the enabling of war by state law. A conscientious objector with left–leaning ideas pleads in vain in front of a panel deciding these cases. His reasons for denying military service are rejected. The state's rules and specific procedures are highlighted in a scene in which Foyle studies the legal text. Later, class injustice is suggested when it turns out that the Magistrate presiding over the panel is guilty of corruption in granting the son of an industrialist conscious objector status. Remarkably, the TV series does not draw an idealist picture of a "*Blitz* spirit" uniting the English people. Countless characters are engaging in cynic and criminal action, driven by cruelty, lust, greed and hatred

---

7 *Ehrlich* 2022, Vorrede.
8 A term by *Luhmann* 1999, p. 304.

of German or Italian neighbours and prisoners of war. Or even by hatred of others who are seen as not contributing enough to the war effort. In the first episode, the failed conscientious objector is led to the police cells where he is attacked by the duty sergeant and his men. The victim takes his own life in desperation. State action and propaganda in war may contribute to bring about the worst in soldiers, police officers, and civilians.

There is, however, usually an additional element involved, such as greed, sadism or lack of empathy for others. Committing a crime is fundamentally a moral decision according to Wikström.[9] His Situational Action Model of crime states that crime happens when people with the propensity to commit crime are in a situation which allows them to follow through. "... acts of crime ... are ultimately an outcome of how individuals perceive their action alternatives and, on this basis, make their choices when confronted with the particulars of a social setting in which they are taking part".[10] Crimes are more likely in the absence of effective controls on criminal behaviour.[11] War sometimes rearranges social power relations, the powerful may be handed more means than they usually have at their disposal, and people without much power normally may find themselves with the tools and opportunity to exercise it. For example, in the Danish television series *1864* (Denmark, 2014, dir. Ole Bornedal), playing in the Danish–Prussian war, Didrich, the mentally disturbed son of the Baron, becomes an officer of the unit in which some of his villagers serve. He goes on to severely abuse his command authority. The normal hierarchies may no longer apply in war. The military prosecutor in *Rosen für den Staatsanwalt* (Germany, 1959, dir. Wolfgang Staudte) threatens the judges with Hitler's wrath if they fail to sentence a soldier to death for stealing a package of army chocolate. In the chaos of the last days of WWII, normal controls on behaviour have become ineffective.

War may lead to a change in the institutions and operation of law. Peter Robson in this volume introduces the Republican courts which for a period replaced regular British courts in Ireland in the 1920s. He discusses how ideas of justice clash with the need to run the war machine. A moneylender asks the court to help collecting an extortionate amount of interest he is charging a destitute woman. When the judge is inclined to decide in favour of the defendant, a unit commander intervenes: the revolution will need the support of the wealthy for the war effort. Robson's contribution highlights also how everyday legal business continues in war and is affected by it.

---

9   *Wikström* 2010.
10 *Wikström/Svensson* 2010, p. 396.
11 *Wikström* n.d. These include self-control of behaviour: *Wikström* 2017, p. 512.

2. Law as a Resource, Law as Limitation

One of many ways in which people encounter law is as a resource. Law opens opportunities for those who can use it in their favour. The point is made in the 1953 American film *The Desert Rats* (dir. Robert Wise). After a raid on a German supply dump in Libya, a wounded Captain MacRoberts is taken prisoner. In the medic's tent, he insists on proper medical treatment, citing international convention. Even more, and rather unlikely in its coincidence, his pluckiness earns him the respect of none other than Field Marshal Rommel, who arrives to seek help from the same medics. In the movie *A Bridge Too Far* (U.K./U.S.A., 1977, dir. Richard Attenborough), about the 1944 Allied offensive culminating in the failed attempt to seize the Arnheim bridge, a field surgeon uses the law to reassert his authority. An American paratrooper had risked his life to bring his badly wounded lieutenant friend to the field hospital. The doctor shrugs him off after a quick look at the lifeless man. The tents are full of injured and medical personnel conducts triage to deal with the avalanche of patients. The paratrooper considers, returns, and forces the doctor to start treating the lieutenant at gunpoint. It turns out that life can still be saved. After a long operation, the surgeon demands an officer of the military police to arrest the perpetrator according to military law, but to count down seconds to release him again. The doctor solves a dilemma with his creative use of the law: he had failed in his initial assessment but could not let discipline slip completely. In the cavalry western *She Wore a Yellow Ribbon* (U.S.A., 1949, dir. John Ford), veterans Captain Brittles and his thirsty Sergeant Quincannon are close to retirement. The officer first encourages the Sergeant to celebrate in the garrison's saloon but then orders soldiers to arrest him, in an attempt to keep the Sergeant out of trouble during the last days of his service.

War films may show that the reach of law is limited and that recourse to military action is needed to resolve a crisis. In *Yangtse Incident: The Story of H.M.S. Amethyst* (1957, dir. Michael Anderson), a U.K. film inspired by a real event in the Chinese Civil War in 1949, a British ship is unlawfully stopped by Peoples' Liberation Army gun batteries opening fire. British soldiers, Chinese stewards and Red Chinese soldiers die in the ensuing exchange of artillery rounds. HMS Amethyst ends up stranded and severely damaged. Red Army Colonel Peng now demands from the British to sign a declaration that they had broken the law and initiated the fight which they refuse. The military and legal standoff is only coming to an end, when the ship starts to sneak away in the dark and escapes the consequential bombardment. Military craft and cunning decide the outcome. The law although invoked by both sides, comes across as toothless.

Also quite typical is the treatment of situations in which the outcome is much bleaker. Iker Nabaskues Martinez de Eulate in his contribution discusses a film on the Srebrenica massacre in which all efforts to use international humanitarian law failed. Controversies around the representation of war in music form the content of John Cunningham's article. Three chapters in this book, by Nathan Abrams and Michael Lipiner, by Michael Asimow and by Ann Ching discuss how films deal with attempts of senior officers to exploit the law for political and personal advantage.

Still another constellation is depicted in John Ford's Western *Cheyenne Autumn* (U.S.A., 1964, dir. John Ford), a compassionate portrayal of the mistreatment and suffering of the American Indians in the 19th century. Law causes the conflict, partially shapes its conduct, and ultimately allows for a cessation of war. The U.S. government had broken earlier treaties with the Indian peoples and forced them to live in inhospitable land. Their sustenance was to be guaranteed by private Indian agents who turned starving out Indians into a business model. The Cheyenne break out and head for Canada. They are then subjected to the hostility of Whites who are acting out of fear and some out of plain lust for murder. And they are persecuted by the mighty military machine of the U.S. Army. The slaughter only stops when the Secretary of the Interior Carl Schurz, a veteran of the failed German revolution of 1848, orders it. To a sociologist of law, *Cheyenne Autumn* is a tale about uses and abuses of state law and a lesson in public administration, which, as Max Weber (1968) showed, is intimately connected to modern law and politics. – It is a testimony to the strength of anti–Indian prejudice which had been fuelled not least by countless Western films, that "Cheyenne Autumn" prominently places a young White woman who is accompanying the Cheyenne and caring for their children. Filmmakers have the means to incite hatred but also to support a more enlightened perspective.

Law also encounters people as – occasionally cruel – limitation of the actions they may want to take. In Verdi's 1871 opera *Aida*, the title character, an Ethiopian king's daughter enslaved in Egypt, wants to marry Radamès, an Egyptian general. Both their people are at war with another and submit the opposing side to indiscriminate killings, plunder, and devastation. Inadvertently, Radamès leaks a military secret to Aida and her father overhears the couple. According to Egyptian law, the general is sentenced to death. What is left to Aida, now that they will not be able to live together, is to die together. The staging of the opera by the Gran Teatre del Liceu in 2003 very effectively contrasted Aida's tormented aria with the off–stage voices of Egyptian priests determining her lover's fate.[12]

Combatants are bound by rules. These may be "soft law", like the maxim of chivalry in Monteverdi's short opera *Combattimento di Tancredi e Clorinda* (1624), discussed by Stefan Machura and John Cunningham in their chapter. They can also

---

12   Opus Arte DVD OA 0894 D, Spain, 2004, dir. José Antonio Gutiérrez.

be Rules of Engagement for modern armies which draw on international humanitarian law. Ann Ching's chapter covers their depiction in film. The ultimate breaking of the norms of war must be war crimes.

3. War Crimes

Many films show the military committing war crimes. The British World War II film *Yesterday's Enemy* (1959, dir. Val Guest) deals with war crimes "in all, or at least most, of its ambivalent and grisly senses".[13] The year before the film, *Yesterday's Enemy* appeared as a "then–controversial" BBC TV play.[14] Remnants of a British unit, beaten and encircled by superior Japanese forces, capture a Burmese village. Here, a Japanese map with mysterious markings and a suspicious local informer of the Japanese are found. The commanding Captain Alan Langford forces the informer to reveal that it is a battle map for future Japanese operations by ordering his soldiers to shoot two random villagers which they did. He then commands his Sergeant to kill the informer to silence him forever. Soon, the tables are turned, Langford and his surviving men are prisoners and at the mercy of Major Yamazaki from the Japanese intelligence service. Now, Yamazaki threatens to execute Langford's comrades to learn if the battle plan was compromised. In the end, Langford chooses rather to die than to speak: he provokes his Japanese guards, earning him the Major's personal admiration. All British prisoners are shot, nevertheless. The poster for the German cinema released under the translated title *Feinde von Gestern*, visually captures the constellation (Picture 1): above the scene of soldiers fighting in the village, towers large Langford's face, behind it and to the left, even larger in size, the face of Yamazaki, in pale white. They both apply the same extreme military logic.

In the film, Langford is repeatedly challenged by a military chaplain and a war reporter to explain himself. It is all about winning the fight and saving British lives, Langford declares. There is no time for ethics: "I am doing what I have to do. No more, no less [...] I am not concerned with the methods I use." Upon uttering "In a war, a man with a gun must always believe he's right, if he thinks otherwise, he's got no business being in uniform", Langford hears from the reporter "A few million Jews would disagree with you" and replies "I am only concerned about my own people, I don't care about anyone else."

Why do the British soldiers obey? When the Padre tells the Sergeant that shooting innocent villagers will constitute a war crime, he hears back that the Sergeant and his men put their trust in Langford completely. As the camera moves along the

---

13 *Pronay* 1988, p. 49.
14 *Johnston* 2018, p. 84.

execution squad, the soldier's faces give away that they find this command hard to follow. Nevertheless, follow they do. Later, when the Sergeant returns from shooting the informer, he cleans his hands in a gesture known from Pontius Pilate in the Bible. The effect on the village population is clearly expressed by a Burmese woman equalising the warring parties: "British–Japanese, Japanese–British. No party good."

Picture 1: German film poster advertising Yesterday's Enemy (U.K., 1959, dir. Val Guest). The British Captain Langford and the Japanese Major Yamazaki follow the same unforgiving logic in their conduct of the war. Source: https://filmcharts.ch/movie/ Yesterday%27s-Enemy-37876 (Accessed on 17 July 2023).

The most thrilling lines are, however, given to the Japanese Major Yamazaki when Langford insists that prisoners of war have rights: "You are a strange people. You decide to fight a war and then try to bind yourselves to rules of conduct because it suits your purposes." Reminding Langford of the fate of the Indians, Sudanese, or Boers at the hands of the British in earlier conflicts, Yamazaki declares:

> "Did you have any rules for them? No. But now that you have someone else just as big as you, now, that you are not fighting spears with guns, you want a code of conduct. This is total war, Captain. No quarters asked, no quarters given."

Yesterday's Enemies not only compares the two powers, the old defending its empire and the upstart trying to take its possessions, the film also shows the soldiers of both sides as equally competent militarily and ready to obey any command, even when it constitutes a crime. The figure of Yamazaki is, even more, painted as that of an educated man, an admirer of English literature. *Yesterday's Enemy*, the film title, gives away that there will soon be, after all of war's cruelty, a time of peace. As the film character of the war correspondent says, yesterday's enemy will be "laying wreaths to honour the dead his country killed. ... It IS ugly." (Emphasis in the film.)

The calculated committing of war crimes, soldiers unquestioningly carrying out criminal orders, the spectre of two warring parties ratcheting up the level of atrocities and desperate people caught up in all this, appear and reappear in countless pop cultural products. *Yesterday's Enemies* indeed condenses what is part of a critical strand in media culture.

In this volume, Ann Ching's chapter shows how American films portray the issue of war crimes and the attempt of international humanitarian law to curb its occurrence. Michael Asimow, dealing with military justice, widens the perspective by also covering moving pictures from other countries. The different ways in which pop musicians reacted to war in Ukraine and in Israel and Gaza, is discussed by John Cunningham.

4. Plundering

The range of war crimes committed in works of popular culture is vast. It includes robbing the cultural heritage of an attacked or occupied country. *The Train* (France, 1964, dir. John Frankenheimer and Arthur Penn) deals with attempts of the *Résistance* to stop the transport of treasured paintings to Germany. The German commander and his troops have no scruples, and at the end the film shows crates with artwork and the corpses of massacred hostages strewn along the derailed train. Saving treasures from Nazis also forms the topic of *The Monument Men* (U.S., 2014, dir. George Clooney). Towards the end of this film, the U.S. and advancing Soviet troops find themselves in a race to who gets to the stolen artifacts first.

Crimes motivated by greed are an easily deployed pattern of storytelling. After all, they are immediately understandable to the widest possible audience. The plundering of enemy lands is depicted in opera, as Machura and Cunningham discuss in their chapter. But the treatment is of course more widespread. In *The Train*, the German Colonel finally confesses that his obsession with the French masterpieces follows from his belief that art should be in the hands of members of an elite knowing to appreciate them. He obviously counts himself among those. More trivial is the taking of small items by conquering soldiers. In the popular West German TV

Sitcom *Ein Herz und eine Seele* (1972–1976 and since repeated), the main character, Alfred, had sent his wife perfume and other goods from occupied France during WWII. When Alfred's socialist son–in–law provokes him that these were stolen, he insists they were "commandeered". With this joke, the comedy effectively mocked veterans basking in their fond war memories. Alfred has once more unmasked himself.

5. Indiscriminate Warfare

The laws of war require the parties to spare civilian lives where possible. Powerful modern war technology produces large "collateral damage" with devastating consequences not only for combatants. Popular culture at times acknowledges those dangers. But sometimes, the focus is on the suffering and sacrifice of own soldiers. A prime example is the British film *The Dam Busters* (U.K., 1964, dir. Michael Anderson). The film about the 1943 Royal Air Force air attack is still regularly shown on British television. At the centre of the film is the engineer who constructs a special bomb which, after being dropped from low–flying aircrafts, bounces on the water's surface, sinks to the bottom of a dam and then makes it collapse. This was a major feat and celebrated extensively in period war propaganda. However, the flooding caused did not just knock out industrial plants. Below the Möhne dam, for example, among the first victims were hundreds of slave workers and prisoners of war kept in the river valley.[15] The story in the film, however, does not reflect the full human cost. At least, *The Dam Busters* ends with the engineer's despair about the many air crews who perished in the attack. Since then, several books and television documentaries have added versions of the story.[16]

The development of the nuclear bomb as a weapon of mass destruction which is bound to be used against civilian populations, forms the background of the film *Oppenheimer* (U.S.A./U.K. 2023, dir. Christopher Nolan) as well as the 1980 BBC TV series of the same title. Initially, the weapon is constructed for the fight against Nazi Germany, and the protagonists find themselves in a race with German scientists. When Germany surrenders early enough to be spared of the nuclear bomb, it is used against Japan whose leaders have vowed to keep fighting to the end. The 2023 film shows how a mix of curiosity, personal ambition and political motivation leads to the development of the device which defined the century. Legal considerations do not matter much.

---

15 Royal Airforce Museum, n.d.
16 *Blank* n.d.

6. Military Courts

While the general impression is that of a dearth of academic literature covering both law and war in popular culture, there is an exemption for one aspect. Military courts in times of war as depicted in film have attracted considerable academic attention. For example, Asimow and Bergman discuss selected court martial films in much detail, providing legal and historic, or political background.[17] A detailed discussion is also found in a chapter of Greenfield, Osborn and Robson's "Film and the Law" and there are contributions to the literature by e.g. Michael Kuzina and Ann Ching.[18] Court–martials offer filmmakers to draw on the political and justice concerns of the public. As early as in 1899, a purpose–built cinema showed a film about Alfred Dreyfus facing court–martial and called it the "sensation of the hour".[19] Generally, the portrayal of military courts in wartime is that of a rather flawed institution. Typically, innocents are sacrificed for the career of superior officers or for general political reasons. They do not enjoy the procedural safeguards expected from an independent court and the sentencing is harsh if not exceedingly cruel.

The Australian film *Breaker Morant* (1980, dir. Bruce Beresford), based on a historic case, exemplifies the genre but with the twist that two of the lieutenants accused of war crimes during the Boer War are clearly guilty of the accused crimes, and one to a minor degree (see Asimow's chapter in this book). Nevertheless, even the youngest of the three whose "crime", according to his lawyer, was to shoot a prisoner in self–defence when attacked, is sentenced to years of penal servitude. The three lieutenants may be saved from the firing squad due to mitigation, the film suggests. As their able lawyer, Major Thomas convincingly argues, there is a rule in the British legal system in favour of those who have shown exemplary bravery in battle. The court has none of it. In *Breaker Morant*, the commanding General Herbert Kitchener even instructs his right–hand man, Colonel Hamilton, to lie under oath, denying that an order was given to the troops to kill prisoners. Witnesses in favour of the defence were transferred to India and witnesses for the prosecution testify out of hatred towards the defendants or under pressure of prosecution. Even the Australian government refuses to side with the defendants. With the execution looming, and having thwarted a final effort of Major Thomas, Hamilton reveals that they will be able to go home soon. Meaning, scapegoating the Australian lieutenants will allow a peace conference to be held.

A different path is followed by the story in *The Caine Mutiny* (U.S.A., 1954, dir. Edward Dmytryk), one in which the court is not to blame. While the Second World War is fought around them in the Pacific, a warship's captain antagonises

---

17 *Asimow/Bergman* 2021.
18 *Kuzina* 2002; *Kuzina* 2005; *Greenfield* et al. 2010; *Ching* 2018.
19 *Dirks* 2016.

his junior officers to the point at which some of them take over command. Charged with mutiny, they appear back home in front of a military court. Their defender, Lieutenant Greenwald, reluctantly provokes the captain on the witness stand to expose the kind of nervous and uncontrolled behaviour that made him unfit for his job. The film's ending is not entirely positive, due to Greenwald appearing at the celebratory party. In a drunken state, he berates the officers that they did not support their captain and that they were responsible for taking a ship out of action when it was needed to fight the war.

For soldiers who have risked their lives to be dragged in front of a manipulated military court must be one of the most desperate situations imaginable. In this book, Nathan Abrams and Michael Lipiner discuss director Stanley Kubrick's seminal work *Paths of Glory* (U.S.A., 1957) and how it reflects military and political events around the two World Wars and the time of its production. With the towering character of Colonel Dax, the lawyer–turned–commander who defends the soldiers of his regiment, Kubrick also wanted to counter the prejudicial portrayal of Jewish soldiers as Abrams and Lipiner argue. That the efforts of Dax are in vain, only serves to underline that law can be subverted in war by an uncontrolled military.

7. Justice Before and After War

Ever versatile, popular legal culture deals with situations in which cruel military justice leads to war as well as with how countries come to terms with armed conflict. Steve Greenfield's chapter discusses the Indian film *Mangal Pandey: The Rising* (2005, dir. Ketan Mehta). Here, the actions of the East India Company's military leadership worsen tensions to the point that locally recruited soldiers begin to mutineer, threatening its operation altogether. The Company that is acting as if it were a state and rightfully ruling India, provoked an uprising (Greenfield in this book). Similarities of this film loosely covering a historic case, with European events and their pop cultural treatment are quite obvious. Machura and Cunningham mention Verdi's opera *I vespri siciliani* (1855) in which French military occupation enrages Italians.

Ferdinando Spina in this volume describes how Italian films in the dying days of the Second World War and the first years after dealt with trials and retribution against fascists. He observes the conduct of three wars simultaneously, the one of Allied forces against the Germans and the fascist Republic, the ensuing civil war between fascists and anti–fascists and a war between social classes. The desperate situation led to lynchings. Then the new Italian state took over with its justice system, including specially created agencies. Spina shows that the "wild purges" eventually stopped, and adjudication moved from show trials to the regular, tranquil criminal court procedure. Three key films covered the spirit of the time and do well to convey the high tension, turmoil, and emotion of the years of transition. Perpetrators of fascist crimes and collaborators of the German occupation were living door to door with their victims. The films simplify the events but are like a time capsule for today's viewers.

Picture 2: In Soweit die Füße tragen (West Germany 1959, dir. Fritz Umgelter), fellow prisoners are conducting the physical punishment of an escapee brought back into the lead mine. Source: https://www.ebay.de/itm/325277586559 (Accessed on 27 June 2024).

The aftermath of war invites further treatments in popular culture. For example, what happens to the soldiers? In *American Sniper* (U.S.A., 2014, dir. Clint Eastwood), the lead character is murdered by an ex–comrade suffering from PTSD. The main antagonists in *The Searchers* (U.S.A., 1956, dir. John Ford) are Ethan Edwards, a veteran of the Confederate army who did not accept peace when his side capitulated in the Civil War, and Scar, a belligerent chief who is equally an outsider among the Comanche. For post–war West German society, the TV series *Soweit*

die Füße tragen[20] had enormous significance as it portrays a German Lieutenant, Clemens Forell, escaping from a deadly labour camp in East Siberia. The audience was reminded of the suffering of prisoners of war. The last German captives were released by the Soviet Union as late as 1956, eleven years after World War Two. Forell, not a Nazi apparently, is introduced as a victim of cruel victor's justice: sentenced in a mass trial. Already the rail transport in freezing freight waggons takes months and claims the lives of a third of the prisoners. The endless march on foot to the penal colony as well as working and living in the mine cost many more lives.

Forell's first attempt to flee is in vain and a particularly cruel punishment is awaiting. The camp authorities had forced the prisoners to work for days with only thin soup as food in reaction to the escape. When Forell is sent back in the mine tunnels, the captives line up with sticks and whatever is at hand. "Go!" a guard commands. A shocked Forell has to run the gauntlet (Picture 2). Forell has not only broken state/camp rules but also an implicit contract, an informal law that prisoners do not make the plight of others worse. As Forell falls on the ground, bleeding and passes out, the beating continues. Then another prisoner shelters Forell with his own body, only to receive a heavy blow to his head. A third man saves the second, wipes the blood of his forehead and shouts on top of his lungs: "What swine has done this?" As Forell's saviour is on his feet again, he repeatedly tells the prisoners: "How can you be so stupid?". Admonishing them how could they beat so hard; he reminds them of the basic rule that prisoners shall not harm each other. Truly, the "living law" can on occasion be unjust, as Eugen Ehrlich knew[21], and it can be exercised cruelly.

In the film, the whole of the Soviet Union appears as a completely securitised society. Without papers, people can go nowhere and armed guards limit everyone's movements. *Soweit die Füße tragen* has a scene in which the escapee attacks and robs a Russian railroad cashier. "Rogue, a criminal is what I have become", he later mutters to himself. Ironically, not the war but the unjust sentence, the prison camp and the conditions on his escape have made Forell a perpetrator of crime.

In 2001, the German cinema resurrected the topic and in this version of *Soweit die Füße Tragen* (dir. Hardy Martins, English title like the 1959 series), the most memorable scene is probably when the labour camp commander Kamenev threatens to shoot an exhausted prisoner. The man presses his forehead against the pistol's muzzle. Challenged by the gesture of a man accepting his inevitable fate, Kamenev does not hesitate to pull the trigger. What is essentially murder will go unpunished in a Siberian mine under Stalin's regime.

---

20 Dir. Fritz Umgelter, six–part TV series after a bestselling book by Josef Martin Bauer, English title *As Far As My Feet Will Carry Me*.
21 *Vogl* 2003, p. 283.

As many examples cited by the authors of this book demonstrate, popular culture in its best moments captures the public's imagination of war and the role of law within it. While it can only approximate the brutal reality of war, there is the chance to infuse the audience with liberal ideas of the rule of law even under the most adverse conditions. After all, the response to seeing injustice is likely to favour better institutions, better rules, better servants of the law and better practices.[22] But products of popular culture can also veil severe abuses of power and mythologise living and dying in war. In this case, law can become void or an auxiliary to crime.

8. Future Research

Inevitably, a view on future research shows ample of opportunities to deepen our understanding of law and war in popular culture. Different types of cultural artifacts could be studied and what they say about law and war. Researchers may also for example study law and war in popular culture in historical perspective, perhaps outlining how the treatment and the public response have changed in one country over time, as a response to experiences of war, or as a reflection of political reforms and revolutions. Likewise, an international comparison can be attempted how law and war have been portrayed in countries of interest. So far, it seems as if the U.S.A. with its prominence of law in political culture[23] and the many wars fought by American soldiers has the most extensive back catalogue.

Like in other studies on law in popular culture, especially film and television, empirical work could be conducted into the audience reaction to products dealing with law and war. What messages do they receive and does it influence their view of law, of war, or the relation of the two. Again, it will be possible that people react differently depending on their own experience with law or war, or the experiences of trusted others. There may also be contrasting impacts on e.g., adolescents and on more mature audiences. At this point in time, little is known and the contributions in this book had to limit themselves to preferred readings which are implied in products of popular culture. But this is varied enough.

9. Chapter Overview

The articles in the first part of this book are dealing with war crimes and military justice in film. The foundation is laid in Ann Ching's chapter on the depiction of war crimes in U.S. films. Ann Ching introduces central laws governing the conduct

---

22 Machura 2017.
23 Ibid.

of war, the international humanitarian law. Michael Asimow's chapter follows with a broader discussion of military justice in films. Here, the perspective is widened to cover films from other countries too. Nathan Abrams and Michael Lipiner are concluding Part 1 with an in-depth analysis of "Law and War in Stanley Kubrick's *Paths of Glory* (1957)". The authors are relating the film set in France in World War One to the experience of the Holocaust which was very present for the director and his star actor.

Part 2 covers war, civil war, and justice in divided societies. First, Ferdinando Spina in his chapter reminds readers of the critical situation Italy was in towards the end of World War Two. Spina uses three film examples to show how popular legal culture can be deeply engaged with the political and legal events of the day. The Bosnian War and the war crime in Srebrenica specifically are depicted in a film discussed by Iker Nabaskues Martínez de Eulate. Events at the advent of the massacre and the actions of those entrapped in the situation are the focus of the film *Quo Vadis Aida?* The creation and functioning of courts in war time form the topic of a film which Peter Robson is introducing. In *The Wind that Shakes the Barley*, the imperative to conduct a war trumps the attempt to conduct fair trials.

The third part of the book leaves films following European or North American patterns behind. Law and war in the opera are the focus of Machura and Cunningham's chapter. It shows that operas have dealt with law and war from a variety of angles and often with a serious political message for the audience. The penultimate book chapter by John Cunningham turns to war crimes in popular music. Contemporary armed conflict has influenced the production of music and the reaction of audiences. The book closes with a look at Indian cinema: Steve Greenfield introduces a film on the historic figure of Mangal Pandey and how it created a national hero but also sparked public and legal controversy. The film depicts the outbreak of war as a response to cultural insensitivity of the colonial powers and blatant injustice in the military.

The editor would like to thank Rüdiger Voigt for offering to edit a volume in his book series "Conceptions of Statehood". Many thanks also to Ann Ching for kindly providing the title picture. Bangor University has generously supported the book preparation with an undergraduate student internship, and I think I can speak in the name of all authors when I express my deepest gratitude to Jade Williams for her thorough language editing and proof–reading of manuscripts.

Bibliography

Asimow, Michael/*Bergman*, Paul, 2021: Real to Reel. Truth and Trickery in Courtroom Movies. Lake Mary, FL, Vandeplas.

Blank, Ralf, n.d.: Die Nacht des 16./17. Mai 1943 – "Operation Züchtigung": Die Zerstörung der Möhne–Talsperre. At: https://www.lwl.org/westfaelische-geschichte/portal/Internet/inp ut_felder/langDatensatz_ebene4.php?urlID=493&url_tabelle=tab_websegmente (Accessed on 30 October 2023).

Ching, Ann B., 2018: Military Justice in Film. In: *Rafter*, Nicole/*Brown*, Michelle (eds.), Oxford Research Encyclopedia of Crime, Media, and Popular Culture. New York, Oxford University Press, pp. 508–525.

Dirks, Tim, 2016: Timeline of Greatest Film Milestones and Turning Points in Film History. AMC Filmsite. At: http://www.filmsite.org/milestonespre1900s_2.html (Ac-cessed 4 February 2024).

Ehrlich, Eugen, 1967: Gutachten über die Frage: Was kann geschehen, um bei der Ausbil-dung (vor oder nach Abschluß des Universitätsstudiums) das Verständnis des Juristen für psychologische, wirtschaftliche und soziologische Fragen in erhöhtem Maße zu fördern? In: *Ehrlich*, Eugen, Recht und Leben, ed. by Manfred Rehbinder. Berlin, Duncker und Humblot, pp. 61–79.

Ehrlich, Eugen, 2022: Grundlegung der Soziologie des Rechts. 5th edition, Berlin, Duncker und Humblot.

Friedman, Lawrence, 1985: Transformations in American Legal Culture 1800–1985. In: Zeitschrift für Rechtssoziologie, 6:2, pp. 191–205.

Greenfield, Steve/*Osborn*, Guy/*Robson*, Peter, 2010: Film and the Law. 2nd edition. Oxford, Hart.

Holzleithner, Elisabeth, 2015: "The Game is Rigged": Fictions of Lawyering. In: *Hie-baum*, Christian/*Knaller*, Susanne/*Pichler*, Doris (eds.), Recht und Literatur im Zwischen-raum/Law and Literature In–Between. Bielefeld, Transcript, pp. 287–303.

Johnston, Trevor, 2018: Hammer Volume Three: Blood and Terror. In: Sight and Sound, 28:10, pp. 83–84.

Kuzina, Michael, 2002: Die amerikanische Militärjustiz im Film: The Caine Mutiny Court–Martial. In: *Machura*, Stefan/*Ulbrich*, Stefan (eds.), Recht im Film. Baden–Baden: Nomos, pp. 126–154.

Kuzina, Michael, 2005: Das Kriegsgerichtsverfahren als Filmsujet: US–amerikanische Erzähl-muster. In: *Machura*, Stefan/*Voigt*, Rüdiger (eds.), Krieg im Film. Münster, Lit., pp. 185–236.

Luhmann, Niklas, 1999: Funktionen und Folgen formaler Organisation. Berlin, Duncker and Humblot.

Luhmann, Niklas, 2000: The Reality of the Mass Media. Cambridge, Polity Press.

Machura, Stefan, 2017: Representations of Law, Rights, and Criminal Justice. In: Encyclope-dia of Crime, Media, and Popular Culture. At: http://criminology.Oxfordre.com/view/10.1093/acrefore/9780190264079.001.0001/acrefore-9780190264079-e-201 (Accessed on 6 December 2017).

Machura, Stefan/*Love*, Thomas/*Dwight*, Adam 2014: Law Students' Trust in the Courts and the Police. In: International Journal of Law, Crime and Justice, 42:4, pp. 287–305.

Parsons, Talcott, 1971: Recht und soziale Kontrolle. In: *Hirsch*, Ernst E./*Rehbinder*, Manfred (eds.), Materialien zur Rechtssoziologie. Kölner Zeitschrift für Soziologie und Sozialpsychologie, special issue no. 11, 2nd edition. Opladen, Westdeutscher Verlag, pp. 121–134.

Pronay, Nicholas, 1988: The British Post–bellum Cinema: A Survey of the Films Relating to World War II Made in Britain between 1945 and 1960. In: Historical Journal of Film, Radio and Television, 8:1, pp. 39–54.

Royal Airforce Museum, n.d.: Casualties of the Dams Raid. At: https://www.rafmuseum.org.uk/research/online-exhibitions/617-squadron-and-the-dams-raid/casualties-of-the-dams-raid / (Accessed on 30 October 2023).

Vogl, Stefan, 2003: Soziale Gesetzgebungspolitik, freie Rechtsfindung und soziologische Rechtswissenschaft bei Eugen Ehrlich, Baden-Baden, Nomos.

Weber, Max, 1968: Economy and Society, ed. by Guenther Roth and Claus Wittich. New York, Bedminster Press.

Wikström, Per–Olof H., 2010: Explaining Crime as Moral Actions. In: *Hitlin*, Steven/*Vaysey*, Stephen (eds.). Handbook of the Sociology of Morality. New York, Springer Verlag, pp. 211–240.

Wikström, Per–Olof H., 2017: Character, Circumstances, and the Causes of Crime. In: *Liebling*, Alison/*Maruna*, Shadd/*McAra*, Lesley, 2017: The Oxford Handbook of Criminology. Oxford, Oxford University Press, pp. 501–521.

Wikström, Per–Olof H., n.d: Overview of the Key Steps in the Perception–Choice Action Process. At: https://www.cac.crim.cam.ac.uk/resou/sat (Accessed on 3 January 2020).

Wikström, Per–Olof H./*Svensson*, Robert, 2010: When Does Self–control Matter? The Interaction Between Morality and Self–control in Crime Causation. In: European Journal of Criminology, 7(2), pp. 395–410.

Part 1

War Crimes and Military Justice in Film

Ann Ching[1]

Depictions of War Crimes in Film

A fundamental concept of statehood is the power to enter into relations with other states, such as being a signatory to an international treaty.[2] A related concept is the willingness to abide by international law. A subset of international law is the law of armed conflict (often referred to as international humanitarian law, or IHL), which serves to minimise as much as possible the deleterious effects of warfare on civilian populations.

The primary source of IHL, the Geneva Conventions, have been ratified by nearly 200 nation–states.[3] Nevertheless, every armed conflict results in violations of IHL— war crimes. Thus, although on a national level, states agree to protect civilians on the battlefield, violations of IHL consistently take place during warfare.

In the United States, the percentage of the population that has served in the armed forces hovers around six per cent.[4] Nonetheless, war films have been a popular American film genre for decades. Indeed, sixteen war films have won Best Picture at the Academy Awards, and several others have been nominated.[5] Unlike other genres, however, war films have an outsize ability to influence public perceptions. Although films are created primarily for entertainment, films about warfare often serve as a person's only point of reference for understanding the military, combat operations, and the law of armed conflict. This holds especially true when the films in question purport to depict real–life events; films tend to gain wider audiences than factual news reports or documentaries.

War films are an enduring genre in part because of their inherent ability to depict dramatic conflict. Sources of external conflict are fairly obvious; the plot could be driven by the clash between two warring armies, or a cat–and–mouse chase between opposing snipers. More often, however, war films hit their dramatic high points by depicting characters' internal conflict. This conflict is often portrayed as a struggle between competing values. For example, a protagonist may be a soldier who questions the morality of war and yet must fight to survive and protect his comrades.

---

1 With thanks to *Kenneth Misajet*, Arizona State University Sandra Day O'Connor College of Law, for his research and editing assistance.
2 Montevideo Convention 1933.
3 International Committee of the Red Cross 2023b.
4 *Faint* 2023.
5 *Baxter* 2023.

This chapter explores how the depiction of war crimes in film serves purposes both within the narrative of the film and in the real world. In particular, this chapter focuses on films portraying violations of international laws that mandate humane treatment of civilians on the battlefield. This chapter begins with a brief overview of the protections that IHL affords to civilians in combat zones. Then, this chapter examines how the standards set by these laws often drive narrative conflict and character development in war films. Next, this chapter looks closely at select war films and how their illustration of war crimes sends specific messages regarding IHL and the nature of war crimes. The chapter concludes by discussing the role of war as entertainment in shaping public perception, both within the United States and globally.

1.1 International Humanitarian Law: Treatment of Civilians on the Battlefield

IHL is defined broadly as a set of rules that aim to minimize armed conflict's effect on civilian populations and property. The development of IHL as a body of law is relatively recent. Early recorded history documented harsh treatment of civilians; belligerent powers regularly pillaged conquered cities and committed atrocities upon the populace.[6] However, certain norms of battle began to emerge as far back as two thousand years ago. Sun Tzu's *The Art of War*[7] stated that captured enemy soldiers should be "kindly treated and kept". Centuries later, Hugo Grotius and Emerich de Vattel, two European jurists, authored treatises covering the Law of Nations in 1620 and 1758, respectively.[8] Their treatises are considered foundational; they addressed many aspects of the law of war as it was understood then.[9] Both Grotius and Vattel discussed captured combatant treatment, civilian rape and murder, and civilian property interests.[10] These treatises, however, reflected common, existing practices; they did not serve as binding legal authority.

The foundation of IHL began to emerge as nation–states developed internal rules governing warfare, such as the United States's Lieber Code, which provided a framework for identifying war crimes during the U.S. Civil War.[11] The mid–nineteenth century also produced a series of international treaties that served as the foundation for modern–day IHL.

The first Geneva Convention (1864) addressed prospective protections for wounded combatants, medical personnel who treated them, and civilians who housed the wounded. This convention's groundbreaking work was expanded at the Hague

---

6   *Brown* 1998, n. 9.
7   *Sun Tzu* 1910, p. 77. *Sun Tzu* lived 484–474 B.C.
8   *Kiel* 2012, p. 45.
9   Ibid.
10 Ibid., pp. 45-46; 48–50.
11 *Ching* 1999, n. 24.

Convention (1899). Prisoners of war would receive humane treatment and retain all personal possessions "except arms, horses, and military papers."[12] Civilians also enjoyed expanded rights. Property confiscations and pillaging were officially banned,[13] and belligerents could not hold civilians collectively responsible for hostile acts committed by unidentified persons.[14]

Prisoners of war received additional safeguards after the Geneva Convention of 1929. World War I had demonstrated earlier agreements were incomplete and flawed.[15] The 1929 convention was arguably similar in scope but provided additional details omitted from the earlier Hague Conventions.[16]

Following World War II, the International Committee of the Red Cross held a conference in Geneva, from which emerged the four modern–day Geneva Conventions.[17] These conventions codified protections for wounded soldiers in the field,[18] wounded sailors at sea,[19] prisoners of war,[20] and civilians on the battlefield.[21] Relevant to this chapter's discussion are certain provisions of these Geneva Conventions.

Protection of enemy soldiers who are no longer "in combat." One fundamental concept in IHL is combatant immunity. This means that a soldier who fights as a lawful combatant can also target and kill other combatants without being subject to prosecution for murder. A corollary of this principle is that a soldier loses combatant immunity if the soldier targets enemy soldiers who are *hors de combat* (outside of combat).[22] Soldiers become *hors de combat* if they are unable to fight due to illness or injury, if they surrender, or if they are captured. So, for example, a soldier commits a war crime by shooting a downed enemy soldier to ensure their death (sometimes called a "double tap" or "security round") if that enemy is unable to continue fighting.[23]

Protection of civilians. Another fundamental tenet of IHL is the protection of civilians, both their persons and their property. A civilian is a person who is not a combatant. Per IHL, military forces should not deliberately target, harm, or kill civilians in combat zones. Four key IHL principles relate to the protection of civilians: military necessity, distinction, proportionality, and humanity.[24]

---

12 Hague Convention 1899, art. 4.
13 Ibid., arts. 46, 47.
14 Ibid., art. 50.
15 *Noone* et. al. 2004, p. 8.
16 Ibid.
17 *Brooks* 2004, p. 689.
18 Geneva Convention (I) 1949.
19 Geneva Convention (II) 1949.
20 Geneva Convention (III) 1949.
21 Geneva Convention (IV) 1949.
22 *Montazzoli* 2021; *Corn* 2023, p. 401.
23 *Montazzoli* 2021.
24 *Floyd* 2023, p. 70.

- The *military necessity* principle deems that warring nations should use only the amount and type of military force that is necessary to accomplish legitimate military purposes. Application of this principle prevents "overkill," which can put civilian life and property in danger.
- The *distinction* principle means that militaries must target only lawful military targets, making indiscriminate attacks illegal.
- The *proportionality* principle recognises that even when applying military necessity and distinction to the fight, some degree of "collateral damage" may be unavoidable. Proportionality means that any inadvertent loss of civilian life must not be excessive when weighed against the expected military advantage.
- Lastly, the *humanity* principle dictates that even during warfare, military forces must avoid means and methods that lead to unnecessary suffering. Outlawing these means and methods indirectly protects civilians, as many inhumane weapons (e.g., certain landmines, chemical weapons) also harm civilian populations.

In theory, properly following the four principles outlined above should limit the loss of civilian life and property, even in a large–scale armed conflict. One way in which armies attempt to adhere to these principles is by implementing and following rules of engagement (ROE). For instance, the U.S. armed forces have standing rules of engagement (SROE) that apply in international armed conflict.[25] The unclassified portion of the SROE states that U.S. forces may lawfully target individuals who are part of a declared hostile force (DHF), i.e., based on status alone.[26] Thus, a member of a DHF who is not *hors de combat* may be targeted, even if that person is not actively engaged in hostilities. Notably, only an "appropriate U.S. authority" may designate a DHF.[27]

The SROE also allows U.S. forces to act in self–defence against anyone who displays "hostile intent" or commits a "hostile act" (as defined in the SROE).[28] Thus, U.S. forces may target civilians who lose their IHL protections by engaging in hostile acts. The SROE also allows U.S. forces to target civilians who display hostile intent. As one can imagine, making targeting decisions based on conduct, especially the manifestation of hostile intent, can prove difficult in practice.[29]

The foregoing discussion of IHL is meant to provide only a backdrop for the discussion of war films. Nonetheless, even this abbreviated synopsis serves to illustrate the dramatic tension that can arise for military forces endeavouring to operate within IHL's bounds. Under the protection of combatant immunity, soldiers are ordered to engage in acts that under any other circumstances would be considered murder.

---

25 *Fisher* 2022, pp. 106–109.
26 Ibid., p. 108.
27 Ibid., p. 123.
28 Ibid., p. 108.
29 *Cherry/Rizzotti* 2021.

Forces engaged in unconventional warfare, where enemies blend in with the civilian population, are tasked with making quick assessments of hostile intent. These and other scenarios provide fertile ground for the development of narrative conflict in war films.

1.2 War Crimes Depicted in Film: Conflict in Combat

For this discussion, the term "war films" refers to movies that show combat on the battlefield and the narrative conflicts that arise therefrom. This particular genre, sometimes called the combat film genre, emerged during and immediately after World War II.[30] Although films about combat could include genres such as fantasy and science fiction, this discussion limits "war films" to those about real–life wars and conflicts, even if the characters and plot are works of fiction. Although films about real–life wars can take many forms, including musicals and comedies,[31] these genres do not depict combat and are therefore excluded from this discussion as well.

War crime films are nested within the war film genre. Films depicting the commission or attempted commission of war crimes are invariably dramatic and often include some representation of the military justice system.[32] Some films are centred almost exclusively around a war crime and the resulting legal proceedings. Examples include *Breaker Morant* (1980, dir. Bruce Beresford), an Australian film about the court–martial of soldiers accused of killing prisoners and a civilian; *Rules of Engagement* (2000, dir. William Friedkin), a U.S. film about the court–martial of an Army colonel who ordered troops to open fire indiscriminately on a protesting crowd; and *Conduct Unbecoming* (2011, dir. Sydney J. Furie), a Canadian film about a U.S. Marine accused of killing civilians in Afghanistan. These examples could be fairly categorised as courtroom dramas rather than war films. Films like these provide insight into popular sentiment about the morality of war and the military justice system.[33] However, in these court–martial films, the war crimes are in some cases not even displayed on screen; rather, they serve as the catalyst for the legal drama.

In other instances, a war crime or attempted war crime serves only an ancillary function in the narrative. For example, the fictional World War II drama *Saving Private Ryan* (U.S., 1998, dir. Steven Spielberg) contains a scene where a U.S. soldier threatens to kill a surrendered German soldier as an act of revenge. This would result in a war crime, a fact that creates conflict between soldiers. Ultimately,

---

30 *Basinger* 2003, pp. 22–23.
31 Ibid., pp. 221–235.
32 *Ching* 2017.
33 Ibid.

the protagonist, an Army captain, releases the German soldier, which in turn leads to the captain's disclosure of his pre–war work as a schoolteacher. Thus, the potential war crime serves as a device to drive narrative and character development; prior to this scene, the captain had refused to disclose his civilian occupation. However, the potential war crime is far from the film's focus.

In contrast, some war films place the commission of a war crime at the centre of the narrative. In *Casualties of War* (U.S., 1989, dir. Brian De Palma), nearly the entire second act portrays the kidnapping, rape, and murder of a Vietnamese civilian woman by U.S. Army soldiers. The depiction is unflinching and brutal, heightened by Ennio Morricone's dramatic score. Although the culpable soldiers stand trial in the third act, the court–martial is portrayed almost wholly off–screen; the prosecutor is a disembodied voice, and the camera focuses only on the testifying defendants. *Casualties of War* is therefore the inverse, narratively speaking, of a film like *Breaker Morant*. The film focuses on the moral breakdown of soldiers in the field. The courtroom scenes, while replete with dramatic tension, focus on the consequences of this breakdown rather than the procedures of the military justice system.

Even without depicting the commission or potential commission of a war crime, in certain films IHL provides a narrative backdrop, often serving as a tool to explore the protagonist's morality. In *American Sniper* (U.S., 2014, dir. Clint Eastwood), the sniper/protagonist, Chris Kyle, is portrayed as engaging only in legally justified killings within the film's universe. Although he kills a child early in the film, he does so seemingly reluctantly, only after confirming the child is targeting U.S. troops with a grenade. Later in the film, Kyle nearly kills another child, taking his finger off the trigger only when the child drops the rocket–propelled grenade he had picked up moments before. Although the film technically does not depict war crimes, it consistently highlights the complexity of insurgent warfare, where targeting must be based on hostile intent or acts, rather than status alone.

This complexity is further explored in *The Kill Team* (U.S., 2019, dir. Dan Krauss). This film, depicting U.S. soldiers in Afghanistan in 2009, makes it clear early on that any civilian could be an undercover enemy. In the first act, the squad leader, an Army sergeant, admonishes his troops to work on winning the hearts and minds of Afghan civilians. But moments after he gives a friendly wave to a group of Afghan children, he is unceremoniously blown up by an explosive. The message is clear: trust leads to death, and survival relies on aggression. The film's main plot mirrors that of *Casualties of War*. Throughout the film, soldiers continually conspire to murder Afghan civilians, planting weapons to make the killings appear to be legally justified. These crimes fuel the protagonist soldier's internal conflict; he wants to report the crimes but fears he will be murdered in retaliation.

The foregoing films are, of course, only a small sample of films that depict war crimes. But, from these films emerge certain narrative themes reflected in myriad other war films. These archetypal themes, in turn, correspond to classic forms of storytelling conflict: man versus man; man versus self; man versus society; and man versus nature.

Man versus man. In many war films, violations of IHL serve as the basis of external conflict between characters. Typically, the story's protagonist is the "good" soldier who refuses to engage in war crimes. The antagonist, in turn, is the "bad" soldier, often an authority figure, who instigates war crimes. Often, the good soldier puts himself in mortal danger by refusing to participate in the bad soldier's war crimes and thereby finds himself fighting for survival against both fellow soldiers and enemy forces. In these films, the criminal conduct creates a dividing line between good and evil characters. In addition to *Casualties of War* and *The Kill Team*, discussed above, other examples include *Platoon* (U.S., 1986, dir. Oliver Stone) and *Redacted* (U.S., 2007, Brian De Palma).

Man versus self. War films almost invariably explore characters' internal struggles to reconcile competing values and beliefs. At times, this conflict manifests as a reluctance to engage in combat at all, reflecting a character's religious beliefs or natural aversion to killing. In many films, the internal conflict relates to a protagonist's recruitment to engage in a war crime with fellow soldiers. This scenario pits the soldier's righteous desire to protect innocent civilians against his self–preservation, often under threat of fratricide for refusal to participate in criminal conduct. The protagonist–soldier may also fear being labelled as a traitor or otherwise isolated from fellow soldiers. This trope almost always accompanies the man–versus–man conflict described above. For example, *Casualties of War* centres exclusively around the moral journey of its protagonist, Private Eric Eriksson. Conflict arises not only between Eriksson and squad leader, Sergeant Meserve; it arises within Eriksson himself, as he reconciles his dependence on Meserve for survival with his disgust at Meserve's brutal mistreatment of a kidnapped Vietnamese woman.

Man versus society. Films depicting war crimes are often intended as commentary on the nature of war itself. In these films, soldiers are often shown to be succumbing to the pressure of the combat environment. When "good" soldiers are drawn into corrupt conduct, these films send a distinctly anti–war message: young people are thrust into impossibly difficult moral scenarios in far–off lands, created by unseen and uncaring national leadership. *The Kill Team* provides an example of this type of conflict. Contemporaneously with the protagonist–soldier's efforts to avoid participating in his sergeant's war crimes, the soldier's parents make futile attempts to

35

report these crimes to U.S. military authorities. In this manner, the insurmountable bureaucracy of the military creates conflict that exacerbates the protagonist–soldier's seemingly impossible moral dilemma. Ultimately, the military's response comes too late, after the soldier has already been drawn into his sergeant's criminal scheme. The film thus sends a message about the senselessness of combat; the military effectively traps a "good" soldier in an impossible situation, provides no escape, then punishes the soldier despite his attempts to bring misconduct to light.

Man versus nature. The fourth type of classical narrative conflict is that between humankind and the natural environment. Although man versus nature is not usually the central source of conflict in war films, it does crop up in films that portray the natural terrain as indifferent, unforgiving, or another form of enemy to be conquered.

A stark example is found in *Apocalypse Now* (U.S., 1979, dir. Francis Ford Coppola) with its iconic opening scene showing the use of napalm herbicide to defoliate the Vietnamese landscape. In films that depict war crimes, another type of man–versus–nature conflict emerges. The civilian population is often characterised in a manner that makes it almost indistinct from the environment. Civilians are usually nameless characters, dressed similarly to each other in (supposedly) native garb, blending into a rugged landscape dotted periodically by rudimentary houses and roaming livestock. For the soldiers in these films, civilians are yet another challenge to deal with as they traverse a foreign land, and often a potential source of hidden danger. Thus, civilians in war–crime films are often portrayed on par with landmines or booby traps — non–human obstacles, indistinguishable from the surrounding landscape.

As the war film examples above illustrate, their depictions of war crimes do not provide any in–depth education on the nuances of IHL. Rather, war crimes serve as a catalyst for narrative conflict, centered around the four classical conflict types. However, a close analysis of U.S. war films reveals several distinct messages about IHL, civilians in combat, and popular attitudes towards war crimes in general.

1.3 Messages that Emerge from War Crime Films

Throughout the history of U.S. war films, their messages have varied depending on a variety of external factors. Films produced during World War II, for example, served to promote citizens' support of the U.S. war efforts. Many films were released almost contemporaneously with the combat events depicted therein, such as

Bataan (U.S., 1943, dir. Tay Garnett).[34] In *Bataan*, the pro–war message is akin to propaganda; although the film ends in the defeat of every main character, the ending voiceover proudly proclaims: "So fought the heroes of Bataan. Their sacrifice made possible our own victories in the Coral and Bismarck Seas, Midway, New Guinea and Guadalcanal. Their spirit will lead us back to Bataan!"[35]

One reason World War II films were able to send such a clear message is the nature of the war itself. The U.S. involvement in World War II was a national effort; indeed, it was the last time that the U.S. government formally declared war.[36] U.S. forces engaged distinct, declared hostile forces in the form of uniformed, Axis military troops. In other words, World War II films could portray a specific enemy which, pursuant to international law, U.S. forces could unambiguously target and kill.

As the genre developed through the mid–to late–twentieth century, war films portrayed U.S. forces engaging in overseas conflicts against unconventional, insurgent fighters who did not wear distinctive uniforms. Moreover, these war films, particularly those exploring the Vietnam War, portrayed conflicts where the U.S. popular sentiment toward the war was mixed, to say the least. Consequently, the messages emerging from these films shifted away from pro–war propaganda. Films like *Platoon* and *Casualties of War* commented on the brutal, senseless nature of combat and its effects on both soldiers and the civilian population in combat zones.

In the twenty–first century, many films depicting the United States' post–9/11 involvement in Iraq and Afghanistan demonstrate an interesting blend of the pro–military stance of World War II films with the anti–war stance of Vietnam war films. This convergence reflects the U.S. population's sentiment toward Operation Enduring Freedom (Afghanistan), Operation Iraqi Freedom, and related conflicts. Many were keen to avoid the mistreatment of returning U.S. troops that took place during the Vietnam era. However, many in the United States also had reservations about U.S. involvement in the Afghanistan and Iraq conflicts. Thus, several films of the 2000s and 2010s both show U.S. forces as heroes and comment on the toll that protracted warfare takes on soldiers and families.

This dual message is reflected, for instance, in *The Hurt Locker* (U.S., 2008, dir. Kathryn Bigelow). In this film, the Explosive Ordnance Disposal (EOD) soldiers are depicted almost as superheroes; aside from defusing bombs, they also defeat a sniper and conduct patrols to find insurgents. However, the protagonist, Sergeant James, is also portrayed as psychologically damaged by his high–pressure combat experiences. Notably, the film does little to tackle the toll of insurgent warfare on

---

34 *Crowther* 1943.
35 *Basinger* 2003, p. 55.
36 U.S. Senate n.d.

the Iraqi civilian population; the focus is on the U.S. soldiers and their wartime experience.

Although *The Hurt Locker* does not purport to depict war crimes by U.S. forces, its messages are echoed in war crime films that depict the Vietnam era and subsequent conflicts. Generally speaking, this specific sub–genre of war films typically examines war crimes from the point of view of the U.S. military perpetrator, rather than the civilians who suffer the consequences. These films also tend to relate the commission of war crimes back to the psychological toll of combat. In this manner, modern war crime films can avoid portraying soldiers in an entirely negative light, while still commenting on the hardships exacted by combat service.

A close analysis of a handful of modern war–crime films (mainly *Casualties of War*, *American Sniper*, and *The Kill Team*) reveals some more specific messaging relating to international law, insurgent warfare, and the nature of combat.

International humanitarian law is simple. War–crime films always allude to the broad outlines of IHL, if only for the purpose of putting the protagonist–soldier's actions into context. But when characters refer to IHL or rules of engagement, they do so in very broad terms. In an opening scene of *American Sniper*, the titular sniper, Chris Kyle, is in Fallujah, Iraq. He aims his rifle at a woman and child, dressed in civilian clothes, walking toward a U.S. convoy. He looks for weapons to determine if they are legitimate targets. His spotter, a Marine referred to in the script as Goat, is at his side. The following exchange ensues:

CHRIS KYLE: You got eyes on this? Can you confirm?
COMMANDING OFFICER (over radio): Negative. You know the ROEs. Your call.
GOAT: They fry you if you're wrong. Send your ass to Leavenworth.

This dialogue communicates to the audience the potential consequences of killing noncombatants. "They" (military authorities) will "fry" the soldier in question, implying excessive punishment, and then send the soldier to "Leavenworth," shorthand for the U.S. Army Disciplinary Barracks (military prison). Here, IHL is presented as black and white—one mistake will lead to indefinite confinement—therefore oversimplifying the consequences of an IHL violation.

A later sequence in the film depicts the second battle of Fallujah. One Navy SEAL, Marc Lee, describes the ROE to the other SEALs and Marines:

MARC LEE: The city was evacuated. Any military–aged male still here, is here to kill you.

This statement echoes a real–life order issued by an Army colonel in the early years of the Iraq war. In 2007, an Army investigation found that Colonel Michael D.

Steele improperly told his troops that they could target any military–aged male.[37] This interpretation of the ROE did not conform to IHL principles, primarily by failing to distinguish civilians from combatants. The investigation further found that this improper ROE interpretation contributed to the unlawful killing of four Iraqi men.

However, in *American Sniper*, this ROE is presented as entirely routine. The Navy SEAL issuing the order does so with authority, and no one questions its legitimacy. Indeed, following this order does not later come back to haunt the SEALs in *American Sniper*; their actions are presented as justified throughout the film's duration. Audiences could easily walk away believing that the "kill all military–aged males" order was entirely lawful—an interpretation of IHL that is both simplistic and incorrect.

Casualties of War, a film predating *American Sniper* by over two decades, contains a similar misinterpretation. Early in the film, one soldier explains the ROE to the protagonist, Private Eriksson, as, "We don't shoot except in self–defence. . . . [but] you get one of these fuckers out in the open, you waste 'em." Although *Casualties of War* is set during the Vietnam War, conflicts in both Vietnam and Iraq involved insurgent warfare where combatants typically did not wear uniforms. Thus, the "waste 'em" order suggests an interpretation similar to "kill all military–aged males," permitting indiscriminate targeting based on status rather than conduct.

Now, in *Casualties of War*, the soldier explaining the ROE possesses less authority than Marc Lee in *American Sniper*. The audience would likely interpret the "waste 'em" order as a crude and inaccurate statement of the rules. However, once again, this order is never questioned throughout the film. Indeed, it is the only discussion of ROE in a film that spans nearly two hours and takes place almost entirely within a combat zone. Although *Casualties of War* does focus on a war crime, it does not focus on the ROE or any particular provision of IHL.

In *The Kill Team*, set in Kandahar in 2009, the protagonist, Specialist Briggman, knows that his fellow soldiers are breaking the law by murdering Afghan civilians. Interestingly, though, the film does not have any explicit discussion of IHL. The culpable soldiers, led by the intimidating Sergeant Deeks, seek to cover their crimes by planting weapons at or near the bodies of slain civilians. The implication is that this is enough to demonstrate that a killing was lawful. However, once again, this is an overly simplified message regarding the nature of IHL.

In total, these three representative examples do not explain much about IHL, even in films that centre around war crimes. What little is communicated regarding IHL is fairly rudimentary: do not kill civilians, unless they have weapons; do kill anyone

---

37   *von Zielbauer* 2007.

who fits a general description of the enemy. Certainly, these films are not created for the purpose of educating the public about international law. However, for a public who has no exposure to the military other than through film, these uncontradicted messages may become the last word on the topic.

Violations of IHL are morally ambiguous. In contrast to the straightforward way in which IHL and ROE are communicated in war films, war crimes are presented in a complex and nuanced manner. For example, *Casualties of War* and *The Kill Team* are based on real–life incidents. In both films, fictionalised elements are added to the storyline to provide a rationale or justification for even the most heinous of real–world crimes. The net effect is to create a degree of sympathy for the soldiers who commit these crimes, even when none would be warranted in real life.

In *Casualties of War*, squad leader Sergeant Meserve is the primary instigator of the kidnapping, rape, and murder of Vietnamese civilian Tran Thi Oanh. The film's story is based on the real–life crimes committed against Phan Thi Mao, documented by reporter Daniel Lang in the New Yorker.[38] In the film's first act, Sergeant Meserve's friend and fellow soldier, Brownie, is mortally wounded during an attack. Onscreen, Sergeant Meserve demonstrates his grief through his anger. Shortly after learning that Brownie has died, Sergeant Meserve formulates the plan to "requisition a girl" from a local village. The implication is apparent; Sergeant Meserve is driven to commit a war crime by his anger, his grief, and the cruel reality of combat in Vietnam.

As reported in *The New Yorker*, however, Sergeant Meserve's squad suffered no such loss directly before his decision to kidnap Phan Thi Mao. Rather, Sergeant Meserve told the squad of the plan with "a straight face" while briefing them on an upcoming mission.[39] No indication is given of any reason why Sergeant Meserve formulated this plan, other than one soldier's report that Meserve had developed "a mean streak toward the Vietnamese."[40] Indeed, he was reported to have committed acts of violence against other Vietnamese civilians prior to kidnapping Mao. Compared to the film, the article provides a less sympathetic view of Sergeant Meserve's unquestionably criminal conduct.

Decades later, *Casualties of War* director Brian De Palma followed a similar narrative arc in his film *Redacted* (U.S., 2007). This film depicts a heinous crime—the rape and murder of a civilian Iraqi girl, and the murder of her family. In *Redacted*, the soldiers/offenders are spurred to act out of grief, anger, and vengeance following the death of another soldier. Like *Casualties of War*, *Redacted* is based on a real–life incident—the 2006 rape and killing of an Iraqi family in Mahmudiyah.

---

38 *Lang* 1969.
39 Ibid.
40 Ibid.

News accounts of the incident, however, do not report that soldiers were motivated by a fellow soldier's death. Rather, according to one soldier, they came up with the crime while playing cards one night.[41] Once again, the fictionalised account gives the offenders some thread of moral justification that did not exist in real life.

Similar questions of morality creep into the narrative in *The Kill Team*. This 2019 movie is based on real–world war crimes that took place in Afghanistan. The director, Dan Krauss, based his film on a documentary he made about the incident, also entitled *The Kill Team* (U.S., 2013). The fictionalised version frames the war crimes as a soldier's choice between competing values: obeying the law and returning home safe to one's family. Or, put another way: in combat, one must be willing to bend (or break) the rules to survive. The opening act of *The Kill Team* sends this message when the soldiers' original squad leader, Sergeant Wallace, falls victim to an improvised explosive device. Shortly before the explosion, Sergeant Wallace admonishes his soldiers to treat Afghan civilians humanely, reminding them that they are there to "win hearts and minds." The implication is clear — soldiers who let their guard down around civilians are "soft" and vulnerable.

This message is further solidified with the introduction of Sergeant Deeks, the new squad leader. In *The Kill Team*, Sergeant Deeks persuades his squad to murder Afghan civilians whilst planting weapons on the bodies to make the killings appear justified. Like his real–life counterpart, Sergeant Deeks commits acts that are unquestionably criminal: murder, conspiracy, and collecting victims' body parts as war trophies. And yet, Sergeant Deeks is portrayed at times as a sympathetic, perhaps even admirable, character. Soon after his arrival, the soldiers discuss the nature of his legendary kills during a previous Iraq deployment, documented by a series of skull tattoos on his body. The soldiers feel their survival is better assured being led by Sergeant Deeks, a person willing to kill or be killed; they agree, "We need guys like Deeks."

Moreover, Sergeant Deeks is portrayed as a caring father. In one scene, the protagonist, Specialist Briggman, interrupts Sergeant Deeks during a video call with his young son. In turn, Sergeant Deeks sometimes takes on a fatherly demeanour when interacting with Briggs, even as he urges him to take part in war crimes. Rendered this way, Sergeant Deeks is not just a cold–blooded killer, a collection of body parts notwithstanding. He is a father who is doing all he can to return home to the family he loves.

Notably, the documentary version of *The Kill Team* does not present this fatherly, sometimes compassionate version of Sergeant Gibbs (the inspiration for Sergeant Deeks). Sergeant Gibbs is not directly featured in the documentary; instead, he is described by other soldiers in the squad. Their description reflects an intimidating

---

41   *MacAskell/Howard* 2007.

leader rather than a father figure. In describing his artistic choices when making the cinematic version of the documentary's story, director Dan Krauss stated: "I relished the opportunity to have the freedom to distil the emotions of the story without having to make a second piece of journalism. Now I was free to explore the story from an emotional standpoint."[42]

Of course, this film, like all others, is a piece of art rather than a piece of journalism. Nonetheless, it still sends a message about the nature of war crimes. In this case, the message is that perpetrators of war crimes act from a position of moral conflict, driven in part by understandable motives like avenging a fallen friend or returning home safely. Even the protagonist soldiers (e.g., Private Eriksson in *Casualties of War*, Specialist Briggman in *The Kill Team*) are conflicted when it comes to participating in or reporting war crimes. The moral complexity of war crimes contrasts with the simplicity of how IHL is explained in the universe of war crime films.

The victims of war crimes are nameless and faceless. As discussed above, popular war crime films provide the perspective of soldiers in combat and their struggles, both internal and external. A casual observer could easily conclude that war crimes affect perpetrators more than victims. In large part, U.S. war crime films do little to humanise the civilians who suffer the effects of warfare, and in particular, those who are subject to war crimes.

Take, for example, Tran Thi Oanh, the Vietnamese woman in *Casualties of War*. The audience sees fairly graphic on–screen depictions of the soldiers' crimes against her. Over the course of the film, she is battered, bloodied, and crying in pain. She pleads with Private Eriksson in Vietnamese, but he has no idea what she is saying. Neither does the audience (unless they speak Vietnamese) – her extensive dialogue is not subtitled. Without a doubt, the audience feels pity, disgust, perhaps even horror at Tran Thi Oanh's treatment. And yet, the audience does not really know anything about her as a person. Her name is not revealed until the final act of the film, during the court–martial scenes.

Perhaps the absence of character development is deliberate. By keeping Tran Thi Oanh fairly anonymous, she can stand in for all Vietnamese civilians who were victims of war crimes (e.g., the civilians killed during the My Lai massacre). It also reinforces the film's protagonist–driven perspective; Private Eriksson would know nothing about Tran Thi Oanh, other than her suffering. Nonetheless, the net effect is to leave the audience knowing nothing about Tran Thi Oanh, her anguished mother, or the other residents of her village.

---

42 *Thompson* 2019.

Post–9/11 war crime films also tend to lack character development of the civilians depicted therein. Rather, their portrayal often relies on broad stereotypes, presenting a Westernised perception of "typical Arab" or "typical Muslim" culture (even in regions that in reality are not predominantly Arab or Muslim). As portrayed in popular films, Afghan and Iraqi civilians are indistinguishable from one another, characterised by shabby garments and rudimentary dwellings. Women and children may be innocents, or may be terrorists in disguise, as depicted in *American Sniper*. Indeed, films like *American Sniper* and *The Hurt Locker* reinforce a negative stereotype: the "secret terrorist."[43] In the universe of war crime films, Afghan and Iraqi civilians are undeserving of trust or sympathy. In *The Kill Team*, local civilians are described as "goatfuckers" and "motherless fucks," a characterisation that goes unchallenged. When civilians fall victim to IHL violations, the audience may perceive grief or outrage, but through the lens of the U.S. soldiers involved. The victims themselves are nameless stereotypes: the elderly cleric, the wide–eyed young boy, the modestly dressed woman.

Synthesising these three messages—international humanitarian law is simple, violations of IHL are morally ambiguous, and the victims of war crimes are nameless and faceless—reveals a template of sorts for U.S. war crime films. A morally conflicted protagonist–soldier fights to survive in a foreign land. His fellow soldiers, grief–stricken over the loss of a comrade, desire to seek vengeance on the local population. In some cases, the protagonist–soldier convinces the others to refrain from killing civilians; in other cases, the protagonist–soldier stands by helplessly, afraid to speak out lest he also be killed. When soldiers commit war crimes, the soldiers themselves feel the greatest effects, victimised by circumstance, the desire to survive, and the horrors of war. The actual victims are anonymous, and it is implied that some of them may have even been enemies in disguise.

It certainly makes sense that films targeted to U.S. audiences would focus on the experiences of U.S. troops, rather than foreign civilians. It also makes sense that these films would gloss over the complexities of international law, choosing to examine emotions over facts. Again, films are art, not journalism. Nevertheless, as discussed below, fictional stories can have real–life effects.

1.4 The Influence of War Films on Perception and Public Policy

Numerous studies have documented how films can shape a viewer's opinions and attitudes.[44] For example, viewing *Argo* (U.S., 2012, dir. Ben Affleck) and *Zero*

---

43 *Gandhi* 2022.
44 *Kubrak* 2020.

Dark Thirty (U.S., 2012, dir. Kathryn Bigelow) influenced one–third of viewers to change their answers to the question, "How would you rate the job being done by the military?"[45] Other studies have recognised a link between the viewer's emotional involvement in the film and the film's effect on the viewer.[46] War crime films contain emotionally charged scenes of combat, along with easily recognised "good" and "bad" characters, which may increase the influence of these types of films on the viewing audience.[47]

Although academic studies tend to focus on small groups of viewers, history reveals instances where the lines between cinema and the real world have blurred. With regard to films depicting the military and combat, several have influenced U.S. military recruitment over the years. A well–known example is the effect of *Top Gun* (U.S., 1986, dir. Tony Scott) on U.S. Navy recruitment, which increased by about 8% after the film's release.[48] Popular media has even influenced U.S. military policy. In an instance of real–life mirroring the silver screen, the 2003 military operation to capture Saddam Hussein was designated "Operation Red Dawn," inspired by the 1984 film *Red Dawn* (U.S., dir. John Milius).[49]

For many reasons, war films can influence audiences more than other genres. For one, the vast majority of viewers will not have firsthand combat experience, and most will not have travelled to the foreign lands that provide the films' setting. Therefore, the films' illustrations of war are not competing with the viewers' lived experiences. Additionally, war films, especially war crime films, are based on real–life events. As discussed earlier in this chapter, war crime films borrow heavily from true stories, while concurrently altering facts to simplify storylines and increase emotional depth. Although audiences could watch news reports or documentaries instead of a dramatisation, many more will turn to a film. For instance, Dan Krauss's film *The Kill Team* (2019) had box office returns of about $372,000; the documentary version (2013) brought in just about $19,000.[50]

Blurring the lines even further, the U.S. Department of Defense (DoD) sometimes plays a role in the development and production of military–themed films.[51] Both *Top Gun* (1986) and its sequel, *Top Gun: Maverick* (U.S., 2022, dir. Joseph Kosinski) benefited from using actual military resources (e.g., aircraft, facilities) and receiving input from military advisors.[52] Other notable films made with DoD support include *Clear and Present Danger* (U.S.,1994, dir. Phillip Noyce), *Black Hawk Down* (U.S.,

---

45 *Pautz* 2015, p. 127.
46 *Kubrak* 2020.
47 *Pautz* 2015.
48 *Hunt* 2022.
49 *Huiskamp* et al. 2016, pp. 502–505.
50 The Numbers n.d.
51 *Timmer* 2014, pp. 327–329.
52 *Hunt* 2022.

2001, Ridley Scott), and *Windtalkers* (U.S., 2002, dir. John Woo).[53] Although viewers might believe that films backed by the U.S. military would be more authentic than otherwise, DoD policy generally only permits support to films when it would be "in the best interest of the Nation," based on factors such as "benefit[ing] Military Service recruiting and retention programs."[54] Thus, a war film may have the feel of a military documentary while presenting as, perhaps even sanitised, version of real–life events.

All these factors contribute to the outsize influence that war films can have on real–life perceptions and policy. When it comes to films that depict war crimes, the primary thematic messages identified earlier in this chapter can affect how the public views IHL, war crime violations, and their victims. Shallow characterisations of civilians in foreign countries can perpetuate stereotypes. In extreme circumstances, the "secret terrorist" trope often applied to Iraqi and Afghan characters can sow real–world mistrust, even hate.[55] War crime films can also simplify complex issues, such as the status of children who are forced to bear arms. In *American Sniper*, a child with a weapon is a target that the protagonist rightfully, if reluctantly, kills. In real life, children are frequently victims of war crimes, and conscripting children into combat is a violation of international law.[56] The film does not explore this latter point, nor is it required to; indeed, such a digression could detract from the primary narrative. However, the absence of a more complex depiction of IHL in war films leaves viewers with an incomplete picture of combat and international law.

To be certain, many films exist that provide a thoughtful, balanced exploration of warfare and international law. Some are documentaries, like *Taxi to the Dark Side* (U.S., 2007, dir. Alex Gibney) and *The Road to Guantanamo* (U.K., 2006, dir. Michael Winterbottom). Others use alternative formats, such as the animated film *Grave of the Fireflies* (Japan, 1988, dir. Isao Takahata), portraying Japanese children in the aftermath of bombings during World War II. However, these films are not as widely viewed as popular U.S. war films. *American Sniper*, for instance, generated box office returns of over a half–billion dollars worldwide,[57] and the film was nominated for several Academy Awards.[58]

Ultimately, this chapter is not an indictment of any particular war film. Popular media, such as film, are a form of art and a source of entertainment. Hollywood directors are not held to the fact–checking standards of journalists. Nevertheless, for many viewers, a "realistic" war film, "based on a true story," will serve as both entertainment and education about warfare and war crimes.

---

53 *Timmer* 2014, pp. 328-329, n. 4–5.
54 U.S. Department of Defense 2015.
55 *Gandhi* 2022.
56 International Committee of the Red Cross 2023a.
57 Box Office Mojo n.d.
58 *Hipes* 2015.

1.5 Conclusion

A fundamental characteristic of a state is the ability to enter into international agreements, such as treaties, with other states. The legitimacy of a system of international laws relies on cooperative concepts such as reciprocity and comity between states. When it comes to the law of armed conflict, a state's willingness to abide by IHL may be influenced by how it perceives the willingness of other states also to obey the law.

In turn, the global perception of U.S. attitudes toward war crimes is shaped, in part, by U.S. war films. The global impact of Hollywood films is well documented.[59] Indeed, when it comes to war films, the U.S. government has at times worked deliberately to influence both domestic and international sentiments toward U.S. military policy.[60] However, as this chapter has discussed, the depiction of war crimes in U.S. films frequently demonstrates a shallow, nationalistic understanding of the protections that IHL affords civilians in wartime. Although the primary purpose of Hollywood films is to entertain, rather than educate, U.S. policymakers should be sensitive to their large–scale influence on public perceptions of warfare and the military.

Bibliography

International Treaties

Convention for the Amelioration of The Condition of The Wounded in Armies in The Field, Aug. 22, 1864, 22 Stat. 940.

Convention with Respect to The Laws and Customs of War by Land (Hague II), July 29, 1899, 32 Stat. 1803.

Convention Relative To The Treatment Of War Prisoners, July 27, 1929, 47 Stat. 2021.

Geneva Convention (I) for the Amelioration of the Condition of Wounded and Sick in Armed Forces in the Field, Aug. 12, 1949, 6 U.S.T. 3114; 75 U.N.T.S. 31.

Geneva Convention (II) for the Amelioration of the Condition of Wounded, Sick and Shipwrecked Members of Armed Forces at Sea, Aug. 12, 1949, 6 U.S.T. 3217; 75 U.N.T.S. 85.

Geneva Convention (III) Relative to the Treatment of Prisoners of War, Aug. 12, 1949, 6 U.S.T. 3316; 75 U.N.T.S. 135.

Geneva Convention (IV) Relative to the Protection of Civilian Persons in Time of War, Aug. 12, 1949, 6 U.S.T. 3516; 75 U.N.T.S. 287.

---

59 *Maisuwong* 2012, pp. 4–6.
60 *Guan* et al. 2023, p. 3.

Montevideo Convention on the Rights and Duties of States, Dec. 26, 1933, 49 Stat. 3097; 165 L.N.T.S. 19.

Other Sources

Basinger, Jeanine, 2003: The World War II Combat Film. Anatomy of a Genre. Middletown, CT: Wesleyan University Press.

Baxter, Robin, 2023: Every war film that has won the 'Best Picture' Oscar. In: Far Out Magazine, Dec. 16. At: https://faroutmagazine.co.uk/every-war-film-won-best-picture-oscar/ (Accessed on 3 January 2024).

Box Office Mojo, n.d.: American Sniper (2014). At: https://www.boxofficemojo.com/title/tt2179136/?ref_=bo_se_r_1 (Accessed on 5 January 2024).

Brooks, Rosa Ehrenreich, 2004: War Everywhere. Rights, National Security Law, and the Law of Armed Conflict in the Age of Terror. In: University of Pennsylvania Law Review, 153:2, pp. 675–761.

Brown, Gary D., 1998: Prisoner of War Parole: Ancient Concept, Modern Utility. In: Military Law Review, 156:1, pp. 200–223.

Cherry, John/*Rizzotti*, Michael, 2021: Understanding Self–Defense and the Law of Armed Conflict. In: Articles of War, The Lieber Institute, West Point, Mar. 9. At: https://lieber.westpoint.edu/understanding-self-defense-law-armed-conflict/ (Accessed on 27 December 2023).

Ching, Ann, 1999: Evolution of the Command Responsibility Doctrine in Light of the Celebici Decision of the International Criminal Tribunal for the Former Yugoslavia. In: North Carolina Journal of International Law, 25:1, pp. 167–205.

Ching, Ann, 2017: Military Justice in Film. In: *Rafter*, Nicole/*Brown*, Michelle (eds.), The Oxford Encyclopedia of Crime, Media, and Popular Culture. Oxford, U.K., Oxford University Press (online version).

Corn, Geoffrey, 2023: The Case for Attempted Perfidy: An "Attempt" to Enhance Deterrent Value. In: Journal of National Security Law & Policy, 13:3, pp. 401–447.

Crowther, Bosley, 1943: 'Bataan,' Film of Heroic Defense of Peninsula, Starring Robert Taylor, Robert Walker and Thomas Mitchell, at Capitol. In: The New York Times, June 4.

Faint, Charles, 2023: What Percentage of Americans Ever Served in the US Military? In: The Havok Journal, October 30. At: https://havokjournal.com/veterans-3/what-percentage-of-americans-ever-served-in-the-us-military/ (Accessed on 3 January 2024).

Fisher, Ryan (ed.), 2022: Operational Law Handbook. Charlottesville, VA: National Security Law Department, The Judge Advocate General's Legal Center & School.

Floyd, Stephen, 2023: The Targeting of Undersea Communications Cables: Armed Conflict, Developing States & the Need for a TWAIL Approach. In: Minnesota Journal of International Law, 32:2, pp. 39–92.

Gandhi, Insiya, 2022: Reel to Real: Harmful Stereotypes of Arabs and Muslims in American Film and Television. In: Rhetorikos: Excellence in Student Writing, Fall. At: https://rhetorikos.blog.fordham.edu/?p=1738# (Accessed on 4 January 2024).

Guan, Miaofang et al., 2023: Winning Hearts and Minds: Soft Power, Cinema, and Public Perceptions of the United States and China in Brazil. In: Global Studies Quarterly, 3:2, pp. 1–10.

Hipes, Patrick, 2015: Oscar Nominations: 'Grand Budapest Hotel' & 'Birdman' Lead Way With 9 Noms; 'Imitation Game' Scores 8. In: Deadline, January 15. At: https://deadline.com/2015/01/oscar-nominations-2015-full-list-academy-award-nominees-1201350619/ (Accessed on 5 January 2024).

Huiskamp, Gerard et al., 2016: Watching War Movies in Baghdad: Popular Culture and the Construction of Military Policy in the Iraq War. In: Polity, 48:4, pp. 496–523.

Hunt, Aaron, 2022: How the US Military Gave Notes on Top Gun: Maverick. In: GQ, June 24. At: https://www.gq.com/story/top-gun-maverick-military-advisor-interview (Accessed on 5 January 2024).

International Committee of the Red Cross, 2023: Child Soldiers. ICRC Casebook. At: https://casebook.icrc.org/a_to_z/glossary/child-soldiers (Accessed on 5 January 2024).

International Committee of the Red Cross, 2023: States Party to the Following International Humanitarian Law and Other Related Treaties as of 25-September-2023. At: https://ihl-databases.icrc.org/public/refdocs/IHL_and_other_related_Treaties.pdf (Accessed on 14 January 2024).

Kiel, John L., 2012: War Crimes in the American Revolution: Examining the Conduct of Lt. Col. Banastre Tarleton and the British Legion During the Southern Campaigns of 1780–1781. In: Military Law Review, 213:1, pp. 29–64.

Kubrak, Tina, 2020: Impact of Films: Changes in Young People's Attitudes after Watching a Movie. In: Behavioral Sciences, No. 10(5). At: https://doi.org/10.3390/bs10050086 (Accessed on 5 January 2024).

Lang, Daniel, 1969: Casualties of War. In: The New Yorker, October 18, 1969, pp. 61–146.

MacAskell, Ewen/*Howard*, Michael, 2007: US Soldier Sentenced to 100 years for Iraq Rape and Murder. In: The Guardian, February 23. At: https://web.archive.org/web/20160820102607/https://www.theguardian.com/world/2007/feb/23/usa.iraq (Accessed on 3 January 2024).

Maisuwong, Wanwarang, 2012: The Promotion of American Culture through Hollywood Movies to the World. In: International Journal of Engineering Research & Technology, 1:4, pp. 1–7.

Montazzoli, Matt, 2021: Down is Not Always Out: Hors de Combat in the Close Fight. In: Articles of War, The Lieber Institute, West Point, July 8. At: https://lieber.Westpoint.Edu/down-not-always-out-hors-de-combat-close-fight/ (Accessed on 27 December 2023).

Nash Information Services, n.d.: The Numbers. At: https://www.the-numbers.com/custom-search?searchterm=The+Kill+Team (Accessed on 5 January 2024).

Noone, Gregory P., 2004: Prisoners of War in the 21st Century. In: Naval Law Review, 50:1, pp. 1–69.

Pautz, Michelle C., 2015: *Argo* and *Zero Dark Thirty*: Film, Government, and Audiences. In: Political Science & Politics, 48:1, pp. 120–128.

Sun-Tzu, 1910: Sun-Tzu on the Art of War. Translated by Lionel Giles. London, Luzac and Co.

Thompson, Simon, 2019: Fact, Fiction and the Importance of Seeking the Truth with 'The Kill Team.' In: Forbes, October 24. At: https://www.forbes.com/sites/simonthompson/2019/10/24/fact-fiction-and-the-importance-of-seeking-the-truth-with-the-kill-team/ (Accessed on 3 January 2024).

Timmer, Joel, 2014: Viewpoint Discrimination in the Military's Filmmaker Assistance Program and the First Amendment. In: Communication Law and Policy, 19:3, pp. 327–365.

U.S. Department of Defense, DoD Instruction 5410.16, DoD Assistance to Non-Government, Entertainment-Oriented Media Productions, July 31, 2015. At: https://www.esd.whs.mil/Portals/54/Documents/DD/issuances/dodi/541016p.pdf (Accessed on 5 January 2024).

U.S. Senate, n.d.: About Declarations of War by Congress. At: https://www.senate.gov/about/powers-procedures/declarations-of-war.htm (Accessed on 29 December 2023).

von Zielbauer, Paul, 2007: Army Says Improper Orders by Colonel Led to 4 Deaths. In: The New York Times, January 21. At: https://www.nytimes.com/2007/01/21/world/middleeast/21abuse.html (Accessed on 3 January 2024).

Michael Asimow

All's Fair in Love and War. Military Justice in the Movies

The title of this chapter is ironic: All is *not* fair, either in love or in war, particularly not in the administration of military justice. This chapter surveys military justice in English–language films (I will save fairness in love for another occasion). A consistent theme that runs through the cinematic representations of this subject is that military justice is inferior to civilian criminal justice.[1] In particular, military justice films often emphasise abuse of the following orders defence and tampering by superiors with the court martial process, especially by exercising command influence.

Pop culture media are designed to entertain mass audiences and turn a profit. At their best, movies and television tell captivating stories about strong and nuanced characters toward whom viewers feel empathy or antipathy. Normally these stories are intended to serve as light entertainment to be pleasurably consumed and quickly forgotten. But all of us who participate in popular culture studies believe that pop culture is much more than slick and forgettable mass entertainment. We believe that pop cultural representations are important and worthy of serious study. Such representations function both as a mirror and a lamp, meaning that they broadly reflect public opinion as well as constructing and reinforcing public opinion. In addition, pop culture is valuable because it highlights societal problems, including defects in the justice system and in the legal profession. And so it is with movies about military justice. These films focus on deep flaws inherent in military justice, including command influence and abuse of the following orders defence.[2]

Part 1 discusses the law of command influence and the following orders defence. Part 2 discusses movie representations of command influence and other forms of

---

1 In fact, the opposite is probably true. The American military justice system contains numerous safeguards for the accused that are absent in the civilian justice system. See *Asimow/Silbey* 2020, pp. 232-34.

2 Of course, these are not the only flaws inherent in military justice as it appears in the movies. *Billy Budd* (U.S. 1962, dir. Peter Ustinov), for example, concerns the injustice of court-martials administered by commanding officers on the spot and the application of military law with extreme severity. For a different analysis of military justice films, see *Khoday* 2018. Khoday's article emphasises films that positively represent military personnel who resist illegal or unwise orders and who expose wrongdoing by superior officers.

tampering by superior officers. Part 3 discusses films that focus on abuse of the following orders defence. Part 4 concludes.[3]

1. The Law of Command Influence and the Following Orders Defence

1.1. Command Influence

Command influence is an enduring problem of military justice. It refers to interference through the exercise of influence or other forms of tampering by superior officers with the witnesses, judges, or jury of a court–martial. In the field of military justice, a commander's power properly includes the discretion whether to convene a court–martial to consider serious forms of punishment for military offences or to accept a plea bargain adjudging some lesser punishment. It also includes the choice of military personnel to serve as prosecutors and jurors. Interference with the court martial process that goes beyond these powers is considered command influence.[4]

The Uniform Code of Military Justice (UCMJ), the U. S. statute that regulates the military justice system, firmly prohibits command influence. Under Article 37(a)(1) of the UCMJ,

> "No court–martial convening authority, nor any other commanding officer, may censure, reprimand, or admonish the court or any member, military judge, or counsel thereof, with respect to the findings or sentence adjudged by the court, or with respect to any other exercise of its or his functions in the conduct of the proceeding."[5]

---

3 The subject of military justice on television is beyond the scope of this chapter. However, it is worth noting that *JAG* (U.S., 1995-2005) was an important American television series about the military justice system. It ran a remarkable ten years and included 227 episodes (*Wikipedia*, *JAG*). It consistently portrayed the military justice system in a positive and patriotic way. Smith points to the pro-military perspective of the show. "Unlike some law shows and films in which negative stereotypes of civilian lawyers are emphasised to attract a larger audience, or lawyers are depicted as politically motivated, *JAG* played to a different audience – one that wanted to see the American military and its lawyers portrayed as just and fair." (*Smith* 2009, p. 153). *NCIS* (U.S. 2003-) is a spinoff from *JAG* that has run for 21 years and is still going strong. It is a military police procedural. The title stands for Naval Criminal Investigative Service. See Wikipedia, *NCIS*.

4 See *Bedi* 2016, which summarises the history of the command influence problem in British and American military justice. Bedi argues that the military law's current protection against command influence is more robust than the comparable doctrines providing for oversight of misconduct by civilian prosecutors.

5 10 U.S. Code § 837(a)(1). This provision spells out additional detailed provisions preventing interference with witnesses or any form of coercion. It also prohibits a commanding officer in the preparation of a personnel report from taking account of the performance of a court-martial member or because of the zeal with which counsel represented any person in a court-martial proceeding. *Id.* § 837(b).

Nevertheless, prohibitions on the exercise of command influence often come into conflict with military culture. The court–martial convening authorities are not lawyers and sometimes resent the constraints imposed on them by the legalistic court–martial system. They have many opportunities to influence court–martials through choosing the jurors and covertly influencing witness testimony. As a result, American court–martial judges and military appellate courts have decided numerous cases dealing with cases of command influence. This body of law is generous to defendants. The government carries the burden of showing command influence did not exist. When it appears, the military judge must fashion an appropriate remedy that might involve a new trial or even dismissal of all charges.[6] While blatant interference with courts–martial is probably infrequent, the reality is that there are many opportunities in the military justice system for the exercise of subtle forms of command influence.

An important change in U.S. military justice procedure occurred in 2023. Command officers no longer have power to convene a court–martial arising out of sexual violence or harassment. The prosecutorial decision is lodged in a new unit of the Judge Advocate General (JAG) Corps, the agency that provides both prosecutors and defence lawyers in the court–martial system.[7] This change occurred out of concern that commanding officers tolerated sexual violence and intimidation among their troops as a lesser evil occurring because of gender desegregation in the military and they did not want to subject their troops to military discipline because of it.

1.2 The Following Orders Defence[8]

The legal issues relating to following orders can arise in three different contexts. First, a soldier might be prosecuted for refusing to follow orders from a superior officer (for example, for refusing an order to kill prisoners). The soldier could defend by arguing that the order was illegal and therefore it would have been illegal to follow it. Second, soldiers might be prosecuted for a crime (such as killing prisoners) and defend by claiming they were following orders to carry out the

---

6 See *United States v. Douglas,* 68 M.J. 349 (Ct..App. Armed Forces, 2010), which involved efforts by the defendant's commanding officer to intimidate the defendant and the witnesses.

7 Fact Sheet: President Biden To Sign Executive Order Implementing Bipartisan Military Justice Reforms (July 28, 2023), 2023 WL 4840631. The Executive Order stated: "The historic reforms announced today will better protect victims and ensure prosecutorial decisions are fully independent from the chain of the command. They follow decades of tireless efforts by survivors, advocates, and Members of Congress, to strengthen the military justice system's response to gender-based violence and build on recommendations from the Independent Review Commission on Sexual Assault in the Military…".

8 See *Khoday* 2018, pp. 388-391.

illegal acts. Third, superior offices could be prosecuted for giving illegal orders.[9] This discussion will concentrate on the second issue – when a soldier claims the following orders defence.

The Nuremberg trials after World War II established that the accused German officials and military officers could not claim a following–orders defence to prosecution for genocide and other war crimes. In the *Einsatzgruppen Case*, the Nuremberg tribunal wrote:

> "The obedience of a soldier is not the obedience of an automaton. A soldier is a reasoning agent…The fact that a soldier may not, without incurring unfavourable consequences, refuse to drill, salute, exercise, reconnoitre, and even go into battle, does not mean he must fulfil every demand put to him…The subordinate is bound only to obey the lawful orders of his superior and if he accepts a criminal order and executes it with a malice of his own, he may not plead superior orders in mitigation of his offence.[10]

Contrary to the implication from the Nuremberg decision, the following orders defence is alive and well.[11] Under the U. S. Manual for Courts–Martial: "It is a defence to any offence that the accused was acting pursuant to orders *unless* the accused *knew* the orders to be unlawful [a subjective standard] *or* a person of ordinary sense and understanding would have known the orders to be unlawful [an objective standard] "[12]

The following–orders defence is inherently problematic. Military discipline depends on soldiers following orders from superior officers.[13] As the Manual states, "an order requiring the performance of a military duty or act may be inferred to be lawful, and it is disobeyed at the peril of the subordinate. This inference does

---

9   See *Majesky* 2013, p.138. Majesky argues that the high-level officials who ordered torture of prisoners in military detention facilities during America's Iraq War should have been prosecuted as well as the low-level military personnel who carried out the orders. In *Rules of Engagement*, discussed in part 2.3, Col. Chiders is prosecuted for giving an illegal order to murder civilians. In *A Few Good Men*, discussed in part 3.1, Jessep and Kendrick are arrested at the end of the film, presumably for perjury and obstruction of justice as well as for giving illegal orders.

10 *Minow* 2007, pp. 17-18. Minow points out that while the Nuremberg tribunal disallowed the defence of following illegal orders, it permitted consideration of whether the defendant followed orders in considering the level of punishment.

11 For discussion of the history and the current status of the following orders defence in international law and U. S. military law, see *Bedi* 2014, pp. 2111-2127; *Hobel* 2011, pp. 578-592.

12 Manual for Courts-Martial, Rule 916(d), p. II-129 (emphasis added). See United States v. Calley, 48 C.M.R. 19 (1973), involving prosecution for war crimes resulting from the My Lai massacre during the Vietnamese War. The *Calley* case held that under the objective test, a person of common sense and understanding would know that an order to murder civilians was illegal. In international law, the objective standard is frequently stated as the order was not "manifestly unlawful" such as orders to commit genocide or crimes against humanity.

13 Art. 90 of the UCMJ provides that a person who wilfully disobeys a lawful command in time of war shall be punished by death or such other punishment as a court-martial may direct.

not apply to a patently illegal order, such as one that directs the commission of a crime."[14]

Consequently, soldiers are very likely to follow orders from superior officers without challenging their legality. Military personnel are trained to follow orders unquestioningly and the consequences of refusing to follow an order in battle can be very serious. This situation is confusing to both officers and enlisted personnel alike. Telling soldiers they face punishment unless they disobey illegal orders means telling them to think for themselves and question authority. Yet, directing them to question the legality of their orders undermines their training and group discipline and risks the lives of all concerned.

The objective standard is equally troubling. Who is this person of "ordinary sense and understanding" who would have known the orders were illegal?[15] Has that person had the same training as the defendant and undergone the same experiences and lived in the same military environment? Does that person of "ordinary sense and understanding" understand the full context of the order?

Psychological research indicates that it is doubtful that ordinary soldiers can resist following illegal orders. The famous Milgram experiments suggests that they are quite unlikely to do so. Milgram set up an experiment in which volunteers thought they were administering electric shocks to students who were supposed to be learning a list of words. They were told to turn up the voltage when the students made a mistake. Of course, the "students" were actors who were not actually receiving shocks. In the experiments, about two–thirds of the volunteers followed orders to turn up the voltage to the maximum despite screams of agony from the "students." Milgram showed that ordinary people will follow morally repellent orders if the person giving the orders seems to be legitimate and authoritative and states that he will take responsibility if any of the "students" are harmed.[16]

Similarly, conformity studies show that most people are likely to go along with the group. Conformity appeals to those who want to avoid being ridiculed or rejected by peers. Conformity pressures increase in groups with cohesive ties built by affection or mutual dependence, as occurs in the military.[17] Thus the realities of

---

14 Manual for Courts-Martial, pp. IV–24.
15 See *Bedi* 2014, pp. 2128–2131.
16 See *Minow* 2007, pp. 30-33. Milgram wrote: "Obedience is as basic an element in the structure of social life as one can point to. Some system of authority is a requirement of all communal living, and it is only the man dwelling in isolation who is not forced to respond, through defiance or submission, to the commands of others. Obedience, as a determinant of behaviour, is of particular relevance to our time. It has been reliably established that from 1933 ... 45 millions of innocent persons were systematically slaughtered on command. Gas chambers were built, death camps were guarded; daily quotas of corpses were produced with the same efficiency as the manufacture of appliances. These inhumane policies may have originated in the mind of a single person, but they could only be carried out on a massive scale if a very large number of persons obeyed orders." (*Milgram* 1963, p. 371).
17 *Minow* 2007, pp. 33–35.

military life as well as psychological data suggest court–martial judges should be receptive when defendants assert the defence that they were obeying orders even when those orders were illegal.

2. Command Influence in the Movies

Numerous court–martial movies have centred on command influence and other forms of tampering by superior officers with the military justice process. This part discusses a number of these films.

2.1. Breaker Morant

Breaker Morant (Aus, dir. Bruce Beresford,1980)[18] provides a powerful account of command influence in military justice as well as disregard of the following orders defence (as discussed in Part 3.2). The Boer War (1899–1902) was a brutal struggle between the British, who wanted to gain control over South Africa and its mineral resources, and the Boers (Dutch settlers now called Afrikaners) who sought to expel the British. The British confined many Boers to concentration camps where the death rate from disease was extreme.

To combat the Boers' guerrilla tactics ("a new war for a new century") the British organise an elite unit made up mostly of Australians called the Bushveldt Carbineers. Lieutenant Harry "Breaker" Morant (Edward Woodward), Lieutenant Peter Handcock (Bryan Brown), and Lieutenant George Witton (Louis Fitz–Gerald) are members of the Carbineers. The Carbineers are lured into an ambush during which Morant's close friend and commanding officer, Captain Simon Hunt, is killed. Morant takes command of the unit and hunts down the Boers responsible for the ambush. In a fury, he orders the execution of a captive, Dennis Visser, who was wearing Hunt's uniform. At a later point, Morant orders the execution of Boer prisoners, including some who surrendered under a white flag. Witton participates in this execution. Morant also orders Handcock to kill Reverend Hesse, a German

---

18 The film *Breaker Morant* is based on historic facts, but there is extensive controversy among historians about many aspects of Morant's life and about numerous aspects of the case. Morant and Handcock have become Australian folk heroes and there have been efforts to obtain a posthumous pardon for them. On the other hand, many South Africans believe that Morant and Handcock's punishment was appropriate and other members of the Carbineers should have been punished as well. There is a thorough summary of the differing historic and popular opinions in *Wikipedia, Breaker Morant.* Further discussion of these issues is beyond the scope of this Chapter.

missionary, who had spoken to the prisoners against Morant's orders and probably would have reported their killing.

Lord Kitchener is the British commander in South Africa. He orders the court–martial of Morant, Handcock, and Witton. Kitchener seeks to placate Germany, which is considering whether to join the war on the side of the Boers and was particularly disturbed by the killing of Hesse. As "colonials with bad habits," Australians are convenient and expendable scapegoats. Even the Australian government supports Kitchener's decision. The country has just been admitted to the British Commonwealth and wants to shed "lingering impressions of a frontier colony, frontier behaviour."

Kitchener is quite clear in his plans for the trial:

KITCHENER: The Boer leaders must see in this court–martial the demonstration of our impartial justice. If these three Australians have to be [pauses shortly] sacrificed to help bring about a peace conference, small price to pay.

Kitchener appoints Major Charles Bolton as the prosecutor. Major J. F. Thomas (Jack Thompson) represents the three defendants. Thomas was an Australian solicitor who specialized in land titles and wills and had never tried a case. Understandably, his clients do not trust him and initially, he appears incompetent. But once the trial begins, Thomas does his thankless job with great skill and courage. He is a true lawyer hero, the one positive character in this sordid story.

Command influence reduces the trial to a formalistic ritual that provides only an illusion of fairness and justice.[19] At a dinner party at the beginning of the film, the presiding judge, Lt. Col. H.C. Denny, expresses his contempt for Australians.

DENNY: It's a matter of discipline and tradition. Do you think this business could've happened with any contingent other than the Australians?"[20]

Thomas is given inadequate time to prepare for the trial. The presiding judge's evidentiary rulings prevent his introducing relevant evidence. Numerous prosecution witnesses testify falsely. As discussed in Part 3.2, the presiding judge reacts with outrage when the defence seeks to show that Kitchener gave illegal orders.

The three Carbineers are sentenced to death. Defence lawyer Thomas rushes to Kitchener's office to seek a stay of execution that would enable him to seek a pardon or a commutation, but Kitchener is conveniently unavailable. At sunrise the next morning, a firing squad executes Morant and Handcock. Witton's sentence is commuted to life at hard labour.

---

19 *Kershen* 1997, pp. 109-111.
20 *Van Patten* 2020, p. 112.

2.2. Paths of Glory

Stanley Kubrick's masterpiece *Paths of Glory* (U.S., 1957)[21] is one of the greatest anti–war films of all time. It also tells a heart–wrenching story of command influence. The film cuts between a gorgeous chateau, where the officers make politicised war plans and throw gala dances, and the filthy trenches where the troops who must fight the ghastly war are barely surviving.

General Broulard (Adolph Menjou) bribes General Mireau (George Macready) with a promotion if his weakened regiment assaults an impregnable German position called the Ant Hill. Mireau in turn entrusts Colonel Dax (Kirk Douglas) with the hopeless task. The attack fails miserably. The German fire is so intense that many of the men never leave the trenches. Most of those that did were slaughtered. In frustration, Mireau orders French artillery to fire on his own positions, but the gunners refuse to execute the order.

Mireau's career is on the line and he must find scapegoats to blame for the disaster. He convenes a general court–martial. At first, Mireau wants to put one hundred men on trial, but grudgingly reduces the number of defendants to three. One soldier is chosen to cover up for his superior officer who had botched a patrol. One is chosen by lot. And a third is chosen because his superior officer considers him a social undesirable. The charge is cowardice in the face of the enemy and the punishment is death. Yet, it is obvious that these soldiers were not guilty of cowardice. They tried to advance, but the suicidal attack had no chance of success and they had to retreat (indeed they were ordered to do so). Colonel Dax (formerly the best criminal lawyer in France) volunteers to serve as defence counsel.

Virtually everything that could be wrong with a military trial occurs in the rushed court–martial the following day. Procedural niceties like a written indictment or a transcript are dispensed with. Mireau observes the trial to make sure the judges follow the script. The judge rules out evidence that might show that the men were not cowards (such as citations for bravery in the past). Nor can Dax introduce evidence of the impossibility of the assault or the incompetence of the generals. His impassioned closing falls on deaf ears.

DAX: The case made against these men is a mockery of all human justice. Gentlemen of the court, to find these men guilty would be a crime to haunt each of you to the day you die.

---

21 For in-depth treatment of *Paths of Glory* and of its star Kirk Douglas, see *Abrams/Lipiner,* 2024. Their chapter analogises the court martial to Nazi justice and the banality of evil as well as to the Dreyfus affair in France. *King and Country* (U.K.,1964, dir. Joseph Losey) is often compared to *Paths of Glory.* It is a grim story of the hasty court martial of a British soldier in World War I. He is tried, convicted of desertion, and shot as an example to the troops, even though he was obviously suffering from shell shock.

The fact that the trial takes place at all demonstrates how trials are important cultural rituals. The process might be a sham, but some sort of trial must take place in order to legitimate the outcome.

Underlying the soldiers' convictions is the theory of collective guilt. Mireau believes the regiment as a whole is guilty of cowardice since it didn't take the Ant Hill or die trying. Three sacrificial lambs must bear the guilt of all. This idea of collective guilt is repellent. Even in conditions of deathly combat, there is no room for collective guilt in a civilised justice system.

2.3 Rules of Engagement

In *Rules of Engagement* (U.S., 2000, dir. William Friedkin),[22] high officials go beyond exercising command influence over a court martial and engage in outright obstruction of justice. The film concerns the court–martial of Colonel Terry Childers (Samuel L. Jackson), a decorated Marine officer, who leads a squad on a rescue operation in Yemen. A number of snipers in adjacent buildings, armed with automatic weapons, besiege the embassy with intense gunfire. In addition, a screaming mob is demonstrating outside the embassy. The squad manages to evacuate the terrified Ambassador Mourain (Ben Kingsley) and his family by helicopter. Mourain is extremely grateful to Childers for his professionalism under fire.

Childers returns to the roof of the embassy where his squad is taking heavy fire from the snipers. In addition, as we learn at the end of the film, Childers (alone among his men who are huddled below the parapet) can observe gunmen in the crowd of demonstrators below firing on the Marines. Several Marines are killed by gunfire coming either from the snipers or the demonstrators.

Childers orders his squad to "waste the motherfuckers," meaning open fire on the civilians below. Captain Lee, Childers' second in command, at first refuses to follow the order, but Childers repeats it. Eighty–three people (including women and children) are killed and many others wounded. This creates an enormous international incident and threatens U.S. relations with moderate Arab regimes. Childers is prosecuted for murder for giving the fateful order. National Security Adviser Bill Sokal (Bruce Greenwood) needs Childers to be convicted in order to provide a scapegoat on whom the massacre can be blamed—a familiar theme in military justice movies. To convict Childers under the applicable rules of engagement, the

---

22 *High Crimes* (U.S. 2002, dir. Carl Franklin) is another rigged court martial story similar to *A Few Good Men* (discussed below under 3.1.) and *Rules of Engagement*. In *High Crimes,* an ex-marine is court-martialled for killing civilians in El Salvador. The case was brought to cover up blunders and wrongdoing by military officials.

prosecution must prove that the only fire was coming from the snipers, in which case Childers' order to fire on civilian demonstrators would have been illegal.

Sokal withholds the facts from discovery and destroys a surveillance videotape that would have shown fire coming from the crowd. Sokal forces Ambassador Mourain to testify against Childers. Mourain falsely states that the crowd was peaceful and that Childers charged into the situation, possessed by a murderous rage. He also testifies falsely that Childers forced him to leave the embassy when he wished to stay. Unlike the more hard–hitting narratives of *Breaker Morant, A Few Good Men, and Paths of Glory,* the movie ends implausibly with Sokal and Mourain disgraced and Childers vindicated.

2.4 Man in the Middle

Man in the Middle (U.S., 1964, dir. Guy Hamilton) involves extreme command influence as well as tampering with evidence and witnesses. The film is situated at a joint British and American outpost in India during World War II.[23] American Lieutenant Charles Winston (Keenan Wynn) shot and killed a British non–com, Sergeant Quinn, in front of numerous witnesses. This caused serious friction between the American and British contingents in India. The American General Kempton desperately wants Winston to be convicted and executed for murder to smooth over the rift.

Lieutenant Colonel Barney Adams (Robert Mitchum) is a career military officer with little legal knowledge. He is forced to defend Winston. Winston is a raving racist who killed Sergeant Quinn because Quinn was seeing Indian women and also because Winston believed Quinn was undermining his own authority. It is apparent that Winston is suffering from severe psychiatric illness.

General Kempton and Colonel Burton, the hospital commander, are concerned that Winston might escape the death penalty by asserting an insanity defence. They do everything possible to prevent Adams from raising that defence. Major Kaufman, a qualified psychiatrist at the base hospital, examined Winston and opined that he was legally insane. Burton orders Kaufman's report destroyed and ships him off to a distant base. Burton appointed a "lunacy board" consisting of himself, a surgeon, and a dentist (none of them experts in psychiatry), that found Winston was sane. And Kempton strongly implies that Adams' promotion depends on his presenting only a token defence of Winston.

---

23 The movie was named *The Winston Affair* in some markets, which was also the title of the novel by Howard Fast from which it was adapted. For an excellent and appreciative analysis of the novel and the film, see *Nevins* 1996.

Early in the film, it appears that Adams is going to play along with his superiors in order to protect his own career. Later, however, Adams inexplicably changes into a zealous and self–sacrificial defender of his detestable client. Adams persuades Kaufman to testify at the trial, but Kaufman dies in a jeep accident on his way to the hearing. Adams stumbles onto a carbon copy of Kaufman's report, but it is unsigned and cannot be authenticated, so the law officer rules that it cannot be admitted. At the trial, Burton testifies that he cannot authenticate the report even though he admits to having read it. Winston leaps to his feet and delivers an insane rant. And British Major Kensington, a psychiatrist who knew Winston, testifies that he was insane. Perhaps uniquely in the courtroom genre, we never learn the court martial's verdict.

2.5. The Conspirator

The Conspirator (U.S., 2011, dir. Robert Redford) involves a military commission formed to try civilians suspected of conspiracy in the assassination of Abraham Lincoln in 1865.[24] Secretary of War, Edwin Stanton (Kevin Kline), orders formation of the commission which consists of nine Union generals.

The defendant, Mary Surratt (Robin Wright), owns a boarding house in Washington frequented by the conspirators including the actual assassin, John Wilkes Booth, and several other men, including Mary Surratt's son John (who has not been found and was a likely conspirator). The defence lawyer, Frederick Aiken (James McAvoy), is a young Union veteran with little legal experience. Aiken detests his client Mary Surratt and is given only one day to prepare. He disregards his client's admonition not to attempt to shift blame to John Surratt. Still, Aiken does a noble job in a hopeless cause, thereby earning the utter contempt of his friends and the entire community.

The military commission is little more than a uniformed lynch mob that provides a ceremonial function. There are no procedural protections for the accused, such as a jury trial, disclosure of the government's evidence, a reasonable doubt standard

---

24 For discussion of the historical basis for the film and of the trial proceedings, see *Lederman* 2018; *Asimow/Bergman* 2021, pp. 400-403. One year after the actions of the military commission, the Supreme Court ruled that civilians are entitled to be tried by civilian courts rather than military commissions, so long as civil courts are functioning. *Ex Parte Milligan,* 71 U.S. 2 (1866). Another devastatingly negative film about military commissions is *The Mauritanian* (U.S. 2021, dir. Kevin Macdonald). The film concerns U.S. military commissions at Guantanamo Bay, Cuba, formed to try detainees suspected of complicity in the bombing of the World Trade Center in 2001. The film concerns Mohamedou Ould Slahi who was detained from 2002 to 2016. He was subjected to torture and sexual abuse and was held without charges for many years. A civilian court issued a writ of habeas corpus that ordered him to be freed, but he was held another seven years pending appeal of that decision. The Guantanamo military commissions have been a total fiasco.

of proof, or any right of appeal. The judges reject Aiken's attempts to discredit prosecution witnesses. Defence witnesses change their stories as the result of pressure from the government. Stanton wants the commission to deliver a quick guilty verdict and a death sentence to appease the population's thirst for revenge. The commission obliges by finding Surratt guilty, but the generals vote to impose life in prison rather than the death penalty – until Stanton changes their minds. Aiken procures a writ of habeas corpus that requires the government to provide a new trial in a civilian court. But President Andrew Johnson suspends the writ and Surratt is hanged.

Due process is of little concern. As Stanton says to Senator Reverdy Johnson, who had persuaded the reluctant Aiken to take on Surratt's defence:

STANTON: This trial will do more to keep the peace than any paper treaty could. … Because justice, swift and firm, will help deter the South from ever conspiring again. As well as discouraging the North from seeking revenge.
JOHNSON: What about the rule of law?
STANTON: My first responsibility is to ensure that this war stays won…
JOHNSON: Abandoning the Constitution is not the answer.

3. The Following Orders Defence in the Movies

Several courtroom movies involved lower–level military personnel who follow the illegal orders given by their superiors. Their attempts to rely on the following orders defence (discussed in Part 1.2) are unavailing.

3.1 A Few Good Men

A Few Good Men[25] (U.S., 1992, dir. Rob Reiner) was a commercially successful and well–reviewed film. It provides a springboard for discussing the following orders defence. The movie is set at the U. S. Marine base at Guantanamo Bay, Cuba. In the film, Private Willie Santiago is an unhappy Marine desperate to transfer out of Guantanamo. Santiago observes Corporal Harold Dawson (Wolfgang Bodison) unlawfully fire a shot over the fence line into Cuban territory. Ignoring the chain of command, Santiago offers to disclose the identity of the shooter to anyone who might transfer him.

Soon thereafter, Dawson and Private Lowden Downey (James Marshall) subject Santiago to a "Code Red" hazing procedure and accidentally kill him. Dawson and Downey are charged with murder. Their defence is that their superior officer,

---

25 See discussion in *Khoday* 2018, pp. 402-404.

Lieutenant Jonathan Kendrick (Kiefer Sutherland) had ordered them to administer the Code Red. Code Red hazing was illegal because the Marines had officially abolished it.

Lieutenant Daniel Kaffee (Tom Cruise) is a brash neophyte in the Navy Judge Advocate General (JAG) Corps. His father was a famous military and trial lawyer who became Attorney General of the U.S. Kaffee has plea–bargained 44 cases and tried none of them. He cares more about the base softball team than about his clients. His superiors appoint him to represent Dawson and Downey, hoping that he will quietly make two more plea deals.[26] The prosecutor Captain Jack Ross (Kevin Bacon) offers Kaffee a favourable plea bargain in hopes the embarrassing case will go away, but Dawson and Downey turn it down.

Kaffee's team includes a seasoned JAG lawyer, Sam Weinberg (Kevin Pollak) and a zealous but rather inept lawyer working in Internal Affairs, Lieutenant Commander Joanne Galloway (Demi Moore). Kaffee, Weinberg and Galloway travel to Cuba to meet with Kendrick and Colonel Nathan Jessep (Jack Nicholson), the base commander. Jessep claims that he ordered that no harm come to Santiago, and Kendrick states he dutifully passed that order on to his men. Jessep also declares that he ordered that Santiago be transferred out on the first available military flight, which unfortunately was not scheduled to depart until the morning after he died. Dawson and Downey tell Kaffee that Kendrick ordered them to execute a Code Red on Santiago.

Ross offers evidence suggesting that Dawson and Downey attacked Santiago with intent to kill. Prosecution witnesses testify that the defendants forced a poisoned rag down Santiago's throat. Santiago's threat to report Dawson for the fence line shooting provided the defendants with a motive to kill Santiago, and the two men ignored Kendrick's order not to harm Santiago.

Kaffee's only hope is to put Jessep on the stand and induce him to admit he ordered the Code Red. Jessep is arrogant and insulting, but he unconvincingly loses his temper when Kaffee confronts him with inconsistencies in his story. Kaffee directly accuses Jessep of ordering the Code Red and destroying the records of a redeye flight that could have safely transferred Santiago out of Guantanamo the night that he was killed.

---

26 It is evident that this appointment was a sign of command influence. Kaffee was clearly unqualified to take on a case of such importance.

When Kaffee demands the truth, Jessep snarls:

JESSEP: You can't handle the truth... Santiago's death, while tragic, probably saved lives. And my existence, while grotesque and incomprehensible to you, saved lives. ...You want me on that wall, you need me on that wall... I have neither the time nor the inclination to explain myself to a man who rises and sleeps under the blanket of the very freedom that I provide, and then questions the manner in which I provide it...
KAFFEE: Did you order the Code Red?
JESSEP: You're goddamn right I did.

This startling and implausible admission causes prosecutor Ross to order that Jessep be arrested. Kendrick is next.[27] Dawson and Downey are found not guilty of murder. However, they are convicted of the "general offence," meaning engaging in conduct unbecoming a Marine, and they are dishonourably discharged.

The murder trial in *A Few Good Men* raises questions about when a soldier should be held responsible for following an illegal order issued by his superior. If Dawson and Downey had refused to administer a Code Red to Santiago, they would certainly have been punished for disobeying Kendrick's order. In theory, they could have defended by arguing that the Code Red was illegal under U. S. law because the Marines had banned Code Reds. However, they would have taken an enormous risk in refusing to follow Kendrick's order, given the stern disciplinary practices at Guantanamo and Kendrick's punishment of Dawson for failing to follow his orders in a prior case.[28]

However, Dawson and Downey did follow Kendrick's order. The question is whether they have a following orders defence to the charges against them. As previously discussed in Part 1.2, the accused in a court–martial proceeding can assert as a defence that the accused was acting pursuant to orders, unless the accused knew the orders to be unlawful *or* a person of ordinary sense and understanding would have known the orders were unlawful. The defence lawyers' debate whether the following orders defence should apply.

WEINBERG: An argument that didn't work for Calley at My Lai, an argument that didn't work for the Nazis at Nuremberg.
KAFFEE: Do you really think that's the same as two teenage Marines executing a routine order they never believed would result in harm? These guys aren't the Nazis.

---

27 For discussion of the culpability of the superior officer who issues an illegal order to subordinates, see *Mohamed* 2022.
28 Kendrick had ordered that Carter Bell be confined to barracks without food for seven days as discipline. Dawson disregarded the order by bringing Bell food. As a result, Kendrick gave Dawson a poor performance evaluation for refusing to follow an order. Kendrick made clear that he believed all superior orders had to be followed, regardless of the situation.

Later Weinberg and Kaffee renew their debate.

KAFFEE: They were following an order, Sam.
WEINBERG: An illegal order.
KAFFEE: You think Dawson and Downey knew it was an illegal order?
WEINBERG: It doesn't matter what they knew. Any decent human being would have refused to.
KAFFEE: They're not permitted to question orders.
WEINBERG: Then what's the secret? Huh? What are the magic words? I give orders every day and nobody follows them.
KAFFEE: We have softball games and marching bands. They work at a place where you have to wear camouflage or you might get shot.

And in his opening statement Kaffee strongly asserts the following orders defence:

KAFFEE: [I]if you're a Marine, assigned to Rifle Security Company Windward, Guantanamo Bay Cuba, and you're given an order, you follow it or you pack your bags. Make no mistake about it. Harold Dawson and Loudon Downey are sitting before you today because they did their job.

At the end of the film, Dawson accepts blame for his conduct. He tells Downey, "We were supposed to fight for people who couldn't fight for themselves. We were supposed to fight for Willie."

Nevertheless, this defence should have been accepted. Dawson and Downey were probably never told that the Marines had banned Code Reds, since these were commonly administered at Guantanamo as a disciplinary tactic. By the same token, a person of ordinary sense and understanding would not have known the order to be unlawful. The overriding fact is that the Marine Corps teaches unquestioning and immediate submission to orders. The Nuremberg precedent seems inapplicable since Kendrick ordered Dawson and Downey to "teach Santiago a lesson." This order relates to Marine Corps discipline, not manifestly illegal activities like the slaughter of civilians or the abuse of prisoners of war.

As a result, Dawson and Downey should not have been convicted of any offence, including the so-called "general offence." They should not, therefore, have been dishonourably discharged from the Marines. The jury's decision seems to be a compromise (not guilty of murder, but guilty of the "general offence"), but the same legal principles apply to all offences.

Under the circumstances of tight Marine Corps discipline – and Dawson's previous problems with Kendrick for not following orders in the Carter Bell case – it seems unfair and unrealistic to punish the two Marines. Had they defied Kendrick's order (which after all came straight from Jessep), they would have been severely disciplined. They would never have an opportunity to assert the defence that the order was illegal because they would never have been prosecuted, just informally punished.

3.2. Breaker Morant

As already discussed under the topic of command influence (Part 2.1), *Breaker Morant* is a classic indictment of military justice. It also provides a good account of the abuse of the following–orders defence. Morant, Handcock and Witton are accused of killing prisoners. Major Thomas' defence is that Kitchener and his subordinates, including Captain Hunt, had issued unwritten orders to take no Boer prisoners.[29]

The court–martial judges are outraged at the suggestion that Kitchener and Hunt might have issued illegal orders to take no prisoners, and they reject the argument out of hand. To Thomas' request that Kitchener be made to appear at the court–martial to testify as to whether such orders had been issued, the presiding judge replies:

PRESIDING   You are impertinent, Major Thomas. Are you suggesting that the
JUDGE: most senior soldier in the British army, a man venerated throughout
              the world, would be capable of issuing an order of such barbarity?

At an earlier point, the court sustains objections to Thomas's questions to a witness, Captain Donald Robertson, on the subject of killing prisoners because the answer might incriminate the witness. Thomas has no way to prove that illegal orders were ever issued. Hunt is dead and Kitchener refuses to testify. Witnesses declare they never heard of such orders. Kitchener's aide, Colonel Hamilton, falsely denies that any such orders were issued or that he had so instructed Captain Hunt. Yet Kitchener's unwritten orders to "take no prisoners" were widely circulated in the Transvaal area and execution of prisoners was common. Indeed, defence witness Captain Taylor (an intelligence officer with the Carbineers) is asked "Did you know of any orders to shoot Boer prisoners?" He replies, "there was … an understanding."[30]

Under military law in effect at the time of the Boer War, the following–orders defence was generally accepted, regardless of the legality of the orders. Under modern law, as discussed in Part 1.2, the defence would be more doubtful because the following–orders defence cannot be asserted if a person of ordinary sense and understanding would have known the orders to be unlawful. However, under the

---

29 Kitchener had issued orders permitting the execution of prisoners "wearing khaki," but the presiding judge ruled that order applied only to prisoners who were intending to impersonate British troops. Visser was wearing Captain Hunt's uniform, but probably just to keep warm, not to impersonate a British soldier. See *Van Patten* 2020, p. 120.

30 *Van Patten* 2020, p. 124.

brutal conditions of guerilla fighting in the Transvaal, a reasonable person might well have believed the orders to take no prisoners were legal.

MORANT: As for rules, we didn't carry military manuals around with us. We were out there on the veldt, fighting the Boer the way he fought us. I'll tell you what rule we applied, sir. We applied rule 303. We caught them and we shot them under Rule 303 [referring to the caliber of their Enfield rifles].

Moreover, a reasonable person might have considered the orders to be lawful because the Carbineers had no way to confine or otherwise care for prisoners captured in the remote areas of the Transvaal where combat took place or to transport them to an area where they could be cared for.[31]

In any case, the killing of Boer prisoners was relatively common, but only Morant and Handcock were executed for it. At a minimum, the judges should have taken the novelty and harshness of guerilla warfare into account in determining the severity of the punishment meted out to Morant and Handcock. As Thomas argues in his closing:

THOMAS: The tragedy of war is that these horrors are committed by normal men in abnormal situations. Situations in which the ebb and flow of everyday life have departed and have been replaced by a constant round of fear and anger and blood and death. Soldiers at war are not to be judged by civilian rules, as the prosecution is attempting to do. Even though they commit acts, which, calmly viewed afterwards, could only be seen as un–Christian and brutal. And if in every war, particularly guerilla war, all the men who committed reprisals were to be charged and tried as murderers, court–martials like this one would be in permanent session, would they not? I say that we cannot hope to judge such matters unless we ourselves have been submitted to the same pressures, the same provocations as these men whose actions are on trial.

4. Conclusion

The military justice movies discussed in this chapter tell a consistent story of injustice arising out of risks that are inherent in the military justice system. So long as military justice is administered by military rather than civilian courts, these problems will continue to recur. Military trials, especially during war, are always part of the war. Superior officers must produce convictions because they need scapegoats to maintain authority or to carry out other tactical objectives. Hence, the non–lawyers in command have reason to exercise command influence or otherwise

---

31 *Kirschke* 2008, p. 52.

tamper with the trials. Similarly, superior officers sometimes issue illegal orders because war is brutal, and the end justifies the means. As the saying goes, "all's fair in love and war" and soldiers at the bottom of the pyramid must sometimes take the blame. Although modern military law strongly prohibits command influence and offers a robust following orders defence, these flaws in the military justice system are inescapable. The movies discussed in this chapter are a timely reminder of this tragic fact.

Bibliography

Abrams, Nathan/*Lipiner*, Michael, 2024: Macho–Menschlichkeit: Law and War in Stanley Kubrick's *Paths of Glory* (1957). In: *Machura*, Stefan (ed.), *Law and War in Popular Culture*. Baden–Baden, Nomos.

Asimow, Michael/*Bergman*, Paul, 2021: Real to Reel: Truth and Trickery in Courtroom Movies. Lake Mary, Florida, Vandeplas Publishing.

Asimow, Michael/*Silbey*, Jessica, 2020. Law and Popular Culture: A Course Book. 3d edition, Lake Mary, Florida, Vandeplas Publishing.

Bedi, Monu, 2016. Unravelling Unlawful Command Influence. In: Washington University Law Review, 93:6, pp. 1401–1460

Bedi, Monu, 2014. Entrapped: A Reconceptualization of the Obedience to Order Defence. In: Minnesota Law Review, 98:6, pp. 2103–2178.

Hobel, Mark W. S., 2011. So Vast an Area of Legal Irresponsibility: The Superior Orders Defence and Good Faith Reliance on Advice of Counsel. In: Columbia Law Review, 111:3, pp. 574–623.

Kershen, Drew L., 1997: Breaker Morant. In: Oklahoma City University Law Review, 22:1, pp. 107–128.

Khoday, Amar, 2018: Valorising Disobedience. In: Cardozo Arts and Entertainment Journal, 36:2, pp. 369–426.

Kirschke, James, J. 2008: Say Who Made Her So: Breaker Morant and British Empire. In: Film and History, Vol. 38:2, pp. 45–53.

Lederman, Martin. S., 2018: The Law (?) of the Lincoln Assassination. In: Columbia Law Review, 118:2, pp. 323–490.

Majesky, Robert, 2013: The Abu Ghraib Convictions: A Miscarriage of Justice. In: Buffalo Public Interest Journal, 32:1, pp. 103–173.

Manual for Courts–Martial, United States, 2023. At https://jsc.defense.gov/Portals/99/Docum ents/MCM%20editions/2023%20MCM%20(2023_08_30).pdf?ver=ungvu5HSVg1_o20I0 XEHwQ%3d%3d (Accessed on 15 November 2023)

Milgram, Stanley, 1963: Behaviour Study of Obedience. In: Journal of Abnormal and Social Psychology, 67:1, pp. 371–378.

Minow, Martha, 2007: Living Up to Rules: Holding Soldiers Responsible for Abusive Conduct and the Dilemma of the Superior Orders Doctrine. In: McGill Law Journal, 52:1, pp. 1–54.

Mohamed, Siara, 2022: Abuse by Authority: The Hidden Harm of Illegal Orders. In: Iowa Law Review, 107:5, pp. 2183–2246.

Nevins, Francis M., 1996: Man in the Middle: Unsung Classic of the Warren Court. In: University of San Francisco Law Review, 30:4, pp. 1097–1110.

Smith, Justin T., 2009. *JAG:* Maintaining the Front Lines of Justice. In: *Asimow*, Michael (ed.), Lawyers in Your Living Room. Chicago, American Bar Association, pp. 151–162.

Van Patten, Jonathan, 2020: The Trial of Breaker Morant. In: South Dakota Law Review, 65:1, pp. 104–144.

Wikipedia, *Breaker Morant*. At: https://jsc.defense.gov/Portals/99/Documents/MCM%20edi tions/2023%20MCM%20(2023_08_30).pdf?ver=ungvu5HSVg1_o20I0XEHwQ%3d%3d (last accessed on 15 November 2023).

Wikipedia, n.d., JAG. https://en.wikipedia.org/wiki/JAG_(TV_series) (Accessed on 15 November 2023).

Wikipedia, n.d., Milgram Experiment. At: https://en.wikipedia.org/wiki/JAG_(TV_series) (last accessed on 15 November 2023).

Wikipedia, n.d., NCIS. At: https://en.wikipedia.org/wiki/NCIS_(TV_series) (Accessed on 15 November 2023).

Nathan Abrams and Michael Lipiner

Macho–*Menschlichkeit*:
Law and War in Stanley Kubrick's *Paths of Glory* (1957)

Stanley Kubrick's landmark 1957 film *Paths of Glory* showcases the conjunction of law and war in the context of the French military during World War One. In exploring the film, this chapter will demonstrate how Kubrick's adaptation of *Paths of Glory* was determined by the circumstances of its making by drawing upon the prevailing cultural trends of the 1950s which include but are not limited to macho–*menschlichkeit*, the Holocaust, the Dreyfus Affair, Hollywood's representation of Jews and lawyers, the House UnAmerican Activities Committee, the war film, and the law film. The film also shows how the powers of the state can employ deeply unjust legal procedures against its citizens in time of war.

1. From Page to Screen

The source of the film was Canadian Humphrey Cobb's bleak, anti–war World War I novel, *Paths of Glory* – the title from a line in Thomas Gray's 1751 "Elegy Written in a Country Churchyard': 'The paths of glory lead but to the grave." Written in 1935, it was inspired by real events in 1915. The plot focuses on the hypocrisy of the French military high command when the general staff were willing to sacrifice an entire division in a hopeless and impossible attack on a fortified and impregnable German position known as "The Pimple" on the Western Front. When the suicidal attack inevitably fails, they need a scapegoat, and five soldiers are selected at random as blood sacrifices for the greater good of France. Court–martialled for cowardice and although ably defended by their commanding officer, the trial is nothing more than a mock formality designed to exonerate those in command. The men are found guilty and executed by firing squad. The innocent soldiers' widows and families then sued the French army for false and unjust accusations. Two decades later, before a military tribunal, the men were eventually acquitted, but their widows received only a pittance and their families nothing at all.[1] Shortly after publication, the novel was adapted for the stage by *Gone with the Wind* (U.S.A., 1939, dir. Victor Fleming) screenwriter Sidney Howard. After its Broadway

---

1 *Cobb* 1935, p. 181.

opening in 1935, it lasted just twenty–three performances. The *New York Times* critic Brooks Atkinson gave it a lukewarm review but presciently added: "Someday the screen will seize this ghastly tale and make a work of art from it."[2] Paramount Pictures initially bought the rights to Cobb's novel. Afraid of offending the French government, however, Paramount proposed changing the army to that of czarist Russia. Top General George Broulard (Adolphe Menjou) and Division Commander Paul Mireau (George Macready) exemplify Nicole Rafter's description of "injustice figures," namely people "responsible for creating or maintaining the gap between justice and man–made law."[3] They haughtily discuss taking the Ant Hill, a heavily fortified German–occupied region, even though this attack will undoubtedly result in losing most of their platoon.

Kubrick was unsure where and when he first read Cobb's novel, perhaps when he was fifteen. "It was one of the few books I'd read for pleasure in high school. I think I found it lying around my father's office and started reading it while waiting for him to get finished with a patient."[4] He remembered that it had "made an impression on me, not because of its literary qualities but because of the troubling and tragic situation of three of its characters – three [whittled down from the five in the novel] innocent soldiers accused of cowardice and mutiny who were executed to set an example."[5]

In 1956, Kubrick and his partner, James B. Harris, a Jewish producer from New York City, bought the rights to Cobb's novel. After Kubrick optioned the rights to *Paths of Glory*, he brought it to Kirk Douglas's Bryna Productions, a company the actor had established and named in honour of his Eastern European Jewish immigrant mother. Impressed by Kubrick's third film, *The Killing* (1956), Douglas agreed to star.[6]

2. The Macho–Mensch

As played by Kirk Douglas, the attacking Regiment's commander Colonel Dax is the embodiment of what Rebecca Alpert called the "macho mensch," which was emerging in Jewish–American popular culture at this time. This figure manifested three features: "he is an outstanding athlete; he is an ethical human being who displays his virtues through gentility and kindness; and he is demonstrably connected to his Jewish identity, marking his *menschlichkeit* through the attributes of loyalty and

---

2 *Atkinson* 1935, p. 24.
3 *Rafter* 2001, p. 10.
4 *Abrams* 2018, p. 46.
5 *Ibid.*
6 *Ibid.*

bravery."[7] He is also a "conqueror with a conscience," combining his power with morality. Broulard refers to "the keenness of [Dax's] mind," and Mireau describes Dax as "perhaps the foremost criminal lawyer in France." Such designations define Dax by his intellect, possessing what is known, approvingly, in Yiddish as *Yiddische kopf* (Jewish brains), tapping into a trend, predating the invention of cinema, whereby Jews are stereotypically defined by their minds.

Nathan Abrams contends that Kubrick was most likely attracted to Douglas for having defied the stereotypically "normal" but "weak, passive, ineffectual, intellectual Jew into one of macho toughness"[8] in the 1950s. This depiction provided a counterpoint to the Holocaust's images of Jewish weakness, victimhood, and passivity by the masculine, sturdy, and muscular Jewish actor.[9] As Kirsten Fermaglich explains,

"The stereotype of the weak or feminised Jewish man is a product of centuries of victimization: Jewish men were constructed as "others" often faced with substantial violence from non–Jews, and legally prevented from participating in traditionally masculine activities, such as bearing arms."[10]

This influenced the film. In Douglas's first scene in *Paths of Glory*, which has no equivalent in either the novel or the play, he is depicted stripped to the waist, as he washes his face from a basin of water, showcasing his muscular physique. The shot emphasises Douglas' build, beginning the full–frontal (pun intended) assault on antisemitic stereotypes of weak and defenceless Jews. (This enlargement of a key role beyond its original significance, occupied by a Jewish star, set a pattern that defined Kubrick's next three films: *Spartacus*, 1960; *Lolita*, 1962; and *Dr. Strangelove*, 1964.

As Dax, Douglas rejects age–old antisemitic stereotypes which traditionally depicted Jews as weak, passive, and averse to military involvement. For centuries, Jewish physiognomy and physiology were intertwined with notions of unmanliness, hysteria, and pathology, all bred by the lack of healthy, outdoor activity. Jewish legs and feet were characterised as unnatural and unsuited to war, making Jews seem "unfit" for military service as foot soldiers in the modern infantries of the newly created nation–states of the late nineteenth and early twentieth centuries. Such demeaning perceptions of Jewish weakness were embedded in U.S. society and its military, as well as having been devastatingly underlined by the Holocaust. Kubrick himself had been deemed unfit for military service,[11] perhaps fuelling his desire to recreate convincingly and accurately battle scenes as a form of compensation.

---

7   *Alpert* 2015, p. 109.
8   *Abrams* 2018, p. 57.
9   *Abrams* 2018, p. 72.
10 *Fermaglich* 2007, p. 33.
11 *Abrams* 2018, p. 47.

This unfitness for military service – where Jewish soldiers are often shady as well as laughable – was reflected in American cinema up to that point. In *Cohen Saves the Flag* (U.S.A., 1913, dir. Mack Sennett), two Jews at Gettysburg put romantic rivalry above the interests of the Union Army. The running joke about the lascivious and cowardly Private Lipinsky in *What Price Glory?* (U.S.A., 1926, dir. Raoul Walsh) is the size of his nose. And Sammy Cohen, who played Lipinsky, also played Sammy Nosenblum in *Plastered in Paris* (U.S.A., 1928, dir. Benjamin Stoloff). Knowledge of the Holocaust did not cause Hollywood to retire these tropes: *Air Force* (U.S.A., 1943, dir. Howard Hawks) finds time for the pratfalls of simpleton Corporal Weinberg. The same year in *Bataan* (U.S.A., 1943, dir. Tay Garnett), craven Corporal Feingold's bunions are the joke; he's still complaining about them as he dies face–down in a puddle. Corporal Gabby Gordon in *Objective, Burma!* (U.S.A., 1945, dir. Raoul Walsh) is a standard–issue daft Jewish soldier. In the film, Lieutenant Jacobs is tortured by the Japanese but passes on a vital message before dying. Jews increasingly die to impart benefit to other characters or even moral instruction to viewers. In *Stalag 17* (U.S.A., 1953, dir. Billy Wilder), Harry Shapiro is unreliable, vulgar and indebted — and lusts after female Russian prisoners. Private Jackie Rabin of Bethnal Green lightens the mood of *A Hill in Korea* (U.K., 1956, dir. Julian Amyes), complaining that he should have bribed his way out of National Service. More darkly, the spinelessness of Sergeant Nate Lewis of *Men in War* (U.S.A., 1957, dir. Anthony Mann) causes him to bolt, fatally, from a minefield. Benjamin Vos adds, "after the revelation of the Holocaust, whether consciously on the part of screenwriters or not, Jewish characters' deaths seem sometimes to take on meaning beyond their individual passing. Jewish deaths are now of universal significance, which is perhaps better than being irrelevant — but, it turns out, not much."[12]

However, Kubrick gives Dax a much bigger role as the sole saviour of these three soldiers. In doing so, he "is the only officer who has not let a gap develop between himself and his men."[13] Dax washes from a decorative porcelain bowl, the one luxury item he possesses, manifesting his desire to remain clean in a morally dirty world. Dax is such a *mensch* that he even selflessly volunteers to be court–marshalled by the generals instead of the men to be made an example.

The embodiment of *menschlichkeit*, Dax is a benevolent and heroic paragon of reason, compassion, virtue, humanity and justice, standing up for his ordinary men in the face of injustice and corruption. Honourable and highly ethical, he naively believes that some semblance of "truth" or "justice" might result from his actions. He believes that "the noblest impulse of man" is "his compassion for another." When Broulard offers Dax Mireau's position as Division Commander, he refuses,

---

12   *Vos* 2022.
13   *Walker et al.* 2000, pp. 51-52.

brazenly stating, "... you're a degenerate, sadistic old man. And you can go to hell before I apologise to you now or ever again!" Broulard simply replies, "You're an idealist, and I pity you as I would the village idiot." Thus, the righteous have no place in a dissolute society which values unfaltering conformity and condemns individuality.

Dax is a heroic and extremely sympathetic officer fighting the sociopathy of the general staff. He "is amplified from the marginal character depicted in the book to the central character." In doing so, Kubrick described Dax as "obviously morally superior" and was concerned with eliciting "the audience's sympathy."[14] Moreover, Douglas's portrayal of Dax defies what had been the traditional Hollywood depiction of lawyers. Stefan Machura asserts that male lawyers on film are frequently portrayed as wealthy with a tasteful lifestyle or as young and just starting their careers. He argues that in American films one's education at an elite law school is often mentioned.[15] Dax befits neither of these descriptions and therefore illustrates a fairly unique and new characterisation of a lawyer seeking justice without a capitalistic angle, which defies traditional Jewish stereotypes.

When given an exit strategy from the doomed attack – Broulard offers to place him on leave – Dax refuses to abandon his men and agrees to lead the charge on the Ant Hill, assuring his superior officer of success. Dynamic and brave, he heads the assault, returning to rally those troops who remained behind. A loyal officer, Dax returns to the front with his troops later on and has "never failed to live up to" Mireau's "credo" of "He's got to fight. He can't do that unless he's where the fighting is."

Later, in cinema, the legal profession became a stereotypical marker of Jewishness. Twice in their initial exchange, Dax trips up Mireau, giving the impression that he is much more intelligent than his superior officer. With lawyer–like precision, he punctures Mireau's circumlocutions forcing him to admit: "You're right on your toes this morning, Colonel. Even sharper than usual." Dax stresses his rhetorical and ethical authority, his blunt language contrasting with Mireau's banal clichés, suggesting Dax earned his rank through merit whereas Mireau obtained his through class privileges.

3. Echoes of the Holocaust

Although set on the Western Front during World War One and about the French military, behind the film lurks the Holocaust. Cobb wrote his novel, in 1935, two years into the regime of the Nazi Party in Germany, as Geoffrey Cocks notes, "at a

---

14   *Abrams* 2018, p. 67.
15   *Machura* 2007, p. 337.

time of renewed German threat from under the new Nazi government."[16] This was also around the same time as the shameful and belated restitution to the soldier's families which was intended to protect the French army's reputation.

Furthermore, Kubrick's film was shot in West Germany's Bavaria Film Studios in Geiselgasteig and the severely damaged Schleissheim castle – an eighteenth–century structure that had been bombed during the war. Located near Munich, just beyond the location of the shoot was the Dachau Concentration Camp memorial which Kubrick and Harris visited. "That was about the only time you started thinking about your Jewishness. It reminds you of all the atrocities and genocide that took place," Harris recalled[17] that Kirk Douglas felt, "the war was too close, and I still had deep feelings that I tried to hide. I kept telling myself that not all Germans had participated in the Holocaust [. . .] all Germans were not like that."[18] The French soldiers were played by German policemen – were any of them old enough to have participated in wartime atrocities? – and the crew included such personnel as Georg Krause who had worked throughout the Nazi period, shooting some of its best pilot films, production manager George von Block, who had served in the Luftwaffe and Hans Stumpf, one of the technical crew who was ex–Wehrmacht. Joe Turkel, who played Private Arnaud, recalled one incident where Stumpf was talking about the war and how great Germany was. He then demonstrated the technique of how to goosestep correctly:

> "[R]ight on the fucking stage, right there and I'm a Jew and Stanley's a Jew and we looked at each other. He [Stumpf] just thought 'I'm just telling you something that happened' and I'm saying to myself, 'This happened and millions died, you cocksucker.' I didn't say that. I thought it and Stanley I think thought the same thing and I said, 'What do you think of this Stanley?' And he said, 'Not good, let's get back to film–making.' And that was it."[19]

If it was a strange experience for these young Jewish men to work with those who may have been implicated in some of the greatest crimes of the twentieth century, they did not speak much about it, even during their trip to Dachau.

If Kubrick had feelings on any of this, we do not know what they were but arguably the context influenced his film. *Paths of Glory*'s opening title credits sequence is accompanied by France's national anthem "La Marseillaise." A natural choice for a film about France, it also ties into an earlier anti–Nazi film that appeared more than a decade beforehand. In Michael Curtiz's *Casablanca* (U.S.A., 1942), Warner Bros.'s attempt to push the U.S. into war in 1941/1942, resistance leader Victor Laszlo (played by Jewish actor Paul Henreid) orders a band to play the piece to

---

16 *Cocks* 2004, p. 93.
17 *Abrams* 2018, p. 54.
18 *Douglas* 1988, p. 329.
19 *Turkel* 2019.

drown out singing by Nazi soldiers. Furthermore, its lyrics uncannily resonate with the Holocaust:

> "They come right to our arms
> To slit the throats of our sons, our friends!
> [...]
> It is us that they dare to consider
> Returning to ancient slavery!
> [...]
> We will enter the pit
> When our elders are no longer there;
> There, we will find their dust and the traces of their virtues."

"La Marseillaise" also symbolised the abuse of power at the Birkenau concentration camp with inmate musicians recalling being forced by Nazi guards to perform the anthem as Jewish victims (among them French) were murdered.[20] Kubrick would likely have been aware of this fact in the late 1950s as he admitted to a "widespread fascination with Nazi Germany."[21] He also did an extensive amount of historical research, as confirmed by actor Richard Anderson during their first encounter on the set in Germany.[22]

The films' generals are housed in "Chateau d'Aigle," a French translation of "Eagle Castle," the bird an archetypal image of Nazi power and domination.[23] It recalls The Kehlsteinhaus (known in English as the Eagle's Nest), a Nazi–constructed building used exclusively by members of the Nazi Party for governmental and social meetings and visited on many occasions by Hitler. Kubrick portrays the French soldiers as victims of their corrupt and evil generals, who act like Nazis. When Dax's soldiers fail to take the enemy position, Mireau chastises him and criticises the fallen soldiers using very callous terms.

DAX: Our troops did attack, sir, but they could make no headway.
MIREAU: Because they didn't try. I saw it myself. Half never left the trenches.
DAX: A third of my men were pinned down because the fire was so intense.
MIREAU: Don't quibble over fractions.

Mireau's disregard for the number of human lives lost as a result of his maniacal actions reverberates with Nazi ideology. He recalls the many Nazis who post–war remained "guilty without feeling any guilt," sealing off the atrocities they committed and thus owing no moral debt to their murdered victims. Likewise, Mireau instead degrades Dax and his men: "They're scum, Colonel. The whole rotten regiment is a pack of sneaking, whining, tail–dragging curs." Dax scornfully retorts, "Why not

---

20 *Grymes* 2014, pp. 120-128.
21 *Ciment* 1983, p. 156.
22 *LoBrutto* 1997, p. 201.
23 *Sax* 2000, p. 158.

shoot the entire regiment?" Equal to Mireau's indifference to human casualties while exhibiting an egocentric taste for power is Broulard.

Behind the film stands the issue of selection. The more politically pragmatic Broulard understands that they cannot afford to garner bad press by executing the entire platoon. He desperately pleads with them to minimise the number of scapegoated soldiers whom Mireau demands be tried for treason. Dax knows that his men will most likely be found guilty by a biased court, and thus executed, to set an example for the platoon for refusing to blindly follow diabolical orders. After surmising the list of victims for selection, Broulard cleverly convinces Mireau to narrow it down to just three soldiers. This selection process forms a "thorny issue" between Kubrick and Douglas, both the sons of Jewish immigrants to the U.S. "In the wake of the Holocaust, which ended only twelve years earlier, the very notion of *selection* must surely have contained echoes of the extermination camps."[24]

Stefan Machura and Stefan Ulbrich categorise courtroom movies taken from an analysis of the frequency of certain programs on German television. They define courtroom movies as films in which scenes essential to the story take place in court,[25] which befits *Paths of Glory*. Machura also asserts, "symbolism often is an important ingredient in law films."[26] Kubrick cleverly shoots his courtroom scenes with wide–angle shots to show a checkerboard floor of black–and–white square tiles, symbolic of chess in which the defence and prosecution are merely pieces in a corrupt judicial game. These scenes mirror the Third Reich's immoral judicial system. Dax tries to use logic and reason to defend the three scapegoated soldiers. He submits hard evidence in their defence but is immediately silenced by the judges. "The dispensing of these means the proceedings are flawed, unjust and amount to a Nazi–style show trial."[27] By placing the two "social undesirables," Férol, a big, clumsy braggart who is the first to break down at the verdict,[28] and Meyer (a Jewish character from Cobb's novel) together on trial, Kubrick evokes Jewish and Other minority persecution. All the while, Dax attempts unsuccessfully to show the court that taking the Ant Hill was futile and suicidal:

DAX: Why didn't you storm the Ant Hill alone?
FÉROL: Just me and Meyer? You're kidding, sir.
DAX: Yes, I'm kidding, Private Férol. Thank you, that's all.
CHIEF JUDGE: I don't see the point of this line of questioning.
DAX: Well, I'm attempting to indicate, sir, the utter absurdity of the
                line of questioning used by the prosecutor.

---

24   *Abrams* 2018, p. 54.
25   *Machura/Ulbrich* 2001, p. 117.
26   *Machura* 2007, p. 333.
27   *Abrams* 2018, p. 53.
28   *Bier* 1985.

To make the courtroom scenes more analogous to Nazism, in Kubrick's film, a total of five judges presides over the military trial. However, seven judges had been the typical number in France during World War One,[29] while in Cobb's novel, Assolant (the model for Dax in the novel) signs a document affirming that only two judges were present.[30] Mirroring the Third Reich's typical five judges in higher courts that dealt with "high treason and political crimes."[31]

These scenes illustrate how a supposed impartial judicial system can easily force otherwise innocent people to corroborate with a fascist–run state. Ingo Müller explains the Third Reich's legal system: "German jurists and lawyers acquiesced in the Nazi seizure of power, collaborated with the regime and legitimated it, became involved in promoting the Aryan ideals of Nazism, meted out justice during the Nazi era, and, in short, violated their professional standards and basic morality."[32]

This description befits Paul Duncan's explanation of *Paths of Glory*'s court scenes, mirroring the Third Reich's judicial system in which "conscientious objectors" were often found guilty without proper counsel and subsequently executed:

> "At the general court–martial, held in a large ballroom within the [German–stylised] château, each man is presented in turn, Major Saint–Auban prosecuting, Colonel Dax defending. The indictment is not read out because it would waste time. Dax protests at the absurdity of the court–martial, that there are no witnesses for the prosecution, that no stenographer is making a record of the trial. 'To find these men guilty would be a crime,' Dax shouts."[33]

Indeed, the real crime committed is the chief judge's support of the corrupt generals as he dismisses all witnesses and the defendants' citations of bravery. Dax futilely explains to him, "Mr. President, no one in the entire regiment got anywhere near the German wire, including myself," to which he simply replies, "call the next accused." Dax's moral standing not only challenges a Nazi–run judicial and military system, but his pleas reach out to a basic sense of decency and humanity. In his closing statement, Dax appeals to the court for possible compassion and ethical justice:

> "Gentlemen of the court, there are times when I'm ashamed to be a member of the human race, and this is one such occasion. It's impossible for me to summarize the case for the defense since the court never allowed me a reasonable opportunity to present my case ... I protest against being prevented from introducing evidence that I consider vital to the defense. The prosecution presented no witnesses. There has never been a written indictment of charges made against the defendants. And lastly, I protest against the fact that no stenographic records of this trial have been kept. The attack yesterday morning was no stain on the honor of France and certainly no disgrace to the fighting men of this

29   *Ferrari* 1918-1919, p. 8.
30   *Cobb* 1935, p. 143.
31   *Loewenstein* 1936, p. 808.
32   *Müller* 1991, p. 1.
33   *Duncan* 2002, p. 32.

nation. But this court martial is such a stain and such a disgrace. The case made against these men is a mockery of all human justice. Gentlemen of the court, to find these men guilty would be a crime to haunt each of you till the day you die. I can't believe that the noblest impulse of man – his compassion for another – can be completely dead here. Therefore, I humbly beg you – show mercy to these men."

Notwithstanding, his words befall upon deaf ears. The judges are determined to remain uninterested in carrying out moral justice. In Cobb's novel, Dax never defends the prisoners in court, nor does he attempt to blackmail Mireau (out of desperation) to save the men from being executed.

The mock trial mirrors the Nazi judicial system as outlined by William F. Meinecke and Alexandra Zapruder:

"Popularly known as the Reichstag Fire Decree, the regulations suspended important provisions of the German constitution, especially those safeguarding individual rights and due process of law. The decree permitted the restriction of the right to assembly, freedom of speech, and freedom of the press, among other rights, and it removed all restraints on police investigations. With the decree in place, the regime was free to arrest and incarcerate political opponents without specific charge, dissolve political organizations, and suppress publications. It also gave the central government the authority to overrule state and local laws and overthrow state and local governments. This law became a permanent feature of the Nazi police state ... Hitler and the Nazi Party used the advent of war—and the claim of rising criminality and 'defeatist provocateurs'—to reject lenient sentences and to demand a far more frequent application of the death penalty."[34]

These descriptions correlate with the Kubrickian running themes of fear and death which make *Paths of Glory* a pessimistic, "sad, and cruel ending with no hope that justice can be achieved."[35] Mario Falsetto asserts that in *Paths of Glory* Kubrick "explores the duality of a rational/irrational world in the brilliant sequence of the court martial of the three enlisted men."[36] On the one hand, the film's mock military trial proves military leaders can get away with negligence and treason. However, they do so by using soldiers as pawns, who are hastily questioned by the prosecutor and chief judge. The prosecutor and judges use Gestapo–like interrogation techniques of harassment to extract information without giving the defendants a chance to explain before they are unjustly sentenced to death. Therefore, the court–martial is "a mockery of justice,"[37] echoing the Nazi court system which also masked justice, proclaiming to do so as a "necessary protection of the community."[38]

Furthermore, by broadening Cobb's parochial "Pimple" key position to the film's more wide–reaching "Ant Hill" location, Kubrick enlarged the scope and context

---

34 *Meinecke/Zapruder* 2014, pp. 10, 38.
35 *Machura* 2007, p. 345.
36 *Falsetto* 2001, p. 39.
37 *Walker et al.* 2000, p. 55.
38 *Meinecke/Zapruder* 2014, p. 54.

both literally and figuratively. In doing so, he attempted to universalise an unseen enemy, anticipating the infamous banality of Nazi evil theory coined by Holocaust survivor Hannah Arendt in which she argued that "most evil is done by people who never make up their minds to be or do either good or evil."[39] As Paulina Segarra and Ajnesh Prasad point out, she suggests "that evil, in many instances, is defined by a lack of reflexivity and thoughtlessness and, therein, represents an incapability to think (critically)."[40] Kubrick illustrates this idea, with self–righteous French generals analogous to Nazis in their casual blindness to and acceptance of daily horrors in favour of power. This is demonstrated when, the morning after they are executed, Mireau and Broulard enjoy a hearty breakfast and casually talk about the soldiers' deaths. Their emotionless, blasé conversations echo the Wannsee Conference where top Nazi officials including Reinhard Heydrich, Heinrich Müller, and Adolph Eichmann met to discuss the Final Solution before staying behind in the guest house "to relax over a glass of cognac and review the minutes of the meeting."[41] This is echoed in *Paths of Glory*'s final scene between the corrupt generals:

MIREAU: I'm awfully glad you could be there, George. This sort of thing is always rather grim. But this had a kind of splendor to it, don't you think?
BROULARD: I have never seen an affair of this sort handled any better.
MIREAU: Your men died wonderfully.

Mireau and Broulard display an inability to think, or feel, beyond themselves, anticipating much of what Hannah Arendt later said of Adolf Eichmann.[42] Broulard proves to be a true Nazi–like master strategist and prudent politician. To save face with the press, he forces Mireau to own up to his heinous crimes in court, a ploy to also show the government and its people that the French army is still powerful in its ongoing war with Germany. Alexander Walker et al. assert that Mireau will most likely meet a similar dark fate to Hitler and many top Nazi officers: "we realize over the generals' breakfast that what Broulard decided was not to save the three scapegoats but to add a fourth to them — Mireau, whom he now throws to a court of inquiry, although with the fair certainty that he will 'honorably' blow his brains out before things get that far."[43]

---

39   *Arendt* 1978, p. 180.
40   *Segarra/Prasad* 2018, p. 552.
41   *Jasch/Kreutzmüller* 2017, p. 9.
42   *Segarra* and *Prasad* 2018. pp. 551-552.
43   *Walker et al.* 2000, p. 56.

4. Echoes of the Shoah

The ending of the film has traces of the Holocaust. In a change from the novel, Kubrick invented a wholly new scene, whereby, following the executions and before they head off to fight again, a captured, terrified German girl is forced to entertain the troops with a German folk song, *Der Treue Husar* ("The Faithful Hussar").[44] The soldiers begin by trying to humiliate her with catcalls and insulting heckling. But the troops are moved to tears by her innocence and suffering and she slowly wins them over. They stop their mocking and carousing, and poignantly, one by one, begin to hum and sing along. To play the role of the girl, Kubrick cast Susanne Christian (*née* Christiane Harlan).

Born in 1932, Harlan grew up in the Third Reich. Along with so many of her peers, at age ten, she was forced to join the *Bund Deutscher Mädel* (BDM), the Nazi organisation for girls that paralleled the Hitlerjugend (Hitler Youth). Her father accepted a job at the German Theatre in the Hague as part of the Nazi policy to strengthen German influence throughout Europe and as part of the Wehrmacht entertainment troupes, he performed more for the troops stationed throughout the Netherlands.[45] From Christmas 1942 until late September 1944, Harlan's parents were living in an apartment that had been seized from its Jewish owners, who had been sent east to an extermination camp in Poland. There, Harlan witnessed Nazi occupation policies first–hand, the systematic and inherent brutality towards the Dutch and their consequent hatred for all Germans, something from which she had been largely sheltered in her native Germany. She later talked about her child's–eye view of the war. "I was the little girl who moved in where Anne Frank was pushed out."[46]

Harlan's uncle was the notorious film director Veit Harlan. In 1939, frustrated with the delays on the notoriously antisemitic propaganda film *Jud Süß*, Joseph Goebbels, chief propagandist for the Nazi Party, ordered Fritz Hippler, the head of his film department, to sack its director Peter Paul Brauer and bring in Veit Harlan instead. Replacing Brauer as director, Harlan's name is forever attached to this film. Released in 1940, its plot, widely known in German literature and plays, revolves around a central Jewish character who was executed in 1738. His version contained all the standard antisemitic tropes: a cowardly, venal, unscrupulous, and immoral Jew who takes over and ruins a German city, stealing and plundering riches, defiling, and exploiting Aryan women to satisfy his lust. The brutal rape of an Aryan girl in London – more horrible given that he transgressed racial laws –

---

44 See Wikipedia 2023 for the literal translation of the song.
45 *Abrams* 2018, p. 13.
46 *Cocks* 2004, p. 68.

leads to his execution. In the lead role, Ferdinand Marian's make–up was based on Nazi stereotypes: greasy hair, hooked nose, and beard.

As a piece of propaganda cinema, the movie had a powerful effect on its audiences,[47] helping prepare the German public for further atrocities against Jews. Many viewed it as a documentary and were driven to acts of violence against Jews in the streets. Heinrich Himmler, the head of the Schutzstaffel, ordered all members of the various organisations under his command to see the movie, including local police and concentration camp guards, thus helping to whip up violence against the fabricated enemy.[48] The film became a runaway success across Europe, screened for Nazi and fascist youth groups throughout Europe, and was shown to concentration camp guards and German soldiers on the front. It was a huge hit at its premiere at the 1940 Venice Film Festival, winning the top accolade of the Golden Lion.[49] Harlan continued to receive assignments from Goebbels, and with considerable directorial license and large budgets, during a period of total war, his star remained ascendant through 1945. After the war, Harlan was arrested and twice placed on trial in Hamburg for crimes against humanity and preparing the ground for genocide, with the film introduced as evidence. He was acquitted both times when he successfully defended himself by arguing that the Nazis controlled his work and that he was obeying their orders and should not be held personally responsible for the content. Although Harlan went on making films in Germany until he died in 1964, at the age of sixty–four, both acquittals remain controversial to this day.[50]

5. L'Affaire Dreyfus

Kubrick, Harris, and Douglas's interest in the film's premise can be read as an allusion to the Dreyfus Affair. Jewish French army Captain Alfred Dreyfus was falsely accused of espionage and found guilty in 1894 by a prejudiced military tribunal for allegedly passing defence secrets to Germany. He was then imprisoned. As Dreyfus was taken away, crowds chanted "death to the Jews."[51] It was a miscarriage of justice so profound that it divided France and beyond – Arthur Schnitzler, whom Kubrick much admired, was an ardent Dreyfus supporter, and closely followed the case.[52] And Dreyfus died the same year Cobb published his novel. Dubbed the "Dreyfus Affair," this monumental event is also regarded as a precursor to

---

47 *Tegel* 1996, p. 516; *Ecke* 2002, pp. 67-68.
48 *Prager* 2021, p. 238.
49 *Etlin* 2002, p. 143.
50 See *Noack* 2016.
51 *Lindemann* 1991, p. 116.
52 *Abrams* 2018, p. 46.

the Holocaust, specifically the deportation by the Vichy government of more than 70,000 French Jews.[53]

Kubrick's film echoes Hollywood's misrepresentation of Dreyfus. William Dieterle's *The Life of Emile Zola* (U.S.A., 1937) cast Austrian actor, Joseph Schildkraut, as Dreyfus, severely limiting any reference to the officer's Jewish heritage due to Warner Bros.'s fear of Germany banning all American films from distribution in the country.[54] Likewise, Kubrick removed explicit references to Dreyfus from Cobb's novel as well as the final interpretations of the screenplay. Even virulent French antisemitism, highlighted by the Dreyfus Affair, was deliberately omitted from the film when one of Cobb's original victims in the novel was Jewish to avoid any overt reference to Jewishness or Alfred Dreyfus.

Abrams has speculated that "after World War II and the era of McCarthyism, it was too soon for a commercial Hollywood product to include explicit references to the Dreyfus Affair and antisemitism."[55] He continues to say:

> "[T]o preserve good relations with the French, or at least not strain them, 'Paths of Glory' was not shown at the Berlin Film Festival in 1958 after the French threatened to withdraw from it. This ban was enforced in Germany until 1959. Likewise, the Swiss called it 'subversive propaganda directed at France refused to screen it for journalists and declared that any prints not immediately exported out of the country would be seized and confiscated."[56]

Similarly, Kubrick's incorporation of the French national anthem into the score serves to highlight the blatant corruption found within ruthless and sadistic governing systems which use and abuse soldiers as victims.

A direct correlation can thus be made between *Paths of Glory*'s portrayal of a military trial conducted during wartime and the 1894 proceedings against Dreyfus. Kubrick's mock trial with corrupt judges who refuse concrete evidence mirrors the Jewish French captain's defence counsel, who was not entitled to attend the interrogation of the prisoner.[57] It took many years for Dreyfus to be exonerated from espionage charges. *Paths of Glory* provides an ulterior motive as to why the State refused to reopen the case.

Furthermore, the judges in *Paths of Glory* continually dismiss the defence and are more concerned with condemning the manifestly innocent men, to save face for the generals' immoral orders. They even reject the defence's call to have the indictment read aloud by Saint–Auban. Douglas pragmatically portrays the honourable Dax, telling the judges, "the defense has a right." He mirrors real–life Lieutenant–Colonel

---

53 *Fishel* 2012, p. 119.
54 *Baron* 2005, p. 72.
55 *Abrams* 2014.
56 *Abrams* 2014; see also *Kelly* 2006, p. 219.
57 *Chapman* 2011, p. 161.

Georges Picquart, "a model for narratives that center on honor as a moral compass," who solely (and futilely) proved Dreyfus's innocence.[58] Nonetheless, the Chief Judge in *Paths of Glory* hastily replies, "Please don't take up the court's time with technicalities." This character is played by German actor Peter Capell, who would go on to play other German characters in Holocaust–related films, including *Armored Command* (U.S.A. 1961 dir. Byron Haskin), *The Counterfeit Traitor* (U.S.A. 1962 dir. George Seaton), *I Deal in Danger* (U.S.A. 1966 dir. Walter Grauman), *Hauser's Memory* (U.S.A. 1970 dir. Boris Sagal), *Holocaust* (U.S.A. NBC 1978), *Son of Hitler* (U.K. 1979; dir. Rod Amateau), and *Wallenberg: A Hero's Story* (U.S.A. 1985; dir. Lamont Johnson).

Despite Dax's gallant and moral efforts, the three accused soldiers are given insufficient due process and are quickly sentenced to death. This controversial ending was pushed by Kirk Douglas, an antiwar and extremely liberal political activist, and finalised by Kubrick. They even defied the Motion Picture Association of America's caution to change the film's ending fearing European censors and protests due to the film's critical representation of the French military.[59]

6. Hollywood Context

Although the 1950s were considered a "golden age" in the United States following the hardships and victories of World War Two and preceding the cultural upheavals of the sixties,[60] it was also a period during which explicit Jewish depictions were avoided by Hollywood. Conditioned by periods of open antisemitism from World War One onwards and in a bid to maximise profits and enhance the popular appeal of their movies, the largely Jewish film moguls did not want to alienate their white working–class audiences by having openly Jewish stars with obviously ethnic names front and centre. This was exacerbated in 1947 by the launch of an investigation into possible communist infiltration of the motion–picture industry by HUAC (the House Un–American Activities Committee which had initially been created in 1938 "to monitor fascist (particularly Nazi) subversion,"[61] in 1947 and again in 1951. The initial chair of HUAC in 1947, avowed segregationist and antisemite, Mississippi Representative John Rankin,[62] specifically targeted Hollywood given its large Jewish population. He described it as "the greatest hotbed of subversive activity in the United States."[63] HUAC historian Walter Goodman once said, "in Rankin's mind, to

---

58 *Barrett/Sarbin* 2008, p. 17.
59 *Fenwick* 2020, p. 83.
60 *Jones* 2016, p. 38.
61 *MacAdam* 2015, p. 88.
62 *Gladchuk* 2013, p. 70.
63 *Goodman* 1968, p. 172.

call a Jew a Communist was tautology."[64] Given that so many Jews did indeed work in Hollywood and had joined the Communist Party during the Great Depression, it did give rise to fears that Hollywood was Communist. In many U.S. states, communism was widely considered a Jewish invention.[65] As a result, the Jewish owners of major studios were afraid of drawing attention to their immigrant Jewish origins for fear of arousing allegations of unpatriotic priorities.[66] This resulted in heavy self–censorship.[67]

The 1950s also saw the release of antiwar films set during World War Two. Like Leon Uris's 1953 novel *Battle Cry*, adapted into a film in 1955, Kubrick showed how officers' self–interest, desire for glory and personal promotion led them to willingly sacrifice their men in battle. Broulard and Mireau are corrupt, immoral, and unethical. They are seemingly much more concerned with propriety, the appearance of the proper conduct of the war, the orderly handling of the court's martials, and decorum during executions, than with the soldiers' welfare, justice, or even victory. The men are also merely statistics, which they will send to their deaths without even blinking, indicating their callousness. On the threshold of death, Corporal Philippe Paris (Ralph Meeker), one of the three soldiers to be executed, is advised, "act like a man."

Some scholars have seen the influence of Robert Aldrich's *Attack* (U.S.A., 1956) on *Paths of Glory*.[68] The former film features innocent victims who attempt to survive in a cold and hostile world of ruthless and sadistic military and political leaders. As a result of their moral actions and "insubordination," these characters are court–martialled and punished by the State, including many being sentenced to death: prevalent themes Kubrick explored in *Paths of Glory*.

Kubrick's particular interest in the horrific calamities of soldiers resulting in mutiny draws speculation that he was greatly influenced by those of Edward Dmytryk, who directed the World War Two films, *Crossfire* (U.S.A., 1947) and *The Juggler* (U.S.A., 1953). *Crossfire* was Hollywood's first film about anti–antisemitism. Captain Finlay (Robert Young) interrogates three soldiers (mirroring *Paths of Glory*) who are possible suspects in the murder of a Jewish soldier named Samuels (Jewish actor Sam Levene). The latter universalises the plight of Jews living in America at the time, stating:

> "I think maybe suddenly not having a lot of enemies to hate anymore. Maybe it's because for four years now we've been focusing on our minds on, on one little peanut. The 'win the war' peanut. That was all. Get it over. Eat that peanut … We don't know what we're

---

64 *Ibid.*
65 *Sorin* 2012, p. 31.
66 *Baron* 2010, p. 91.
67 *Ibid.*
68 *Fenwick* 2020, p. 86 and *Landon* 1989, p. 38.

supposed to do. We're too used to fighting but we just don't know what to fight ... A whole lotta fight and hate that don't know where to go."

Moreover, like Mireau, Sergeant Montgomery (Robert Ryan) slaps around his fellow soldiers and concocts an "enemy," unabashedly admitting, "I don't like Jews and I don't like nobody who likes Jews," before murdering Samuels and Floyd (Steve Brodie). Ginny (Gloria Grahame) anticipates the young German woman in *Paths of Glory* as a young, attractive woman who entertains soldiers at a tavern. Meanwhile, a detective shows that Samuels was honourably discharged on August 28, 1945 (when the Allied occupation of Japan began) "upon recommendation of a Medical Board because of disability from wounds received at Okinawa." His war record mirrors the chief judge's support of the corrupt generals in *Paths of Glory* as he dismisses all witnesses and the defendants' citations of bravery much like Dreyfus's "virtues were glossed over"[69] by the French Army during his trial. Finlay befittingly tells a taunted hillbilly soldier named Leroy (William Phipps), "they don't teach it in school but it's real American history just the same."

The Juggler starred Kirk Douglas as a German–Jewish Holocaust survivor named Muller who experiences severe post–war traumatic stress after surviving Nazi concentration camps and losing his wife and children in the war. When Muller is asked where he is from, he says, "Munich, a beautiful city," where Kubrick had shot the generals' meetings at the Schleissheim Palace in *Paths of Glory*. Like Kubrick's scapegoated soldiers, Muller is falsely accused and suffers postwar trauma. In Israel, a doctor tells the head of police: "he's no criminal in the police sense of the word." Both films have English–speaking actors playing Europeans so that the plight of the Holocaust is universalised. When an amicable Israeli police officer asks Muller for identification after he suspiciously flees, he tells him: "you policemen are always the same: hunting, searching, asking questions. You won't let us live. You're all Nazis." In another scene, an Israeli boy asks Muller where he is from and he sardonically replies, "I used to live in Hollywood," evoking the movie industry's limited depiction of Nazism and the Holocaust.

In *Paths of Glory*, Douglas's Dax survives the horrors of World War One and can be read as what Nicole Rafter refers to as a 'justice figure,' the "hero who tries to move man–made law ever closer to the ideal until it matches the justice template."[70] Both in court and in meetings with top generals, Dax fights against the immoral French military, and his soldiers suffer PTSD due to the atrocities of a world war. Dmytryk's follow–up film, *The Caine Mutiny* (U.S.A., 1954), mirrors *Paths of Glory* more closely and features a U.S. Navy mutiny formed against an irrational captain (Humphrey Bogart, a vocally staunch anti–McCarthy advocate much like Douglas). This cowardly captain's inane orders result in disaster and a court–martial

---

69 *Behr* 2018, p. 523.
70 *Rafter* 2001, p. 10.

trial for which he avoids blame and files a false report. Both Dmytryk and Kubrick's films respectively feature innocent victims who attempt to survive in a cold and hostile world run by ruthless and sadistic military and political leaders. As a result of their moral actions and "insubordination," these characters are punished by the State, including many being sentenced to death. Filmmakers like Dmytryk, Aldrich, and Kubrick had to tread carefully by allegorically challenging the "golden age" of 1950s America.

In addition, Hollywood released courtroom drama films about judicial injustice directed by Jewish filmmakers: Zoltan Korda's *Cry, The Beloved Country* (U.K. 1952); Billy Wilder's *Witness for the Prosecution* (U.S.A., 1957); Otto Preminger's *Anatomy of a Murder* (U.S.A., 1959); and Richard Fleisher's *Compulsion* (U.S.A., 1959). Of great significance was Jewish filmmaker, Sidney Lumet's, debut film, *Twelve Angry Men* (U.S.A., 1957), written by Jewish playwright Reginald Rose in 1954, which contained many implicit Jewish allusions. Juror 11 (Jewish actor George Voskovec) is possibly Jewish, although not stated explicitly. He is a polite, logical, and intelligent European immigrant, a refugee who fled persecution, and a naturalised U.S. citizen who illustrates deep respect for the American judicial system and its democratic values, such as due process. He is also one of three jurors who can sway the jury's votes to split six to six, ultimately resulting in saving an innocent adolescent from death row.

Furthermore, the Jewish actor, Martin Balsam, portrays Juror 1, as the jury foreman, who is soft–spoken, calm, and assertive. Despite being an assistant high school football coach, he adheres to long–standing Jewish stereotypes when he makes an effort to keep order, telling the jurors, "all right, gentleman, let's take our seats ... Now, please, I don't want any fights in here" a line repeated almost verbatim in a future Kubrick film, *Dr. Strangelove* (U.S.A., 1964). Jewish actor, Lee J. Cobb, portrays the film's antagonist, Juror 3, as a hot–tempered owner of a courier business who is estranged from his son. Uneducated and crass, he often shouts, bullies, and belittles others to vote for a "guilty" verdict, deflecting his insecurities onto the jurors: "you're not goin' to intimidate me. I'm entitled to my opinion!" In contrast, Jewish actor, Jack Klugman, portrays Juror 5, who grew up in the slums and attests to his poor background. His dialogue is analogous to the defendant in the murder trial and of the (Jewish) immigrant experience: "I used to play in a backyard that was filled with garbage. Maybe it still smells on me." *Twelve Angry Men* must have informed Kubrick's search for his breakout Hollywood film.

7. Conclusion

Stanley Kubrick's *Paths of Glory* is one in a long line of Hollywood films that depict a wide gap between justice and the law. But his representation of a strong male lead who battles corrupt judicial systems can be read as a protest against centuries of Jewish victimisation. As its star, Kirk Douglas, a masculine, sturdy, and muscular Jewish star, who rejects ago–old antisemitic stereotypes which traditionally depicted Jews as weak, passive, and averse to military involvement, *Paths of Glory* set a pattern that defied Hollywood tropes and defined Kubrick's next three films. The embodiment of *menschlichkeit*, Douglas's Dax is not only a moralistic attorney, but a benevolent and heroic paragon of reason, compassion, virtue, humanity, and justice, standing up for his ordinary men in the face of injustice and corruption. Honourable and highly ethical, he naively believes that some semblance of "truth" or "justice" might result from his actions within a seemingly democratic system of law and order.

Dax defies what had been the traditional Hollywood depiction of lawyers. Historically, they had been portrayed as wealthy with a tasteful lifestyle or very young and just starting their careers. In American films, education at an elite law school was often mentioned.[71] Dax's depiction befits neither of these descriptions and therefore illustrates the characterisation of a lawyer seeking justice without a capitalistic angle, which defies traditional Jewish stereotypes.

Furthermore, traces of the Holocaust can be read in Kubrick's film. It was shot in West Germany's Bavaria Film Studios, including using a castle that had been bombed during World War Two. Located near Munich, *just beyond the location of the shoot* was the Dachau Concentration Camp memorial which Kubrick and his producer, James B. Harris, visited. Moreover, behind the film stands the issue of *selection* with echoes of the extermination camps. The more politically pragmatic general in the film understands that they cannot afford to garner bad press by executing the entire platoon. He desperately pleads with them to minimise the number of scapegoated soldiers to be tried for "treason." In doing so, the film's mock military trial of flawed and unjust proceedings amounts to a Nazi–style show and evokes the Dreyfus case and many scenes illustrate how a supposed impartial judicial system can easily force otherwise innocent people to corroborate with a fascist–run state.

---

71 *Machura* 2007, p. 337.

Bibliography

Abrams, Nathan, 2014: "Paths of Glory" Revisited: A Still–palpable Jewish Subtext. Haaretz, May 19. At: https://www.haaretz.com/israel-news/culture/2014-05-19/ty-article/.premiu m/paths-of-glory-revisited/0000017f-e7f6-d62c-a1ff-ffff20f10000 (Accessed on 25 May 2023).

Abrams, Nathan, 2018: Stanley Kubrick: New York Jewish Intellectual. New Brunswick, NJ: Rutgers University Press.

Alpert, Rebecca, 2015: The Macho–Mensch: Modelling American Jewish Masculinity and the Heroes of Baseball. In: *Rein*, Raanan/*Sheinin*, David (eds.), Muscling in on New Worlds. Jews, Sport, and the Making of the Americas, vol. 5, Leiden, The Netherlands: Brill, pp. 101–120.

Atkinson, Brooks, 1935: The Play; Treachery in the High Command Is Theme of "Paths of Glory," Adapted from The Novel. In: The New York Times, September 27.

Baron, Lawrence, 2005: Review of "Imaginary Witness: Hollywood and the Holocaust." In: Film and History, 135, pp. 72–74.

Baron, Lawrence, 2010: The First Wave of American 'Holocaust' Films, 1945—1959. In: The American Historical Review 115:1, pp. 90–114.

Barrett, Frank J./*Sarbin* Theodore R., 2008: Honor as a Moral Category: A Historical–Linguistic Analysis. In: Theory & Psychology 18:1, pp. 5–25.

Behr, Harold, 2018: Captain Alfred Dreyfus: A Case Study in the Group Dynamics of Scapegoating. In: Group Analysis 51:4, pp. 515–530.

Bier, Jesse, 1985: Cobb and Kubrick: Author and Auteur: (*Paths of Glory* As Novel and Film). In: VQR, Summer 1985. At: https://www.vqronline.org/essay/cobb-and-kubrick-aut hor-and-auteur-paths-glory-novel-and-film (Accessed on 25 May 2023).

Chapman, Guy, 2011: The Dreyfus Trials. London: Bloomsbury.

Ciment, Michel, 1983: Kubrick. Glasgow: Collins.

Cobb, Humphrey, 1935: Paths of Glory. London; Penguin Books.

Cocks, Geoffrey, 2004: The Wolf at the Door: Stanley Kubrick, History, and the Holocaust. New York: Peter Lang.

Douglas, Kirk, 1988: The Ragman's Son: An Autobiography. Bath: Chivers.

Duncan, Paul, 2002: Stanley Kubrick. Vermont: Trafalgar Square Publishing.

Ecke, Felix, 2002: Braune Leinwand. Antisemitische Rechtspropaganda im Film des Dritten Reiches. In: *Machura*, Stefan/*Ulbrich*, Stefan (eds.), Recht im Film, Baden–Baden: Nomos, pp. 54–69.

Etlin, Richard A., 2002: Art, Culture, and Media under the Third Reich. Chicago: University of Chicago Press.

Falsetto, Mario, 2001: Stanley Kubrick A Narrative and Stylistic Analysis. Westport, CT: Greenwood Publishing Group.

Fenwick, James, 2020: Stanley Kubrick Produces. New Brunswick, NJ: Rutgers University Press.

Fermaglich, Kirsten, 2007: American Dreams and Nazi Nightmares: Early Holocaust Consciousness and Liberal America, 1957–1965. Lebanon, NH: UPNE.

Ferrari, Robert, May 1918–February 1919: Military Courts of Paris. In: Journal of Criminal Law and Criminology 91, pp. 5–31.

Fischel, Jack, 2012: Review of The Dreyfus Affair in Retrospect by *Harris* Ruth/*Frederick* Brown/*Begley*, Louis. In: Shofar 302, pp. 119–122.

Gladchuk, John J., 2013: Hollywood and Anticommunism: HUAC and the Evolution of the Red Menace, 1935–1950. New York & London: Routledge.

Goodman, Walter, 1968: The Committee: The Extraordinary Career of The House Committee on Un–American Activities. New York: Farrar, Straus and Giroux.

Grymes, James A., 2014: Violins of Hope: Violins of the Holocaust—Instruments of Hope and Liberation in Mankind's Darkest Hour. New York: Harper Perennial.

Jasch, Hans–Christian/*Kreutzmüller*, Christoph, 2017: Introduction. In: *Jasch*, Hans–Christian/*Kreutzmüller*, Christoph (eds.), The Participants: The Men of the Wannsee Conference, New York/Oxford: Berghahn Books, pp. 1–20.

Jones, Robert P., 2016: The End of White Christian America. New York: Simon and Schuster.

Landon, Philip J., 1989: From Cowboy to Organization Man: The Hollywood War Hero, 1940– 1955. In: Studies in Popular Culture 12:1, pp. 28–41.

Lindemann, Albert S., 1991: The Jew Accused: Three Anti–Semitic Affairs (Dreyfus, Beilis, Frank) 1894–1915. Cambridge University Press.

LoBrutto, Vincent, 1997: Stanley Kubrick: a Biography. New York: D.I. Fine Books.

Loewenstein, Karl, March 1936: Law in the Third Reich. In: The Yale Law Journal 45:5, pp. 779–815.

MacAdam, Henry I., 2015: Michael Gold & Dalton Trumbo on *Spartacus*, Blacklist Hollywood, Howard Fast, and the Demise of American Communism. In: Left History 19:1, pp. 57–91.

Machura, Stefan, 2007: An Analysis Scheme for Law Films. In: University of Baltimore Law Review 36:3, pp. 329–345.

Machura, Stefan/*Ulbrich*, Stefan, 2001: Globalizing the Hollywood Courtroom Drama. In: Journal of Law and Society 28:1, pp. 117–132.

Meinecke, William F. and Alexandra *Zapruder*, 2014: Law, Justice, and the Holocaust. Washington, DC: The United States Holocaust Museum.

Müller, Ingo, 1991: Hitler's Justice: The Courts of the Third Reich. Cambridge, Mass: Harvard University Press.

Naremore, James, 2019: On Kubrick. New York: Bloomsbury Publishing.

Noack, Frank, 2016: Veit Harlan: The Life and Work of a Nazi Filmmaker. Lexington, KY: University Press of Kentucky.

Prager, Brad, 2021: Trial by Documentary: the Harlans, Between *Jud Süss* (1940) and *Notre Nazi* (1984). In: *Holocaust Studies*, 27:2, pp. 235–256.

Rafter, Nicole, 2001: American Criminal Trial Films: An Overview of Their Development, 1930–2000. In: Journal of Law and Society 28:1, pp. 9–24.

Sax, Boria, 2000: Animals in The Third Reich. Pittsburgh: Yogh & Thorn Books.

Segarra, Paulina/*Prasad*, Ajnesh, 2018: How Does Corporeality Inform Theorizing? Revisiting Hannah Arendt and the Banality of Evil. In: Human Studies 41, pp. 545–563.

Sorin, Gerald, 2012: Howard Fast: Life and Literature in the Left Lane. Bloomington/IN, Indiana University Press.

Tegel, Susan, 1996: Veit Harlan and the Origins of 'Jud Süss', 1938–1939: Opportunism in the Creation of Nazi Anti–Semitic Film Propaganda. In: Historical Journal of Film, Radio and Television 16:4, pp. 515–531.

Turkel, Joe, 2019: Working with Stanley Kubrick. Kubrick's Universe – The Stanley Kubrick Podcast, June 7. At: https://skas.podbean.com/e/26-working-with-stanley-kubrick-with-joe -turkel/ (Accessed on 25 May 2023).

Vos, Benjamin, 2022: SAS Rogue Heroes Continues the Tradition of Joke Jewish Soldiers. The Jewish Chronicle, December 1. At: https://www.thejc.com/lets-talk/all/sas-rogue -heroes-continues-the-tradition-of-joke-jewish-soldiers-4STA7jV14bnxHktzwyp9mG (Accessed on 25 May 2023).

Walker, Alexander/*Taylor,* Sybil/*Ruchti*, Ulrich, 2000: Stanley Kubrick, Director: A Visual Analysis. New York: WW Norton.

Wikipedia, 2023: The Faithful Hussar. At: https://en.wikipedia.org/wiki/The_Faithful_Hussar (Accessed on 24 May 2023).

Part 2

War, Civil War and Justice in Divided Societies

Ferdinando Spina

Through the Law, Beyond the Law.
Dealing with Fascism and Civil War in Italian Cinema. 1943–1948.

1. Introduction

In Western political thought, theoretical perspectives that are either too realist or too idealist have treated the concepts of law and war as oxymoronic, and the fields of law and war as mutually exclusive.[1] However, historical and legal experience suggests that the Gordian knot of war and law can never be completely untied, nor can the foundational link between violence and law.[2]

Aware of this ambivalence, the socio-legal perspective flies lower than the philosophy of history. Abandoning the normative perspective of morality and the formal framework of international law, it is interested in the historical and social processes of legal institutionalisation of war and peace. A war in its full swing partially suspends the law by establishing, within states and between states, exceptional legal regimes in which laws and codes serve only to authorise, not to oppose or limit, political and military decisions. Conversely, it is in the transition from peace to war or from war to peace that the fate of law is particularly visible, either in the direction of its triumph or in that of its defeat. Moreover, the fluid phases between peace and war are also those in which public hopes for the role of international law in limiting the violence of conflicts are at their highest.[3]

Such uncertain war/peace scenarios as I am discussing here, are historically not the exception but the rule. Think of the Cold War and how it affected the application of constitutional guarantees of civil rights and personal liberties, even in nations with more deeply rooted traditions of the rule of law. Think again of the more recent war on terror against the threat of global terrorism, and the violations of the fundamental values of the rule of law that it has entailed in many Western democracies, particularly the United States.[4] As Norman Dorsen stated, "a nation threatened from without is rarely the best guardian of civil liberties within".[5] Finally, consider the transition periods between war, civil war, military dictatorship, totalita-

---

1 *Douglas* et al. 2014, p. 4.
2 *Benjamin* 2021.
3 *Garapon* 2002.
4 *Abel* 2019.
5 *Dorsen* 1989, p. 843.

rian regime, and the phase of reconstruction of the political and social order. In times of transition, the expectations of justice, peace and freedom entrusted to the law emerge with greater force and drama.[6]

This essay explores transitional justice through the lens of some films that represent a trial, focusing on the case of Italy after the fall of Mussolini's regime in 1943. As I summarise in Chapter 2, the Italian case presents similar aspects to what occurred in other European countries after the end of the Second World War and to other experiences of transitional justice. But it is also unique in several respects, highlighting the liquidity between war and peace that puts transitional justice under scrutiny. Indeed, in the period between 1943 and 1948, and in some cases even beyond, three different wars were fought in Italy, at certain moments simultaneously:[7] The Second World War between the Allied army and the German army with the Italian Social Republic; the civil war between fascists and antifascists; and a class war between workers and peasants on one side and agrarians and bourgeois on the other.

It is in this convulsive phase, in which homicides reached the highest rates ever recorded in the history of the unified nation, in which the state and the administration of justice were on the rise, that the films I will discuss in this essay must be placed. These films offer a glimpse into the lived experience of transitional justice in Italy.

2. Transitional Justice in Italy

I will very briefly reconstruct the complicated period of the Italian experience of transitional justice in the aftermath of Fascism.[8] Transitional justice in Italy began with the fall of Mussolini in July 1943, thus, before any other country engaged on either side in the Second World War.[9] Until the end of the war in Italy (April 1945), three different authorities ruled the country: the German army and the puppet government of the Italian Social Republic, the military government of the Allies, and the Italian government of the National Liberation Committee formed by the antifascist parties but still appointed by the monarchy. Each of these authorities tried to impose its own laws on civilians and enemies. In the areas occupied by the Germans and fascists, the antifascist military movement of the Resistance fought.

In this chaotic context of institutional uncertainty, widespread violence and anomie, efforts to identify and condemn the abuses and crimes committed by mem-

---

6 *Teitel* 2000; *Elster* 2004; *Portinaro* 2011; *Wouters* 2014.
7 *Woller* 1996, p. 166.
8 *Domenico* 1991; *Woller* 1996; *Dondi* 2008; *Focardi/Nubola* 2015; *Nubola* 2017; *Caroli* 2022; *Meniconi/Neppi Modona* 2022.
9 *Elster* 2004, p. 55.

bers of the fascist regime took different forms, sometimes succeeding each other, sometimes operating simultaneously. The first type of purge was carried out by the Allies through military tribunals in the liberated areas, partly in collaboration and partly in confrontation with the Italian governments.[10] The second type has been termed "spontaneous purge" or "wild purge": these terms refer to the extensive process of retribution and revenge carried out by the civilian population, in the form of unofficial purge committees, fascist hunts, private vendettas carried out by individuals or armed groups, and lynchings. There were also partisan tribunals formed by Partisans and citizens aiming to achieve sure and certain justice in punishing the fascist enemy.[11] According to historians' estimates, there were between 10,000 and 12,000 victims of the wild purges between 1943 and 1946.[12]

The third type of purge occurred through the courts set up by the governments in office, the 'bureaucratic' purge as defined by the German historian Hans Woller. The first government after Mussolini's fall, the Badoglio government (from 26 July 1943 until the liberation of Rome in June 1944), passed a first purge law in December 1943. Subsequent governments, led by Bonomi (18 June 1944–12 June 1945), promulgated other measures, including the Legislative Decree of the Lieutenant of the Realm of 27 July 1944, No. 159, titled *Sanctions against Fascism*, which Woller has defined "the Magna Charta of Italian transitional justice".[13] The decree not only established the general framework for the political purge and punishment of high-ranking members of the Fascist Party, but also announced the political will of the Italian government to carry out the purge rigorously and efficiently, taking it away from Anglo–American control. The penalties provided could go as far as life imprisonment or even the death penalty. Article 5 of Title 1 of the decree established the crime of *collaboration* with the German invaders. The High Commission for Sanctions against Fascism and a new special court called the High Court of Justice[14] were set up to prosecute members of the Fascist government and other *gerarchi*.[15]

It is not of interest here to mention the logistical difficulties and the legal and regulatory uncertainties that these bodies had to face. It is worth recalling, however,

---

10 *Woller* 1996, chs. 1–2.
11 *Rovatti* 2015.
12 *Woller* 1996, pp. 279–280; *Dondi* 2008, pp. 91–93.
13 *Woller* 1996, pp. 134–144.
14 The High Commission for Sanctions against Fascism oversaw the work of all agencies responsible for implementing sanctions. It controlled and intervened in the purge commissions operating within both central and peripheral public administrations. The Commission's efforts were directed at cleansing the state administration and confiscating the assets of collaborationists. Additionally, the High Commission acted as the prosecutor in trials for Fascist crimes conducted by the High Court of Justice. The High Court was composed of a president and other members who had not been part of the Fascist regime, some of whom had extensive judicial experience.
15 A *gerarca* (plural: *gerarchi*) was a high-ranking official of the National Fascist Party (PNF). The term is used in a more general sense to refer to a fascist leader, both local and national.

that the trials held were few in number and involved second–level fascists (a total of 99 defendants were tried, of whom 31 were convicted, including 4 who were sentenced to death).[16] Domenico's assessment of the work of the High Court is significant:

"As only one court, its scope was necessarily limited and could not possibly have been devised with the idea of punishing all *gerarchi*. A single bench was established for show trials, not for effective, broadly based sanctions. The proceedings, one trial at a time, went slowly and were complicated by the enormous amount of attention focused on them".[17]

In April 1945, a new decree established the Extraordinary Courts of Assizes (later transformed into Special Sections of the Courts of Assizes) in each Italian provincial capital. These special courts were to prosecute offences of collaboration with the enemy, such as the rounding up of civilians, the deportation of Jews, and the harassment and denunciation of civilians and Partisans. Once again, the aim was to punish fascist crimes exemplarily through trials, in order to meet the people's expectations of justice and to gradually reduce the wild purges and vendettas.[18]

It is worth noting that the trials were passionately followed by the public. The press published extensive legal reports on the proceedings. Some trials were broadcast on the radio and through loudspeakers in the squares.[19]

Between 1946 and 1947, the process of coming to terms with fascism came to an end. The gradual establishment of the institutional structure of the new Italian State, the tensions of the Cold War reflected in the divisions among the political parties of the Anti–Fascist Front, the need to rebuild peace materially and psychologically were all factors that led to the Togliatti Amnesty of June 22 1946, which granted amnesty for common, political, and military crimes. The Togliatti amnesty was "the first relevant moment when Italy had to face the fundamental choice between prosecution and punishment on the one hand, and renouncing both of these on the other hand."[20]

The amnesty of 22 June 1946 had such political and psychological consequences that the phase of prosecutions and purges was progressively reduced. This phase could already be considered closed at the beginning of 1948 with a decree approved on 5 February.[21]

This brief description of events and legislation may have given an idea of the complexity of transitional justice in Italy. It illustrates the unstable understandings of peace and conflict, old and new regimes, guilt and innocence, justice and revenge

---

16   *Dondi* 2008, p. 33.
17   *Domenico* 1991, p. 90.
18   *Rovatti* 2015.
19   *Dondi* 2008, p. 50.
20   *Caroli* 2022, p. 18.
21   *Woller* 1996, p. 373.

that ran through the moral climate of Italy in those years. In a country emerging from twenty years of dictatorship and the devastation of war, inhabited by masses of illiterate people, cinema played a fundamental role in offering stories, symbols and emotions to deal with the past and imagine the new future.

3. *Representing the Trial: Making Transitional Justice Visible*

My approach in this essay is aligned with the Law and Film movement,[22] as the main focus is on the representation that Italian cinema of those years made of the criminal trial for crimes committed during the war. I will explain why I believe this topic is interesting and how it can contribute to the understanding of the concrete implementation of transitional justice.

Theories and research on transitional justice have largely reflected on the practices through which new political regimes and social movements have dealt with the past. These practices include truth commissions, administrative purges and amnesties, reparations, nation–building, the construction of museums and monuments, and commemoration and reparation ceremonies.

However, since Nuremberg, the symbolically representative practice of transitional justice has been the trial. "Successor trials are commonly thought to play the leading foundational role in the transformation to a more liberal political order. Only trials are thought to draw a bright line demarcating the normative shift from illegitimate to legitimate rule."[23] Trials detail the violence of the past, reawaken memories of hidden and forgotten horrors, and manifest their public condemnation. At the same time, trials consolidate the legitimacy of the rule of law and demonstrate that the new order of freedom and democracy cannot be realised outside of it.[24] The courtroom dramas staged in the courts contribute to the reconstitution of social solidarity and even national identity.[25]

Among all the challenges and dilemmas raised by war crimes tribunals and the use of criminal justice in transitional justice, the relationship between the ceremonial procedures of the courts and the social and moral context in which they are performed is of particular interest here, viewed through a sociologist's lens. Indeed, "criminal prosecutions and truth commissions share symbolic celebration of rule of law principles but these institutions do not in and of themselves perform the work of building the rule of law culture and its supporting institutions".[26] The challenge of the courts is to respond to moral dilemmas, political interference, and

---

22 *Robson* 2005; *Greenfield* et al. 2010; *Machura* 2016.
23 *Teitel* 2000, p. 7.
24 *Bass* 2000.
25 *Osiel* 1997.
26 *Fletcher* et al. 2009, pp. 219–220.

drives for vengeance. "Successor trials walk a remarkably thin line between the fulfilment of the potential for a renewed adherence to the rule of law and the risk of perpetuating political justice".[27] More generally, the end of a conflict poses a dilemma for the transitional justice system: whether to pursue justice at all costs or to build democracy and peace as quickly as possible, even if this means foregoing the punishment of perpetrators.[28]

Based on Durkheim's fundamental insight that the punishment of criminals strengthens social solidarity,[29] Stefan Machura explained the role of the media in the construction of social cohesion through the representation of crime, investigation, trial, and punishment.[30] It is through the narrative of crime and justice in popular culture that people see the reinforcement of their shared values and norms. This function of the media's representation of criminal justice, which indicts the crimes of the past regime, is therefore even more important in transitional and post–conflict societies.[31]

In these divided societies, as in the case of post–war Italy, there is a need to rebuild. "Structural and normative requirements are not in place for punishment to actually function as reinforcement and affirmation of norms within communities, as a mechanism to establish solidarity with victims, censure perpetrators and 'outlaw' impunity".[32] In times of transition from war to peace and from dictatorial to democratic regimes, popular legal culture can be one such mechanism. Together with trials and other transitional justice practices, popular representations of crimes and trials in defeated regimes can help to rebuild a sympathetic moral climate and recognise victims' expectations of justice in a long and troubled trajectory.

However, to do so, popular culture can also abandon the principles of due process and even delegitimise the rule of law. Popular narratives may favour show trials that celebrate the political justice of the victors rather than "pure legal justice," as John Elster has put it.[33] Or they may accept that trials are rigged to hide evidence and absolve individuals of guilt and responsibility. Additionally, stories from popular culture may reject the verdict of a court by justifying private revenge.[34]

In this article, just a few examples draw from the depiction of the criminal trial in the postwar Italian films I am about to discuss. There are many different ways

---

27 *Teitel* 2000, p. 30.
28 *Bass* 2000, pp. 404–406.
29 *Durkheim* 2014. See also *Erikson* 1966.
30 *Machura* 2011; *Machura* 2017.
31 Among the studies on the relationship between transition justice and film. See *Benavides Vanegas* 2014; *Menkel-Meadow* 2016; *Punzi* 2019; *Elander* 2024.
32 *Karstedt* 2016.
33 *Elster* 2004, pp. 86–90.
34 *Robson/Spina* 2022, with several examples of revenge stories in transitional periods in Argentina, Italy, Greece, and Portugal.

of dealing with dictatorship and war, but all are necessarily told through the trial. Paradoxically, through the law, but beyond the law.

4. Facing a Terrible Past and an Uncertain Future: The Courtroom Show in Italian Cinema (1943–1948)

In this part, I will examine the films and documentaries that narrated how courts tried and condemned the crimes of Fascism. The sample of films was constructed by selecting the main titles reported in studies on cinema and the Resistance.[35] I then cross–referenced these titles with an analysis of the plots of films produced between 1943 and 1948, available in various repertories.[36] I believe I have a fairly accurate count of the films from this period that contain trial scenes. Watching them has allowed me to identify those that are relevant to the themes and problems of transitional justice. For this reason, I will not discuss a notable judicial film such as *Il testimone* (*The Testimony*, Italy, 1946, dir. Pietro Germi), which deals with themes of trial, miscarriage of justice, and guilt, but from an existentialist perspective and without any reference to the historical reality of the period. Similarly, I must overlook an important film such as *Caccia tragica* (*Tragic Hunt*, Italy, 1947, dir. Giuseppe De Santis). Although it is an extraordinary document of the post–war situation in Italy, narrating the crimes of the fascists and the problem of banditry, *Caccia tragica* is a "lawless" film in which the call to overcome feelings of revenge for the sake of national reconciliation is made through a kangaroo court.

Therefore, I will focus on three films that, in my opinion, provide a comprehensive picture of the representation of the process of transition from Fascism to the Republic, through the war and the Resistance. These films are (in the order in which I will discuss them): *Giorni di gloria* (*Days of Glory*, Italy, 1945, dir. Mario Serandrei, Giuseppe De Santis, Luchino Visconti and Marcello Pagliero); *Un uomo ritorna* (*Revenge*, Italy, 1946, dir. Max Neufeld); and *La vita ricomincia* (*Life Begins Again*, Italy, 1945, dir. Mario Mattoli). The trial scenes in these films involve Italian defendants and take place in special or ordinary courts, not military tribunals.

Three films may seem very few to the international reader, who may have in mind the plethora of examples of American courtroom films. However, as Tomeo has

---

35 *Casadio* 1997; *Ben-Ghiat* 1999; *Cavallo* 2019; *Ghigi* 2009; *Lichtner* 2013; *Zagarrio* 2015; *Zinni* 2015.

36 Sources: Wikipedia, IMDB, the Cinedatabase of Fondazione Ente dello Spettacolo (At: https://www.cinematografo.it/trova-film), the archive of the leading Italian daily newspaper "Il Corriere della Sera", the film periodicals available in the Luigi Chiarini Digital Library (At: https://www.fondazionecsc.it/biblioteca-digitale-biblioteca-luigi-chiarini/), and *Morandini* et al. 2021.

shown and subsequent analyses have confirmed,[37] the courtroom is not a genre that can be found in Italian cinema, except in rare cases and with the exception of hybrid approaches typical of Italian popular legal culture, such as the courtroom comedy or films about the mafia. It should not be underestimated that, in just two years, it has been possible to count several films that place the trial at the centre of their narrative structure. Even considering the production, commercial, and technical factors that may have influenced the decision to include trial scenes, one cannot fail to grasp the connection between this choice and the practices of transitional justice at the time.

This is confirmed by another set of considerations. During the twenty years of the Fascist regime (1922–1943), there were very few films that were in any way interested in judicial themes or that contained explicit references to trials or executions. Of course, with the advent of sound film in mind, we can count only a handful of films that make a more or less extensive mention of judicial procedures and prosecutions. These include *Corte d'Assise* (*Before the Jury*, Italy, 1931, dir. Guido Brignone), which is one of the rare examples of an Italian courtroom film, *Un colpo di vento* (–, 1936, dir. Carlo Felice Tavano and Jean Dréville), the comedy *Gatta ci cova* (–, 1937, dir. Gennaro Righelli), and finally another comedy with a farcical trial, *Imputato, alzatevi* (–, 1939, dir. Mario Mattoli).

To this assessment of cinema, we should add a consideration of the newsreels. Through the nationalisation of the Istituto LUCE, the Fascist regime produced and distributed all Italian newsreels and documentaries. Throughout the 1930s, the Institute released an average of nearly two hundred newsreels a year, covering nearly every topic of current interest, from major news events around the world to the latest fashions in popular culture, from the movements of well–known politicians and movie stars to coverage of sporting events.[38] The focus was always on propaganda about the regime's achievements in economic policy, modernisation of the country, and foreign policy, especially the wars of colonial expansion. Of course, this propaganda also had to emphasise the regime's successes in fighting crime and providing security for its citizens. This explains why, when researching the historical archives of the Luce Institute, it turns out that until 1944 the Institute did not produce any newsreels on criminal cases, on the Mafia, and even less on criminal trials.[39] The only exception I found is the coverage of the Hauptmann trial with five newsreels, between 1934 and 1936, dedicated to the case of the kidnapping of aviator Lindbergh's son, through the use of footage.

---

37 *Vitiello* 2013; *Amodio* 2016; *Spina* 2016; *Tomeo* 2024.
38 *Ricci* 2008, p. 70.
39 The historical archive of the Istituto Luce provides research of 77,270 films, available for watching: At: https://www.archivioluce.com (Last accessed on 31/05/2024).

Apart from this American high–profile crime case, the first newsreel about a trial will be that of the fascist Pietro Caruso, which is also the focus of the first film we will now discuss.

4.1 Giorni di gloria

Despite its rhetorical emphasis, *Giorni di gloria* effectively describes the national tragedy of the war, the violence suffered by the population, and the extensive destruction in many parts of the country. The film also expresses the expectation of national rebirth attributed to the Italian people. In this sense, *Giorni di gloria* conveys a simple ideological and political message meant to be understood by the masses. The film documents the climate of conflicting emotions during the period: on one hand, uncontrollable desires for revenge, and on the other, trust in the state and the law. It is an account of the most notorious instance of the wild purge, as well as the first attempts at judicial punishment.

To be precise, *Giorni di gloria* is a documentary edited by editor and screenwriter Serandrei using archive material, and sequences shot by directors De Santis, Pagliero and Visconti, who contributed to the rise of neorealism. It was produced by the National Association of Italian Partisans. Presented to the public as a document and testimony to the reality of the war and the Resistance, it includes some staged scenes to emphasise the actions of the Partisans.

Giorni di gloria is an interesting movie in many respects, as highlighted by critics, I will dwell on these aspects briefly.[40] The film was released in October 1945, a few weeks after *Roma città aperta* (*Rome, Open City*, Italy, 1945, dir. Roberto Rossellini). This detail is significant because both films promoted the idea of the Resistance as a national liberation movement from the foreign oppressors, and together with the condemnation of Fascism, avoided any problematization of the civil war that had taken place in the country.[41] To illustrate the popularity of these films, consider that *Roma città aperta* grossed 125,000,000 lire, while *Giorni di gloria* grossed 28,820,000 lire.[42] Furthermore, *Giorni di gloria* is one of the few documentaries about the Resistance, a movement that had limited opportunities to tell its own story through images and film, thus increasing its value as a historical document and source of collective memory.[43]

The first part of the film depicts the dramatic events of the war within Italy: the destruction of cities and industries, the drama of the civil war, and the killings

---

40 *Cooke* 2011, pp. 34–35; *Brunetta* 2009, pp. 69–70; *Ciammaroni* 2012; *Pucci* 2013; *Serandrei* 1998.
41 *Parigi* 2015.
42 *Chiti* et al. 1991, pp. 313, 171.
43 *Parigi* 2015.

perpetrated by Nazis and Fascists in the occupied areas of northern Italy in 1944 and the early months of 1945. It then describes the Italian reaction: the partisan war, the role of women in the Resistance, strikes and terrorist actions. These include the Via Rasella episode in Rome and the subsequent German reprisals leading to the Ardeatine Caves massacre of 335 Italian prisoners (24 March 1944).[44] The film shows for the first time to the public the discovery of the slaughtered bodies and the painful work of identifying the corpses. This is how the new government responds to such cruelty, and the response comes through the spectacle of the trial. In fact, we witness the filming of the various stages of the Caruso trial, which took place in Rome between September 18 and 21, 1944.[45] The trial was the first to be held by the High Court of Justice. It was certainly the most high–profile.

Pietro Caruso, Rome's chief of police in early 1944, was accused of organising roundups and collaborating with the German occupiers. The most serious of these collaborations was the reprisal that led to the carnage in the Ardeatine Caves.

The trial of Caruso took place in the Palace of Justice in Rome in an atmosphere of great excitement. On the first day, hundreds of people gathered in front of the Palace of Justice, demanding that the accused be handed over for summary execution, without being allowed to enter the courtroom. At one point, over three hundred people managed to breach the gates and enter the courtroom, which was built to hold sixty people.[46] The crowd consisted mainly of women: mothers, wives, and sisters of the victims of the Ardeatine Caves massacre. It was here that the most notorious lynching of the period was committed.[47] A witness called by the prosecution to testify against Caruso, Donato Carretta, former director of the Regina Coeli prison in Rome, was attacked by the crowd in the courtroom. Notwithstanding his compromised position with the fascist regime, he was innocent of crimes against civilians and political opponents. Despite the efforts of the prosecutor and the police who were present, Carretta was brutally beaten and, dragged out of the Palace of Justice into the street in front of an even larger and more violent crowd, and thrown into the Tevere River where he drowned. His body was hung upside down, naked, from a window of the prison where he had been warden.

Due to this terrible episode, Caruso's trial resumed two days later in a different location with much better police protection. The trial lasted only two days and the sentence was carried out the day after the verdict. The severity and speed of the punishment were meant to serve as a deterrent for any collaborationists.

The Caruso trial is what John Elster calls "show trial", where the appearance of legality is mere fiction because the outcome is predetermined.[48] Woller describes

---

44 *Portelli* 2003.
45 *Domenico* 1991, pp. 92–97; *Woller* 1996, pp. 184–187.
46 *Domenico* 1991, p. 92.
47 *Ranzato* 1997.
48 *Elster* 2004, p. 86.

it as an *Inszenierung*, a staging rather than a trial conducted according to the due process principles.[49] All the events described, from Caruso's arrest to Caretta's lynching, from the trial debate to the execution, are present in the central part of the documentary, lasting 14 minutes out of a total duration of 106 minutes. The trial received extensive press coverage at the time. Its visibility was certainly amplified by the footage shot by Luchino Visconti and his crew, later edited into *Giorni di gloria*. It is evidence of the performative urge to make justice visible and public that the Allied Psychological Warfare Branch chose Visconti to film Caruso's trial.[50]

Throughout the film, the images of the trial are accompanied by an emphatic and rhetorical voiceover, contrasting with the documentary images, which remain particularly vivid and effective. Yet, it is the off–screen commentary that reveals the interpretation of events intended by the authors and received by the audience, and it is on this that we will focus. The lynching is justified not only by the violence of Fascism and the pain of the victims but also by the slowness and ineffectiveness of the legal system to punish those responsible. Among these weaknesses, one must also consider the evasion of some of the accused, who managed to escape justice.[51]

Of the lynching, which was also filmed entirely outside and up to its conclusion, *Giorni di gloria* only shows the scenes inside the courtroom, but it is already clear that Carretta's sad fate is at the mercy of the crowd's brutality. The editing is striking, alternating large overhead shots of the unfortunate man and the entire courtroom with close–ups of the faces of those present, mostly women, expressing dismay, uncertainty or anger. We see lips moving, but the sound is that of the entire crowd, creating a particularly effective portrayal of the confusion of the moment. The voiceover repeats that "even the blood of a single man who has not yet been judged is too much" and insists that this episode of crowd revenge was an isolated incident in the Resistance, denying what historical research has shown, about the wild purges that occurred especially in 1945.

De Santis, one of the film's directors, explained why the lynching footage was not used in full in the final cut:

> "Perhaps we were wrong, but it was both a political and a poetic decision. This was an isolated episode — the Italian people were completely different. We wanted to show another Italy, the Italy of the Resistance, the Italy that had rolled up its sleeves".[52]

---

49 *Woller* 1996, p. 185.
50 *Pucci* 2013, p. 361.
51 The off-screen commentary refers to the case of General Roatta, who fled shortly before his trial. See *Domenico* 1991, pp. 135–138.
52 *Cooke* 2011, p. 35.

Cook commented:

> "It is very easy today to hold De Santis and his colleagues up as an example of dishonesty, but it is necessary to remember that the war had only just finished. Their "censorship" needs to be understood in the context in which the film was made".[53]

After commenting on the first stages of the lynching, the images return to the proceedings of the Caruso trial before the High Court of Justice. The main figures of the trial are captured: the President and the other judges, the defendants, the defence lawyers, the prosecutor, and the head of the Allied police, British Colonel John R. Pollock. The faces of the two defendants are often filmed, while the commentary emphasises their anguish and awareness of their guilt. The lawyers and judges are dressed in robes, the general in uniform, the carabinieri in full parade uniform. Everything is very orderly, in contrast to the brawl and confusion of the lynching moment. The military police imposed restrictions on lighting and the use of cameras, adding the sense of an austere courtroom.[54]

The footage follows the "normal pace of a sensational trial" as the narrator explains. We experience the various stages of a trial that must appear procedurally correct, although the verdict is already known to all. Here are the testimonies of policemen, the chief of police underway, and a bishop. The prosecution is inflexible, and the task of the defence is arduous. The closing statement of the prosecutor, the lawyer and anti–fascist politician Mario Berlinguer, reminds the whole courtroom what the Italian people and the civilised nations of the world expect from justice. He recalls that the task of the trial is to show that Italy is reborn because it is capable of redeeming and liberating itself by punishing those responsible for the crimes of the past. As the prosecutor calls for the death penalty, the film shows images of slaughtered bodies filmed at Fosse Ardeatine: "the dead" – says the voiceover – "are here in the courtroom".

The defence attorneys are now on camera, making long and tedious pleas for mercy for the accused, using, as the commentary says, "the most astute tropes" of rhetoric. The death sentence is read as the condemned man is framed. Soon we see the shooting behind him, that of Caruso and then of other condemned men shot in June 1945. When we return to the mourning of the relatives of the fascist victims, the voiceover proclaims: "it is the just punishment of the crimes committed that has brought down those most directly responsible. Serious and thoughtful justice is the best antidote to the outbursts of revenge".

---

53   Ibid., p. 35.
54   *Ciammaroni* 2012, p. 21.

4.2 Un uomo ritorna

Giorni di gloria concludes with the bodies of Mussolini and the *gerarchi* on the Piazzale Loreto in Milan, surrounded by the crowd. That film ends with images of workers operating machines again and trains moving again, symbolizsing the reconstruction after the war.

The second film I analysed, *Un uomo ritorna*, conveys a similar message of hope, with electric light finally returning to the homes of Italians. This film serves, in my opinion, as a melodramatic counterpoint to *Giorni di gloria*. While the documentary presents crimes and war from a collective perspective, *Un uomo ritorna* focuses on the needs of the individual experiences of its protagonists, shifting from grand historical events to the personal stories of everyday life.

Narrative cinema is well–suited to exploring an often overlooked aspect of transitional justice. This operates on two levels: micro justice, which focuses on the needs of the individual victim and concerns the relationship between individuals, and macro justice, which concerns the needs of society as a whole and concerns the development of the social order.[55] The intersection between personal emotions and the broader community's emotional climate is highly problematic and often leads to judicial outcomes that disappoint victims, driving them into despair and anger. This complex situation is effectively addressed in *Un uomo ritorna*.

The film tells two intertwined stories, that of a man and a woman, destined to intersect in a sentimental relationship. Sergio, the male protagonist, is a technician at a hydroelectric plant crucial for post–war reconstruction. As a war veteran, his primary goal is to repair what the war has destroyed: the power plant, the minefields, and his family, with his sister at risk of becoming a prostitute and his brother involved in smuggling.

Adele, the female protagonist, is a widow who accepts Sergio's courtship while awaiting the return of her son, Giorgio, who was deported by the Repubblichini, Italians loyal to the RSI who fought alongside the Germans. The fascist squad leader responsible for Giorgio's kidnapping lives in the same block as Adele, representing the civil war's spatial contiguity. When this fascist returns home, he is discovered, denounced, and a crowd, including an enraged Adele, gathers to take justice into their own hands. However, the police intervene and arrest the fascist to put him on trial.

The trial scenes, lasting about ten minutes, focus primarily on the defence lawyer, who is the true protagonist, rather than the prosecutor. Moreover, the movie does not have a satirical intention towards lawyers and justice, as is often the case in Italian cinema. The film realistically portrays the course of trials against fascist crimes.

---

55 *Karstedt* 2021.

The defence lawyer's speech during the trial invokes justice, not revenge: "if revenge can be blind, justice cannot and must not be blind". The accused is guilty of being a fascist, but the lawyer questioning whether being a fascist can be a crime for someone who grew up under that dictatorship. The defendant was "unfortunately" guilty of "believing in his ideal" and defending it even after the fall of the regime. The lawyer insists that his client did not use violence ("neither torture nor beatings") and that he did not carry out the combing operation of his own free will ("despite himself"), but "because he was forced to do so" by his superiors. In short, he acted "as a mere clerk".

This defence argument mirrors the actual trials that were held during the same period in the various Extraordinary Courts of Assizes throughout the country. The extenuating circumstances that allowed criminals and collaborators to escape the death penalty, light sentences, and even acquittal of the accused are accurately mentioned in the film trial. These circumstances were the absence of acts contrary to the conventions of war, that is, violence against civilians, and the exclusion of command responsibility in the action.

However, the accused's serious responsibilities emerge within the trial, with an act that is informal but functional to the story. A man from the audience interrupts the defence lawyer's plea to disprove such as exculpatory picture, and then he recounts the torture carried out by the fascist on various prisoners and the death of some of them. And among these is Giorgio, Adele's young son. We and the mother learn the tragic news, she despairs and shouts 'murderer' supported by the other women, the judge adjourns the hearing. This revelation leads to a dramatic confrontation, reminiscent of actual episodes in trials against fascist criminals, for example in the Bologna trial against Tartarotti.[56]

We are left in uncertainty about what the collaborationist's sentence will be: the death penalty, hoped for by his mother and the crowd, or a prison sentence, hoped for by the accused's wife, also present in the courtroom. This narrative detail is certainly functionnal to the film's plot and maintains suspense as we await the verdict. However, it is important to note the difference between this movie and the previous one: in the former, the verdict against the fascist was already known; here, it is unpredictable. As Niklas Luhmann explained, one of the sociological preconditions for the legitimacy of law is precisely the uncertainty about the outcome of a procedure.[57] A minimal indicator of a functioning legal system, even in transitional justice, is the unpredictability of the trial's outcome.[58]

The little fascist is not sentenced to capital punishment (which would have equalled the death of the young man according to a retributive logic) but instead receives

---

56   *Dondi* 2008, p. 53.
57   *Luhmann* 1969.
58   *Elster* 2004, pp. 88, 90.

a twenty–year imprisonment (in line with the jurisprudence of the special courts). The pronouncement of the sentence is not filmed. The viewer understands what the verdict was through the murmur of the crowd outside the courthouse. The sentence seems extremely lenient to the incredulous mother.

Overcome with anger, she confronts the judges as they leave the courtroom:

> "Twenty years you gave him. To the murderer of my son, twenty years. You took pity on him. But who took pity on my son? Who? Aren't you ashamed? That's why you wear these rags" – she says tugging at the astonished judge's robe – "to mock poor people like me. We had to get justice ourselves, ourselves ... That murderer has returned. We must shoot him, shoot him like a dog".

In this case, merely transcribing the monologue does not suffice to convey the emotional force of the scene, as Adele is played by the great Anna Magnani, the renowned actress from *Roma città aperta*. These simple sentences are a synthesis of the narrative already present in *Giorni di gloria*, as well as the historical interpretations of many episodes that took place in Italy during those years. Faced with the lenient and merciful punishments meted out to fascist criminals, punishments that were legally correct, fantasies of revenge and real acts of private justice were unleashed.

The movie continues with Adele's intent for revenge. Armed with a gun, she goes to the apartment of the person responsible for her son's death, which is, as mentioned, next to hers. Her intention is to apply a special law of retribution: a son for a son. But she stops out of pity for the child and does not commit the infanticide. She does not take justice into her own hands, even though she remains in her infinite despair.

Un uomo ritorna can be considered an insightful account of the events and sentiments surrounding transitional justice in Italy. The event that triggers the trial and the desire for summary justice is the return of the fascists to their hometowns, the places where they had previously oppressed the civilian population. This return sparked violent reactions and private vendettas.

In *Giorni di gloria*, the pain and the desire for justice are emphasised through the faces and cries of women, represented in groups as simulacra of Italian mothers, wives, and daughters who have experienced the pain of loss. In this film, too, the female protagonist, the incomparable Anna Magnani with her expressiveness and commitment, is tasked with conveying the anguish of waiting for her sons to return from the front, the despair of death, and the desire for true justice against the fascists.

In both films, the ritual of the trial is solemnly emphasised through the shooting and editing, the seriousness of the actors, the presence of police and carabinieri in full uniform, the backdrop of Rome's monumental Palace of Justice, the furnishings of the courtroom, and the lingering focus on the faces and emotions of the defendants, victims, and audience. Both films also contain a message of hope for the future, represented in the finales by the reopening of factories and the reconstruction of the basic infrastructure of daily life.

However, one notable divergence that is relevant to our discourse is the different levels of trust in the law and the possibility of coming to terms with the past. *Giorni di gloria*, through its portrayal of the trial, aims to convey a message of trust in justice, even though it depicts a form of political justice that diverges from the principles of due process. In contrast, *Un uomo ritorna* reverses the narrative path of the documentary. In *Giorni di gloria*, do–it–yourself justice, in the form of the group lynching of Caretta, takes place while waiting for the law to take effect, culminating in the epiphany of the Caruso trial. The final message there is that only effective justice and certain punishment can defuse the wild purges. In *Un uomo ritorna*, however, the attempt to take justice into one's own hands is triggered precisely by the correct and realistic functioning of the trial and a legally unquestionable verdict.

The film proposes a finale of reconciliation and hope as a different way of coming to terms with the past—a way that goes beyond the law, beyond do–it–yourself justice, and takes an uncertain direction, as uncertain and barely hinted at as Anna Magnani's smile in the last shot of the movie. That of forgetting.

4.3 La vita ricomincia

After the end of the Second World War, Europe embarked on a path of collective but selective amnesia, without which, according to Judt, "Europe's astonishing post–war recovery would not have been possible". Judt continues:

> "To be sure, much was put out of mind that would subsequently return in discomforting ways. But only much later would it become clear just how much post–war Europe rested on foundation myths that would fracture and shift with the passage of years. In the circumstances of 1945, in a continent covered with rubble, there was much to be gained by behaving as though the past was indeed dead and buried and a new age about to begin. The price paid was a certain amount of selective, collective forgetting".[59]

This selective obliteration of the past has had serious consequences for European societies. In Italy, it has contributed to the reproduction of divided memories and irreconcilable narratives about Fascism and the Resistance, making it very difficult to reach consensus even on the fundamental values of democracy.[60] Moreover, it has progressively reinforced in Italians those strategies of neutralisation of responsibility, both individual and collective, that have made them forget the persecution of

---

59 *Judt* 2005, pp. 61–62.
60 *Focardi* 2005; *Foot* 2009.

the Jews, wars of aggression and war crimes committed in occupied and colonised countries.[61]

What interests us here is how this complex game of collective amnesia was represented in cinema when this process had just begun in 1945. Furthermore, this was done through the representation, or rather the lack of representation, of a criminal trial. In fact, the movie's title already describes the need to move beyond war and trials.

La vita ricomincia was one of the very first films released in Italy immediately after the war, in September 1945. It is a popular melodrama, not a courtroom film and does not present a depiction of a trial. However, it tells the story of a prosecutor's investigation into a murder case involving a woman who is clearly guilty. Throughout its narrative, albeit in the schematic and simple terms of the genre, the film poses the problem of guilt and amnesia/amnesty.

The story revolves around Paolo, a war veteran trying to return to Rome, where his wife Patrizia and their child are waiting for him. He finds a fortunate ride from two black marketeers travelling in a truck overloaded with smuggled goods. The journey home passes through Cassino, a completely destroyed city symbolising the destruction of bombing and the front line. The ruins of the city represent the ruins of the state, law, and morality. As his fellow travellers say to him, "sir, today in Italy you are the only one under the law". When he returns to his family, everything seems normal, as if the war had never happened. But his wife is arrested for killing a man with several shots. When Paolo visits her in prison, Patrizia reveals the truth: by giving herself to the man she killed, she had obtained money to pay for an operation to save their seriously ill child. The profiteer wanted to resume the affair and blackmailed her by threatening to reveal the betrayal to her husband. It was for this reason that Patrizia killed him.

The husband feels betrayed and wounded in his honour and reacts with indignation. But the wife responds by explaining her determination as a mother to save their son with the only means at her disposal. She points out that she is not the only one guilty and responsible for this situation; everyone is guilty, including her absent husband.

Stricken with remorse, Paolo goes to see the prosecutor (incorrectly referred to as a judge in the movie) and tries to convince him that he is the murderer in order to acquit his wife. The magistrate understands the falseness of his statement and seems unwilling to betray the fairness of the investigation and misrepresent the truth of the facts. At Paolo's urging, the prosecutor turns against him:

61 *Ben-Ghiat* 1999; *Focardi* 2013.

PROSECUTOR:	Then you want me to help you cheat justice.
PAOLO:	And what does justice care if the killer is me or my wife? Justice wants a guilty person, one who will pay. I'll pay anyway.
PROSECUTOR:	No, justice must punish only the one who committed the crime.
PAOLO:	And who can say, Mr. Judge, who is the real guilty one?

This passage is important. The responsibility for the crimes committed during the war lies not only with individuals, but with society as a whole. At least on a moral level, everyone is absolved. But what happens on the legal level? We learn this by following the prosecutor's reasoning in response to the previous question.

PROSECUTOR:	Yes, it's true, you may be right. I also understand that in these cases we need a higher, more compassionate justice, perhaps above men, who knows how to judge more than our miserable laws. But we are men, we have been given these laws in our hands as a weapon with which we must strike. It is our duty to strike, to punish. ...
PAOLO:	Mr. Judge, please, I have to do something for my wife.
PROSECUTOR:	No, you must not, you cannot do anything. Have faith. Justice is not, as many believe, an enemy thirsting for revenge. Justice knows how to judge, it knows how to understand. It is a hard, painful test that must be endured with a strong heart. I repeat, have faith.

What verdict will distinguish justice from vengeance? What verdict will confirm faith in the law? On the day of the sentencing, Paolo and a close family friend are at home anxiously awaiting the court's decision. Friends at the courthouse call on the phone: Patrizia has been acquitted. After much doubt and torment on Paolo's part, full family reconciliation eventually arrives. The message addressed to the audience, thanks to the melodrama genre, is the need to overcome the drama of the war, with its burden of suffering, betrayal and even crimes. The invitation is to start again, to reconcile by pretending that everything never happened: "nothing happened, there was nothing" the protagonists repeat to each other.

A few months after the end of the Second World War, the Fascists and the Nazis, the collaborationists and the Partisans — they have disappeared in this film. Moreover, reconciliation is symbolically achieved through an acquittal that erases all guilt. An Italian historian, aware of the role of cinema as an "agent of history", has commented on *La vita ricomincia* as follows:

> "It is not unreasonable to read in this absolution of the woman the self–absolution of an entire nation that could thus remove a long and painful war, a twenty–year dictatorship (which the film easily ignored) and — last but not least — the trauma of 8 September. In short, the future could only be built on the basis of the removal of the past".[62]

---

62 *Cavallo* 2019, p. 48.

War has made everyone guilty, as the wife says to her husband and as the husband repeats to the magistrate. Therefore, true justice, which is higher and nobler than the mere application of laws and procedures, can only grant everyone a general amnesty. The amnesty of June 22, 1946, would not be long in coming.

5. Conclusion

When we approach popular culture, we know that we are dealing with fictional narratives that are simplified or distorted in relation to actual events. Nonetheless, we recognise that popular culture can help us better comprehend certain complex relationships, especially those between the broader levels of history and law and the personal experiences and emotions of individuals.

The films analysed here are quite different: they belong to various genres; were produced for different purposes, be it educational or commercial; and their ideological intentions might even be contradictory. Yet, each of these films can be said to reflect the daily lives of millions of Italians during the years of transition from Fascism to war to the Republic.

Giorni di gloria, *Un uomo ritorna* and *La vita ricomincia* express the fundamental need of any society emerging from war to come to terms with the past and begin to live again in a period of peace. In each of these films, the concepts of revenge and justice challenge each other; ultimately, a certain kind of justice (political, legal, moral) is affirmed, always through a trial and with the seal of a judge.

This aspect cannot be underestimated. These films testify to the need to show the community that in the new state justice will be done based on values different from those of the fascist past, values of truth, freedom, and mercy. After years of disinterest, the dramatic dimension of the law, so opposed to the foregone conclusions of the regime's political justice, has reappeared, perhaps responding to a need for reflection and adversarial debate that only courtroom drama can satisfy.

Through their focus on trials, the films analysed in this essay echo the dilemmas of transitional justice, transferring them from legislative decrees and courtrooms to the perspectives of ordinary people. Through their ideological messages and emotional narratives, these films attempted to resolve those dilemmas for the Italians at the time. Did they succeed? What was their role, and that of novels or radio programmes, in enhancing or counteracting the acceptance of the verdicts of purges and convictions? What was their impact on the courts, on the victims, on the witnesses? Further research should explore the impact of films and popular culture products on transitional justice more thoroughly, possibly from a comparative perspective.

These are just some of the questions that popular culture studies can help raise by examining the complex relationship between law and war. These insights can address both the past and the present. Indeed, it remains to be seen how the stories and themes of the films discussed have been transmitted and readapted over the years, how they survive in collective memory, and whether they are remembered at all. Unfortunately, these minor films, as well as the masterpieces of Italian Neo-realism, have almost disappeared from the programming of mainstream television and streaming channels, for purely commercial reasons or perhaps due to veiled ideological censorship. Thankfully, these films have found a new chance to escape oblivion thanks to video–sharing platforms on which they are miraculously available. Watching *Giorni di gloria, Un uomo ritorna* or *La vita ricomincia* could certainly help Italians today to reassess the value of freedom, democracy, and the rule of law.

Bibliography

Abel, Richard L., 2019: Law's Wars. The Fate of the Rule of Law in the US "War on Terror". Cambridge, Cambridge University Press.

Amodio, Ennio, 2016: Estetica della giustizia penale. Prassi, media, fiction. Milano, Giuffrè.

Bass, Gary Jonathan, 2000: Stay the Hand of Vengeance. Princeton, N.J., Princeton University Press.

Benavides Vanegas, Farid Samir, 2014: Film and the Reconstruction of Memory. In: *Wagner*, Anne/*Sherwin*, Richard K. (eds.), Law, Culture and Visual Studies. Dordrecht, Springer, pp. 992–1010.

Ben–Ghiat, Ruth, 1999: Liberation. Italian Cinema and the Fascist Past 1945–50. In: *Bosworth*, Richard J. B./*Dogliani*, Patrizia (eds.), Italian Fascism. London, Palgrave Macmillan, pp. 83–101.

Benjamin, Walter, 2021: Toward the Critique of Violence. Stanford, CA, Stanford University Press.

Brunetta, Gian Piero, 2009: Il cinema neorealista italiano. Da "Roma città aperta" a "I soliti ignoti". Roma–Bari, Laterza.

Caroli, Paolo, 2022: Transitional Justice in Italy and the Crimes of Fascism and Nazism. London, Routledge.

Casadio, Gianfranco, 1997: La guerra al cinema. I film di guerra nel cinema italiano dal 1944 al 1996. Ravenna, Longo.

Cavallo, Pietro, 2019: La storia sul grande schermo: Risorgimento e Resistenza nel cinema italiano tra ricostruzione e miracolo economico (1945–1965). Napoli, Liguori.

Chiti, Roberto/*Poppi*, Roberto/*Lancia*, Enrico, 1991: Dizionario del cinema italiano. Dal 1945 al 1959. Roma, Gremese.

Ciammaroni, Stefano, 2012: Giorni di gloria e la retorica della violenza nel cinema italiano del dopoguerra. In: *Colleoni*, Federica/*Parmeggiani*, Francesca (eds.), Forme, volti e linguaggi della violenza nella cultura italiana. Lonato del Garda (BS), EDIBOM.

Cooke, Philip E., 2011: The Legacy of the Italian Resistance. New York, Palgrave Macmillan.

Domenico, Roy Palmer, 1991: Italian Fascists on Trial, 1943–1948. Chapel Hill, University of North Carolina Press.

Dondi, Mirco, 2008: La lunga liberazione. Giustizia e violenza nel dopoguerra italiano. Roma, Editori Riuniti–L'Unità.

Dorsen, Norman, 1989: Foreign Affairs and Civil Liberties. In: The American Journal of International Law, 83:4, pp. 840–850.

Douglas, Lawrence/*Sarat*, Austin/*Umphrey*, Martha Merrill, 2014: Law and War. An Introduction. In: *Sarat*, Austin/*Douglas*, Lawrence/*Umphrey*, Martha Merrill (eds.), Law and War. Stanford, CA, Stanford University Press, pp. 1–22.

Durkheim, Émile, 2014: The Rules of Sociological Method. And Selected Texts on Sociology and its Method. New York, Free Press.

Elander, Maria, 2024: 'The Working of Time'. Transitional Justice and Body Memory in Rithy Panh's Cinema. In: *Crawley*, Karen/*Giddens*, Thomas/*Peters*, Timothy D. (eds.), The Routledge Handbook of Cultural Legal Studies. London, Routledge, pp. 255–268.

Elster, Jon, 2004: Closing the Books. Transitional Justice in Historical Perspective. Cambridge [U.K.], New York, Cambridge University Press.

Erikson, Kai, 1966: Wayward Puritans. A Study in the Sociology of Deviance. New York, John Wiley.

Fletcher, Laurel E./*Weinstein*, Harvey M./*Rowen*, Jamie, 2009: Context, Timing and the Dynamics of Transitional Justice. A Historical Perspective. In: Human Rights Quarterly, 31:1, pp. 163–220.

Focardi, Filippo, 2005: La guerra della memoria. La Resistenza nel dibattito politico italiano dal 1945 a oggi. Roma–Bari, Laterza.

Focardi, Filippo, 2013: Il cattivo tedesco e il bravo italiano. La rimozione delle colpe della seconda guerra mondiale. Roma–Bari, Laterza.

Focardi, Giovanni/*Nubola*, Cecilia (eds.), 2015: Nei tribunali. Pratiche e protagonisti della giustizia di transizione nell'Italia repubblicana. Bologna, il Mulino.

Foot, John, 2009: Italy's Divided Memory. New York, Palgrave Macmillan.

Garapon, Antoine, 2002: Des crimes qu'on ne peut ni punir ni pardonner. Paris, Odile Jacob.

Ghigi, Giuseppe, 2009: La memoria inquieta. Cinema e Resistenza. Venezia, Cafoscarina.

Greenfield, Steve/*Osborn*, Guy/*Robson*, Peter, 2010: Film and the Law. Oxford, Hart.

Judt, Tony, 2005: Postwar. A History of Europe since 1945. New York, Penguin.

Karstedt, Susanne, 2016: The Lives and Times of Sentenced Nazi War Criminals: Re–negotiating Guilt and Innocence in Post–Nuremberg Germany 1950–1975. In: *Bell*, Christine (ed.), Transitional Justice. London, Routledge, pp. 33–50.

Karstedt, Susanne, 2021: Between micro and macro justice: Emotions in transitional justice. In: *Bandes*, Susan/*Madeira*, Jody/*Temple*, Kathryn/*Kidd White*, Emily (eds.), Research Handbook on Law and Emotion. Cheltenham, U.K., Northampton, MA, Edward Elgar, pp. 460–476.

Lichtner, Giacomo, 2013: Fascism in Italian Cinema since 1945. London, Palgrave Macmillan.

Luhmann, Niklas, 1969: Legitimation durch Verfahren. Neuwied am Rhein, Luchterhand.

Machura, Stefan, 2011: Media Influence on the Perception of the Legal System. In: *Papendorf*, Knut/*Machura*, Stefan/*Andenaes*, Kristian (eds.), Understanding Law in Society. Developments in Socio–Legal Studies. Berlin, LIT, pp. 239–283.

Machura, Stefan, 2016: The Law and Cinema Movement. In: *Picart*, Caroline Joan "Kay" S./*Jacobsen*, Michael Hviid/*Greek*, Cecil (eds.), Framing Law and Crime. An Interdisciplinary Anthology. Lanham, Rowman & Littlefield, pp. 25–58.

Machura, Stefan, 2017: Representations of Law, Rights, and Criminal Justice. In: Encyclopedia of Crime, Media, and Popular Culture. At: http://criminology.Oxfordre.com/view/10.1 093/acrefore/9780190264079.001.0001/acrefore-9780190264079-e-201.

Meniconi, Antonella/*Neppi Modona*, Guido (eds.), 2022: L'epurazione mancata. La magistratura tra fascismo e Repubblica. Bologna, Il mulino.

Menkel–Meadow, Carrie, 2016: In the Land of Blood and Honey. What's Fair or Just in Love and War Crimes? Lessons for Transitional Justice. In: *Picart*, Caroline Joan "Kay" S./*Jacobsen*, Michael Hviid/*Greek*, Cecil (eds.), Framing Law and Crime. An Interdisciplinary Anthology. Lanham, Rowman & Littlefield, pp. 105–133.

Morandini, Laura/*Morandini*, Luisa/*Morandini*, Morando/*Morandini Tassi*, Michele, 2021: Il Morandini. Dizionario dei film e delle serie televisive. Bologna, Zanichelli.

Nubola, Cecilia, 2017: Governare la transizione attraverso la giustizia. In: *Bernardini*, Giovanni/*Cau*, Maurizio/*D'Ottavio*, Gabriele/*Nubola*, Cecilia (eds.), L'età costituente, Italia 1945–1948. Bologna, Il Mulino, pp. 27–51.

Osiel, Mark, 1997: Mass Atrocity, Collective Memory, and the Law. New Brunswick, N.J., Transaction Publishers.

Parigi, Stefania, 2015: L'immagine di guerra. La Resistenza nel cinema italiano dell'immediato dopoguerra. In: Cinema e storia. Rivista annuale di studi interdisciplinari, IV, pp. 35–50.

Portelli, Alessandro, 2003: The Order Has Been Carried Out. History, Memory, and Meaning of a Nazi Massacre in Rome. New York, Palgrave Macmillan.

Portinaro, Pier Paolo, 2011: I conti con il passato vendetta, amnistia, giustizia. Milano, Feltrinelli.

Pucci, Lara, 2013: Shooting Corpses. The Fosse Ardeatine in Giorni di gloria (1945). In: Italian Studies, 68:3, pp. 356–377.

Punzi, Corrado, 2019: La memoria ostinata. Il cinema di Patricio Guzmán come ricerca sociale. Trento, Tangram.

Ranzato, Gabriele, 1997: Il linciaggio di Carretta. Roma 1944. Violenza politica e ordinaria violenza. Milano, Il Saggiatore.

Ricci, Steven, 2008: Cinema and Fascism. Italian Film and Society, 1922–1943. Berkeley, University of California Press.

Robson, Peter, 2005: Law and Film Studies. Autonomy and Theory. In: *Freeman*, Michael (ed.), Law and Popular Culture. Oxford, Oxford University Press, pp. 21–46.

Robson, Peter/*Spina*, Ferdinando (eds.), 2022: Vigilante Justice in Society and Popular Culture. A Global Perspective. Lanham, Md, Rowman & Littlefield/Fairleigh Dickinson University Press.

Rovatti, Toni, 2015: Tra giustizia legale e giustizia sommaria. Forme di punizione del nemico nell'Italia del dopoguerra. In: *Focardi*, Giovanni/*Nubola*, Cecilia (eds.), Nei tribunali. Pratiche e protagonisti della giustizia di transizione nell'Italia repubblicana. Bologna, il Mulino, pp. 15–52.

Serandrei, Mario, 1998: Giorni di gloria. Un film. Mario Serandrei. Gli scritti. *Gaiardoni*, Laura (ed.), Roma, Centro Sperimentale di Cinematografia.

Spina, Ferdinando, 2016: Italy. In: *Robson*, Peter/*Schulz*, Jennifer L. (eds.), A Transnational Study of Law and Justice on TV. Oxford, Hart, pp. 145–162.

Teitel, Ruti G., 2000: Transitional Justice. Oxford, New York, Oxford University Press.

Tomeo, Vincenzo, 2024: The Judge on the Screen. Judiciary and Police in Italian Cinema. *Robson*, Peter (ed.), Lanham, Md, Rowman & Littlefield/Fairleigh Dickinson University Press.

Vitiello, Guido (ed.), 2013: In nome della legge. La giustizia nel cinema italiano. Soveria Mannelli, Rubbettino.

Woller, Hans, 1996: Die Abrechnung mit dem Faschismus in Italien 1943 bis 1948. München, R. Oldenbourg Verlag.

Wouters, Nico (ed.), 2014: Transitional Justice and Memory in Europe (1945–2013). Antwerpen, Intersentia.

Zagarrio, Vito (ed.), 2015: Cinema e antifascismo. Alla ricerca di un epos nazionale, special issue of Cinema e storia. Rivista annuale di studi interdisciplinari, IV.

Zinni, Maurizio, 2015: La storia incompiuta antifascismo e Resistenza nel cinema politico italiano dal boom agli anni Settanta. In: Cinema e storia. Rivista annuale di studi interdisciplinari, IV, pp. 51–81.

Iker Nabaskues Martínez de Eulate

War, Film, Memory and Trauma: the Bosnian Case in *Quo Vadis Aida?*

1. Introduction

The conflicts of modern war have come down to us through television images. Modern wars need the mass media and the media need wars. The support of the population depends on the belief in the necessity of military action and its emotional rewards. The role of communication as a strategic tool meets a media demand for any spectacular event, live television has become a 'must' in the modern media world. In this context, the Gulf war was probably the first war in history to be announced in television guides. After the Gulf War in 1991 television was described as one of the most important means of military strategy. Modern media play a substantial role in the construction of reality as well as in attitude formation in the audience. While propaganda has always played a crucial role in military activities, it has reached new professional levels with the occurrence of global television and the development of increasingly differentiated public relations' strategies.[1]

Without having to go that far in time, we have the example of the Gaza war caused by the October 7 attacks in southern Israel. The criminal attack on defenseless civilians was recorded with go pros carried by the perpetrators in their helmets and weapons. With this, they made evident their specific interest in uploading the scenes of terror to the Internet and promoting a state of terror among the civilian population, in addition to providing a media loudspeaker for their war action. In the case of Israel, the interest has been the opposite. The recordings of the October 7 attacks were broadcast on closed channels to a duly accredited public of politicians and journalists. With this, the Israeli government intended to convey the horror of that day to the actors it wanted, without contributing to spreading the feeling of fear and terror among the civilian population.

The invasion by the Israeli army of the Gaza Strip in 2023-2024 is also played out in the media field. The Hamas government counts the number of civilian victims and, by tightly controlling the information channels, manages the information for its own interests. Likewise, the consequences of the Israeli attacks are broadcast on all television channels to spread the idea of the massacre on the civilian population.

---

1 *Groebel* 1995, pp. 11-12.

The destructive power of war cannot be glimpsed only in television images. The war produces personal ruptures in relationships that, in the case of the Balkan War, reached leading protagonists in the film world. Emir Kusturica, one of the most awarded Serbian filmmakers, and his favorite screenwriter Abdulah Sidran broke up their relationship as a result of the disastrous war that confronted their nations, Serbia and Bosnia.

During his long career, Sidran received numerous awards for his work in literature and television. He was given the 'Freedom Award' by the PEN Centre in France for his impactful poetry collection, 'Sarajevo Coffin', which was published during the 1992-95 war in Bosnia and Herzegovina. Sidran made a significant contribution to the cinema of the former Yugoslavia and was celebrated for his outstanding screenplays for Kusturica's critically acclaimed films.

Sidran and Kusturica's friendship ended in acrimony over the war in Bosnia and Herzegovina when the filmmaker took a Serb stance while the poet opposed attempts to create a 'Greater Serbia'. He made wonderful scripts for Kusturica's films, but war separated them. After the Serbian aggression against Bosnia, Sidran cut off almost all contact with Kusturica, whom he called a former friend.

The important link between war and media finds its fullest expression during those wars, the Balkan wars (1991-2000). In fact, it was also the subject of reflection by many film directors from the war-torn countries, in addition to Kusturica.[2] *Quo Vadis Aida?* (Bosnia, Jasmila Žbanić, 2020) is a film that contains all the elements of what the Balkan wars represented. The film is dedicated to young people by the Bosnian director.

---

2 Balkan cinema has given voice to many stories with important film works during the last decades. Chiara Vitucci (2021) made a compilation of films that deal directly or indirectly with the Yugoslavian-Balkans wars. The work is an indispensable source for gauging the impact of these wars on the filmmakers and producers of the former republic of Yugoslavia and beyond its borders. It develops the plot of each film and is a more than interesting compilation for the Law and Cinema analysis. This is the list: *Before the Rain* (North Macedonia, 1993, dir. Milcho Manchevski); *Underground* (Serbia, 1995, dir. Emir Kusturica); *Pretty Village, Pretty Flame* (Yugoslavia, 1996, dir. Srdjan Dragojević); *Welcome to Sarajevo* (U.K., 1997, dir. Michael Winterbottom); *The Perfect Circle* (Bosnia, 1997, dir. Ademir Kenović); *Beautiful People* (U.K., 1997, dir. Jasmin Dizdar); *Savior* (U.S.A., 1998, dir. Predrag Antonijević); *The Knife* (Yugoslavia, 1999, dir. Miroslav Lekić); *No Man's Land* (Bosnia, 2001, dir. Danis Tanović); *Behind Enemy Lines* (U.S.A., 2001, dir. John Moore); *Midwinter Night's Dream* (Serbia and Montenegro, 2002, dir. Goran Paskaljević); *Life Is a Miracle* (Serbia and Montenegro, 2002, dir. Emir Kusturica); *Fuse* (Bosnia, 2003, dir. Pjer Žalica); *The Secret Life of Words* (Spain, 2005, dir. Isabel Coixet); *Grbavica* (Bosnia, 2006, dir. Jasmila Žbanić); *The Hunting Party* (U.S.A., 2007, dir. Richard Shepard); *Resolution 819* (France, 2008, dir. Giacomo Battiato); *The Tour* (Serbia, 2008, dir. Goran Marković); *The Whistleblower* (Canada, 2010, dir. Larysa Kondracki); *In the Land of Blood and Honey* (U.S.A., 2011, dir. Angelina Jolie); *Killing Season* (Belgium, 2013, dir. M. Steven Johnson); *The High Sun* (Croatia, 2015, dir. Dalibor Matanić); *A Perfect Day* (Spain, 2015, dir. Fernando León De Aranoa); *Quo vadis, Aida?* (Bosnia, 2020, dir. Jasmila Žbanić).

After a wait due to the pandemic, the film could be seen in some countries from the end of February 2021. Also in February 2021, the "Valencia Film and Human Rights Festival" in Spain awarded *Quo vadis, Aida?* with the prize for best film and best screenplay in its 12th edition. The film was one of the five Oscar nominees for Best Foreign Film for the 93rd edition of the 2021 Oscars. It did not win the award due to competition from other equally successful films, but it can certainly be used in schools and university classrooms to talk about the atrocious event known as "the Srebrenica Massacre" and, above all, the terrible social consequences of war in the Balkan societies.

Both art and any theorization about reality have a double function that is only contradictory in appearance: on the one hand, to explain reality a little more and better and, on the other, to complicate it so that new questions arise for the recipient. In this way one remains in a certain state of perplexity regarding the topic in question, but already from a higher level of understanding. This is precisely what *Quo Vadis Aida?* fosters. A brave approach to the ghosts of the past – the Srebrenica Events – that appeal directly to the deepest sensations of Bosnians.[3]

2. *The events*

We must look back to the distant 1995. The process of decomposition of Yugoslavia, after the fall of communism and the Berlin Wall, triggered different independence processes in the countries that had formed the republic. The UN, seeing the turn the conflict was taking, decided to send humanitarian aid troops to the territories in conflict. Dutch blue helmet troops under the command of Commander Thomas Karremans were deployed in Bosnia–Herzegovina. The UN was trying at all costs to prevent a large–scale humanitarian crisis with unforeseeable consequences in the centre of the continent. During the summer of that year, the Serbian troops of General Ratko Mladić advanced into Bosnian territory.

The bloodiest events of all those that took place in the early 1990s in Yugoslavia occurred in Bosnia–Herzegovina. The Bosnian war began one year after the Slovenian and Croatian wars, in 1992, and lasted until 1995. Bosnia–Herzegovina proclaimed its independence on April 6 1992, in a referendum (99% positive votes) in which Muslims and Croats participated, but not Serbs — Serbians from Bosnia— which generated a conflict of incalculable dimensions. The "Yugoslav People's Army" had stated that it would not allow any attempt to found independent republics that would change the borders, based on the principle that wherever Serbs lived, that space would be part of Serbia. This led the Serbs to reclaim much of the territory

---

3   Casals 2021, p. 5.

occupied by Bosnia, which resulted in a violent attack, just two days after the referendum, on the Bosnian population of Zvornik. Thus, began what was to become an ethnic cleansing.

It is important to analyse the important role played by Serbian media in the way of portraying the Serbs from Bosnia as victims of the barbarian Bosnian Muslims.[4] Ideologues were very present in the media, participating in the extension and acceptance of the measures adopted by the Serbian government, and making the crime of genocide tolerable for the population. Belgrade television did an enormous job in producing hatred towards other ethnic groups, constantly exposing different cases of Serbian victims of World War II and encouraging Serbs to take revenge on Muslims for the acts committed. The past and the present were united within a single discourse, becoming inseparable. The willingness of a large part of the Serbian population to commit such a serious crime as genocide was the result of manipulation and mythologising by political leaders and the media. Through the conjunction of a historical memory — mass murder of Serbs during the development of World War II — and a sophisticated ideology that dehumanised Muslims, the Serbian population ended up perceiving Bosnian Muslims as Turks and murderers of Serbian Orthodox.[5]

The brief sequence of events in the Bosnian mountain village of Srebrenica was as follows: on July 11, the Serbian Army General Mladić's troops entered Srebrenica with hardly any military opposition; the "theoretical" requests for NATO air support made by the Dutch Commander Karremans were not heeded so as not to endanger the Dutch blue helmets.[6] The following day, after the flight of part of the civilian population through the adjacent forests and with the movement of about 25,000 people[7] to Potocari (headquarters of the Dutch troops) Mladić and Karremans met and made an agreement to release women and children in the UN headquarters.

---

4   This role pursued the path of works such as that of Miodrag Jovičić, who wrote *Serbs and Albanians* in the 20th Century, where he promoted the idea that Albanians were genetically predisposed to violence due to their Muslim condition. Works such as Vuk Drašković's *The Knife* (1982), which described the violence of Bosnians against Serbs during World War II; or Danko Popović's *The Book on Milutin* (1985), which told the tragic story of a Serbian peasant who fought in both world wars and lost everything. The information in the Serbian media reinforced this view, which was already beginning to take strong root in the imaginary of society, that Muslims were the enemy that had to be destroyed. *Moreno Ruiz* 2020, p. 20.

5   Ibid., p. 22.

6   The UN peacekeepers — often referred to as Blue Berets or Blue Helmets because of their light blue berets or helmets — can include soldiers, police officers, and civilian personnel. Chapter VII of the United Nations Charter gives the United Nations Security Council the power and responsibility to take collective action to maintain international peace and security. Most of these operations are established and implemented by the United Nations itself, with troops obeying UN operational control. In these cases, peacekeepers remain members of their respective armed forces and do not constitute an independent "UN army", as the UN does not have such a force. In the case of the Bosnian war, a platoon of Dutch army soldiers under the command of UN personnel were deployed in different enclaves of the territory.

7   *Martín Hernández* 2008, p. 28.

The separation of the men and the deportation of the women in buses staged the beginning of the massacre. The Bosnian refugees who remained in the enclave were transported to different places in the area and tortured and shot.

There is a telling moment in the movie during the negotiation scene with General Mladić. He puts a cigarette in his mouth, and Colonel Karremans, the commander of the UN forces and visibly nervous throughout the meeting, is on the spot to light it for him, as if he cannot help trying to ingratiate himself (Picture 1). Also telling, about his extremely weak position and resources, is the fact that the lighter misfires twice before producing any result.[8]

Picture 1: Negotiations between General Mladić (on the left) and Colonel Karremans (centre). Source: Film still from Quo vadis, Aida? (Bosnia, 2020, dir. Jasmila Žbanić).

3. Srebrenica: safe enclave

The lessons identified in the Report of the Secretary–General on the fall of Srebrenica show the serious mistakes made both in relation to the decision to declare this city as a safe area. As well as in relation to the successive extensions of the United Nations Protection Forces — UNPROFOR — Mandate, in relation to the protection of the town. The decision to declare Srebrenica as a safe area was not without controversy even before its establishment. Thus, the disagreements among the members of the Security Council were evident as to the decision to establish it; as to the concept of the safe zone to be adopted and the means to be used for the protection of the zone.[9]

---

8 *Sødtholt* 2021.
9 *De Tomás* 2016, p. 121.

Events in Bosnia and Herzegovina set in motion a wave of pessimism among European states and the U.S.A. regarding UN peacekeeping operations as a suitable outlet for deploying peacekeepers. According to the media and many policymakers, the conflict in Bosnia followed a logic albeit evil.[10]

The events in the Srebrenica enclave caused a real national upheaval in the Netherlands. The situation on the ground of the Dutch UNPROFOR contingent with the mandate to protect the safe area and all the events after July 11 provoked a cascade of work, investigations, parliamentary debates and even the resignation of the entire government as a whole. To the point of becoming a real collective exercise of self–criticism of the political class, of the Dutch armed forces in the framework of peacekeeping operations, of the media and of the role of the Netherlands in the international community.[11]

The Bosnian War brought pain, barbarism and oppression to thousands of Muslims and Croats. It left an indelible mark on the minds of communities traumatised by the violence they had suffered. A large part of the refugee population was not able to return to homes that reminded them of the atrocities they had suffered. This led to a regrouping of the refugees in localities inhabited by members of the same ethnic group, which eventually resulted in ethnicity, which eventually led to the creation of a small state, such as Bosnia– Herzegovina, fragmented along ethnic lines.

If we think of the title of one of the earliest texts of international law, the well–known *De iure belli ac pacis* by Grotius, it becomes clear that classical international law organized relations between states also during armed conflicts. Previously, the law of war — *ius in bello* — was distinct from the law of peacetime, the latter encompassing the right to use armed force — *ius ad bellum*. However, since the Charter of the United Nations prohibited the use of armed force, a new terminology has been imposed. Contemporary international law deals with armed conflicts both to try to prevent wars and to regulate conduct throughout hostilities. Today, the international law specifically devoted to conflicts is called "International Humanitarian Law." One of the basic principles is to differentiate between the combatant, who is a legitimate target, and the civilian or person who — because he is wounded, imprisoned or otherwise — does not take part in the hostilities and has to be protected. Another difference, developed over the last fifty years, is that between international armed state conflicts and non–international armed conflicts — civil wars as the Bosnian. According to the UN charter, the UN aims to:

---

10 *Van der Lijn* 2014, p. 4.
11 *López Jimenez* 2016, p. 104. In June 2022, the Dutch Prime Minister Mark Rutte, officially apologised to the Blue Helmets Dutchbat soldiers for the lack of support over Srebrenica, saying that they were sent on an impossible mission to protect the so-called UN "safe haven" of Srebrenica.

"Save succeeding generations from the scourge of war, to reaffirm faith in fundamental human rights, to establish conditions under which justice and respect for the obligations arising from treaties and other sources of international law can be maintained, and to promote social progress and better standards of life in larger freedom."[12]

The mission of the UN blue helmets deployed in the Bosnian enclave, was "to protect the civilian populations of the designated safe areas against attacks and other hostile acts, through the presence of troops and, if necessary, through the application of airpower, in accordance with agreed procedure."[13] The airpower never came. But this was not the only mistake. The UN had made a serious mistake in deploying only a few thousand troops around the country — far fewer than necessary to ensure mission objectives. The Dutch peacekeeper army to protect civilians in the enclave of Srebrenica, were lightly armed and lacked ammunition, there were few in number, and totally unable to confront the Serb forces led by General Mladić.

In July 2015, marking the 20th anniversary of the Srebrenica genocide, the United Nations Security Council put forward a draft resolution to officially condemn the killing of the 8,000 Bosnian men and male children as a genocide. However, Russia, on behalf of Serbia, vetoed the resolution. Russia firmly believes that what happened in Srebrenica was not genocide. That is why, the UN failed to provide the survivors any hope of a formal global acknowledgement of their suffering and all they had lost.

The war in the Balkans marks an important step for international criminal law. Indeed, in response to the violations of international humanitarian law perpetrated during the war in Yugoslavia, the United Nations Security Council created an *ad hoc* Tribunal with the task of punishing those guilty of crimes against humanity and the environment. Almost 40 years from the Srebrenica genocide, it was clear that the UN refrained from taking measures to prevent the horror which was yet to come during those terrible days in Bosnian history. In the Netherlands, the government fell due to the political crisis that came from the Srebrenica events and many years later the Supreme Court in that country established the political responsibility of Dutch dignitaries.

Everything portrayed in the film may relate to the current events in Ukraine. The cinematographic narrative provides us with a paradigm where Europe faces its spectres and turns it, into cultural product. Culture, in this case opens us to new becomings where the European Union questions its recent past, its role as a political actor and active agent in the invasion of Ukraine. As the former vice–secretary of UN Mark Malloch–Brown said:

"For most of its 75–year existence, the United Nations has struggled to strike a balance between its lofty founding aspirations and realities on the ground. But in today's fast–

---

12 United Nations Charter.
13 *Herman* 2006, p. 415.

changing geopolitical environment, the organisation may be facing its biggest challenge yet."[14]

The European continent is currently experiencing the greatest war crisis since the Balkan War. Now it is not the implosion of a state like the former Yugoslavia, but the aggression of one state, against another.[15] The refugee crisis provoked by the Russian invasion poses an unprecedented challenge to the European Union. The Union has launched an unprecedented package of political, economic and financial sanctions against Russia. It is also putting in smuggling or illegal adoption. All this makes it clear that the Union is scrupulously complying with the mandate of the international treaties.

4. The Bosnian director who touched the topic no one else wanted to: the role of film to overcome trauma

The Bosnian director Jasmila Žbanić, a young woman in her twenties during the Yugoslavian War, portrays in *Quo Vadis, Aida?* a stark reality for the citizens of the European Union. The Srebrenica genocide, the largest massacre in Europe since Second World War. The film portrays the traumatic episode of the role of the Dutch UN Blue Helmets in the events. Jasmila Žbanić was a direct witness and victim of the terrible events that unfolded as a consequence of the disintegration process of the Republic of Yugoslavia. The director explains in an interview for the Council of Europe:

"It is a tragedy that took my heart and soul. During the war in Bosnia I was living in Sarajevo under the siege. It was 2.5 hours from Srebrenica. There was no electricity, the internet did not exist and information about Srebrenica and what was happening there was not coming regularly. Srebrenica was a United Nations protected zone and we Bosnians all hoped it was at least safe. We trusted the UN. But, after 30,000 people were expelled from their houses and the UN did nothing, then we all got scared — a sense of security completely disappeared. For me, the story of Srebrenica is an incredible drama of human beings that this institution failed to protect. The more I dug into it, the more I was shocked that it was possible that it could happen in modern–day Europe."[16]

The movie is set in the days of the massacre (11–22, July 1995). The Serbian army takes control of the town of Srebrenica, where Aida lives with her husband and two children. Before the war, she was a teacher and now works as a translator for the

---

14 *Malloch-Brown* 2020.
15 There are a lot of evidence of war crimes in Ukraine, as attacks on children's hospitals, school buildings and the use of lethal weaponry against the civilian population. There were found civilians in mass graves in the Ukrainian towns of Bucha, Irpin and Gostomel. Some human rights organisations spoke of 500 — handcuffed and defenceless executed.
16 *Hurtes* 2020, p. 1.

UN. Almost all the inhabitants have fled the town getting away from the Serbian army. People are crowding near the blue helmets' camp asking for her help. Aida will try to use her privileges as UN worker to try to save her family. Then came the massacre.[17]

The very title of the film asks where Aida, the main character is going. She is a schoolteacher turned UN translator, since the beginning of the conflicts in the Balkans, who must carry out her very important and sometimes invisible work as an interpreter, being present in the decision–making process in a moment of uncertainty and tension. The scenes of the film take place at the exact moment when Commander Karremans becomes aware that he will not receive military aid of any kind, and that he cannot carry out the mission for which he has been appointed. Žbanić puts the microscope where it hurts the most. The moment when the cold and calculated decisions of the UN must be applied. The Bosnian director perfectly portrays the gap between the defence of humanitarian values and the human frailty to carry them out. Žbanić wonders where Aida is going. But what we see in the film is that neither Aida nor anyone else can go anywhere. An ethnic cleansing is being prepared, which is projected throughout the film like a ghost over the seemingly trivial events we observe. No one speaks clearly, there are no exact determinations. The only ones are on Karremans' office table, but those determinations are precisely the only ones that cannot be applied.

But Aida is not neutral during the confinement of the Bosnian population in the UN refugee camp. Aida is Bosnian, and so are her husband and son. She is the interpreter and knows the direct consequences of what she is translating. During this sensitive context, she must do what she can to save her husband and her two children from possible execution.

In the film, we see how the UN turned into a negligent body, and its authorities close to the ground must muddy themselves and at the same time maintain their composure in the face of an authority weakened by the events. *Quo Vadis, Aida?* is a realistic representation of events that marked a turning point in the UN's pacification policy. It portrays the fragility of military structures based on the defence of a peace, that, without the use of force, becomes an empty promise.

In this sense, the film is a perfect exercise in awareness of the events surrounding a tragedy such as the one in Srebrenica. Our imagination constructs realities that are

---

17 *Suljacić* 2001, p. 19. Srebrenica was described in these terms by Judge Fouad Riad, member of the Criminal Tribunal for the former Yugoslavia: "After the fall of Srebrenica following the siege by Serb troops in July 1995, a terrible massacre of the Muslim population took place; the evidence shown by the Prosecution describes scenes of unimaginable savagery: thousands of men executed and buried in mass graves, hundreds of men buried alive, men and women mutilated and massacred, children murdered in full view of their mothers, a grandfather forced to eat his grandson's liver. These are truly scenes from hell, written in the darkest pages of human history." Report of the Secretary-General pursuant to General Assembly resolution 53/35: The fall of Srebrenica (A/54/549).

consonant with the tragic consequences of the events being analysed. In *Quo Vadis Aida?* we observe that the most mundane circumstances are the prelude to tragedy. It does not take much more to trigger ethnic cleansing. There is no need for noise or scandal. It can be built from the most everyday events, such as waiting for a phone call that never comes or translating a statement in a way that matches one's interests.

The massacre happens in the middle of town. Boys are seen playing football before they run away at the sound of the guns, and we have already seen people on a balcony nearby. We do not see the killings. We only hear the sound of the machine–gun fire (Pictures 2 and 3). Like the victims, the gunfire as a concrete manifestation of a massacre having here taken place has disappeared, as if never having existed.[18] If what Žbanić wanted was to portray the coldness, crudity and banality of the events that foreshadow mass crime, we can say that she succeeds.

Pictures 2 and 3: Quo vadis, Aida? Does not show the killings directly. Only the sound is heard. Source: Film stills.

---

18   *Sødtholt* 2021.

Although Aida is a fictional character, her story could easily have happened to anyone in that terrible war environment with the United Nations looking the other way. What makes *Quo Vadis, Aida* stand out is its willingness to introduce, in the middle of a distressing, hopeless story, a feeling of rage and indignation. The film raises an accusing finger against all those who chose to look the other way, who chose not to see what was happening, who ignored reality even when it was happening in front of their eyes. The film, shaken by heartbreak, brings us closer to recent history and makes a moving plea against forgetting.

There is a very suggestive ambivalence between publicity and secrecy in relation to *Quo Vadis Aida?* We all know that one of the most basic concepts of the Rule of Law is the fact that citizens know the institutions, their decisions and the procedures they put in place to make them work properly. In relation to publicity, it can be said that the Srebrenica massacre is an event today, known worldwide. And, if this is so, it was because there are numerous testimonies of Bosnians, witnesses of the massacre, who managed to report information on the facts to the war journalists deployed in the area during that time.

Subsequently, both the UN and the Dutch government and judiciary conducted their own investigations. The International Criminal Tribunal for the former Yugoslavia — ICTY— conducted a brilliant investigation that lasted more than 20 years.[19] General Mladić was sentenced by the tribunal in November 2017 to life imprisonment for genocide and war crimes in Bosnia. Of the eleven charges against him, the International Criminal Tribunal for the Former Yugoslavia convicted him on ten, including the Srebrenica genocide, the most important one. This judgment was the last one handed down by the ICTY, which ceased to function on December 31, 2017, after more than 20 years in which it tried a total of 161 cases.[20] Special mention deserves the great documentary (*The Trial of Ratko Mladić*, U.K., 2018, dir. Henry Singer/Rob Miller) where an exhaustive and detailed analysis is made of the case heard by the Special Tribunal for Yugoslavia and which concluded with the conviction of the Serbian general.

Similarly, the Dutch government and judiciary were involved very seriously in determining the responsibility of Dutch soldiers for the Srebrenica massacre and whether they did everything in their power to prevent it. It can certainly be said in this regard that the Srebrenica massacre not only became known far beyond the

---

19 The International Criminal Tribunal for the former Yugoslavia was a body of the United Nations that was established to prosecute the war crimes that had been committed during the Yugoslav Wars and to try their perpetrators. The tribunal was an *ad hoc* court located in The Hague, Netherlands. It was established by Resolution 827 of the United Nations Security Council, which was passed on 25 May 1993. It had jurisdiction over four clusters of crimes committed on the territory of the former Yugoslavia since 1991: grave breaches of the Geneva Conventions, violations of the laws or customs of war, genocide, and crimes against humanity.

20 United Nations Security Council, 2023.

borders of the Balkans, but also led to a chain of legal actions with far–reaching consequences.

But Srebrenica does not only imply, in this sense that we have just developed, publicity, as a fundamental element of democracy and Human Rights culture. It also involves secrecy. For many years, Srebrenica became a secret. But, what is a secret? In psychoanalytic terms, a family secret implies a prohibition, a taboo, something that is not allowed to be alluded to and, that often becomes a pact of silence. Everything that is not allowed to be said falls into the shadows to avoid to threaten someone´s reputation.

The final scene of *Quo Vadis Aida?* points precisely to the idea of secrecy. In the film's last scene of the school performance, the camera is picking out some of the children for close–ups with them looking straight into the camera. The rhythmic alternation between the children hiding their eyes and looking straight into the lens can be seen as a metaphor about the conflicting impulses of denial and facing the truth (Pictures 4 and 5).

Pictures 4 to 6: The rhythmic alternation between the children hiding their eyes and looking straight into the lens and the flashback with the adults. Source: Film stills from Quo vadis, Aida?

The scene is very touching in itself but becomes even more resonant, however, if we consider the flashback with the adults, many of them cut down in their prime, also gazing into the lens (Picture 6). The flashback show us Bosnian innocent people, victims of the massacre, with a common past shared with their murderers, many of them neighbours. All of them are staring at the camera. They demand to be taken into account, to be respected in their memory. All of them are people with their memories and vicissitudes in their eventful lives. As a counterpoint to these gazes, we have some school children, who after the war, carry out a performance at the school party. On the other side of the audience are the protagonists of the Srebrenica story. There, executioners and victims of the massacre share a seat. Jasmila Zbanić portrays in a plastic and effective way a reality that exists but does not want to be taken into account. The children open and close their hands pretending to look and not wanting to do so. That is the tragedy of civil wars in too many places on earth and in history. At the end of the day, we must get on with our lives. The ambivalence between publicity and secrecy is a tremendously suggestive moral aspect in relation to the real legal consequences of the genocide and the real social situations that human beings, victims of it, must face up to. Publicity is a guarantee of democracy and the principle of legal certainty. Secrecy is the symptom of what we are afraid to face.

It makes intuitive sense that people's memories of traumatic events such as those experienced in Bosnia and Herzegovina during the War will continue to affect the social fabric in some perhaps intangible but nevertheless important way.[21] A number of anthropologists have built on these intuitions and tried to illuminate the role that personal memories and "transmitted memories" of the Second World War may have played in fueling the war in Bosnia.[22] These scholarly approaches take seriously the authenticity and power of personal memories and transmitted memories in shaping events. Beyond academic circles, the aid and policy-making world has acted on the same intuitions. Large sums of money have been spent on psycho-social programmes which aim to soothe or resolve painful memories of the atrocities of the recent war, partly for the benefit of the individual sufferers but sometimes also in the hope of avoiding future conflicts by intervening in the process of trans-generational transmission of trauma. [23]

Individuals' narratives are never solely personal memories but always include a social component, a wider social framework in which the memories are placed and told. Once past experiences are verbalised, personal memories are no longer exclusive and can be exchanged, corrected, disputed, confirmed and even appropriated. Moreover, in endeavouring to make the past meaningful, individuals do not draw

---

21 *Sorajbi* 2006, p. 1.
22 *Bax* 1995; *Hayden* 1994; *Simic* 2000.
23 *Sorajbi* 2006, p. 19.

strict distinctions between "historical facts" and "personal experiences"; the two are closely interwoven in people's narratives. The personal history that allows people to develop a sense of individual identity is socially contextualised in wider frameworks and is always constructed in relation, even in opposition, to others, since "people live in, and deal with, a world that extends beyond themselves".[24]

Memories are created, manifested, but also contested in social fields, through direct or indirect exchange, but also through individual and collective silences. The most common practice for keeping memories alive is to share them with others, with schoolmates, colleagues and friends. But, we can say that, in Bosnia, the intimate space required for keeping shared experiences alive were lost for many. This also concerns the material space to which memories are bound. The houses and flats people inhabited and the personal objects they treasured, a valuable pillar for nurturing memories often had to be left behind during the war.[25]

Different modes of silences and forgetting arouse in Bosnia after the Balkan Wars as pathological symptoms.[26] Silences concerning the war in the 1990s in Bosnia-Herzegovina were especially prominent in the analysis of the Post-Yugoslav generation. Eduard Klain develops the different problems that arise after the traumas produced in the context of civil wars such as that of the former Yugoslavia. Among many others, phenomena such as "parentalization", where the child takes on a parental role with the orphaned father or mother. The "anniversary syndrome" in which the anniversary of the death of the family member involves a traumatic experience. The "savior attitude" due to which helping professions are common among the descendants of victims of civil wars such as doctors, nurses, psychologists, social workers, etc. The so-called "replacement child syndrome", similar to the phenomenon that occurs when a child is born after the death of a newborn, and receives the name of the deceased child. A son or grandson replaces the personality of the deceased. Episodes of "shame and guilt" cause many descendants to hide the story of their father or mother being killed in the war. The "idealization of the dead" that assigns imaginary identities to deceased people. The "frozen grief," an unresolved grief that can be passed on to future generations. The "silence in the families of the aggressors" that can be transmitted as unconscious guilt. The "candle syndrome" in which a descendant acts as a scapegoat. And, finally the better known "Stockholm syndrome" as the identification with the aggressor. Thus, marriages between orphans and soldiers and civil guards who represent the aggressor are frequent.[27]

Secrecy, silence, wanting to look to the future while avoiding looking at the painful past, are not the path to anything productive. Secrecy does not end the

---

24 *Palmberger* 2016, p. 235.
25 *Tochman* 2009, p. 50.
26 *Shaw* 2010, p. 255.
27 *Klain*, pp. 279-296.

conflict, it is simply swept under the carpet. The secret of Srebrenica not only affected Bosnians. Also implied is the guilt on the powerlessness of the United Nations for not defending a defenceless population having deployed its armed forces to prevent a genocide in the heart of Europe. This secret has also haunted different generations in the Netherlands. It is well known that some of those young Dutch soldiers deployed in the Srebenica–Potocari enclave committed suicide some years later after the events.[28]

As we approach the 40th anniversary of the Srebrenica massacre, the UN adopted a historic resolution in May 2024. The United Nations General Assembly voted to establish an annual day of remembrance for the 1995 Srebrenica genocide despite strong opposition from Bosnian Serbs and Serbia. The resolution, written by Germany and Rwanda, received 84 votes in favour and 19 against with 68 abstentions. It makes July 11 the International Day of Remembrance of the Srebrenica Genocide.[29] In the same way, works are still being published about the incessant search by the relatives of the missing for the remains of people who disappeared forty years ago.[30]

The Bosnian director Jasmila Žbanić belongs to a generation of Bosnians who lived through the trauma of Srebrenica. Talking about the approach she was interested in for her film, Žbanić, alluded to a fact that interests us powerfully. And it is clear that Žbanić portrays in the film what she wanted. When we see the film, we see that everyone in the UN safe area has something to do. Commander Karremans must talk to his superiors in Sarajevo and New York. The Serbs must count the men under UN protection — who will then be separated from the women and executed over the next days.[31]

The main character, Aida, uses her skills as a translator to make the decisions of the Dutch commanders coincide with saving the lives of her husband and son. The film raises a terrible idea that points to the pernicious implications of bureaucracy. When everyone has something to do, when everyone is busy doing something, it seems that the terrible is postponed, it seems that an orderly and bureaucratised world as described by Weber[32] ensures that we do not fall into uncertainty. We have come to assimilate the instrumental rationality of our society, of our rule of law over the values and principles that underlie it. And, above all, the most important: the value of human dignity. But none of the efforts that were made, tasks in which so many people were involved, prevented the genocide in Srebrenica.

It is worth watching *Quo Vadis Aida?* It is a bureaucratic, cold, distant and uncompromising chronicle of human misery, as it was portrayed before by Hanna Arendt in her masterpiece *Eichmann in Jerusalem. A Report on the Banality of Evil*

---

28 *Ryngaert/Schrijver* 2015, p. 222.
29 United Nations General Assembly. A/78/L.67/Rev.1. 20 May 2024.
30 *Tervonen* 2024.
31 *Hasanović* 2016, p. 72.
32 *Weber* 1968, pp. 220-223.

(1963). Have we learned anything from Srebrenica to Ukraine? I believe, we do. We Europeans know that we can no longer stand passive when a civilian population is killed close to our borders.

Jasmila Žbanić's cinematographic work does not seem to want to reduce itself to showing that the most terrible aspects of the human condition can germinate from the banal and the mundane. She is interested in the moral analysis of the facts. In this sense, *Quo Vadis Aida?* it is a modern rather than a postmodern film. It can be presented as a reflection open to the viewer's understanding. This does not seem to be the intention of the young Bosnian director. She aspires to the moral condemnation of those who, although they did what they could, "someone" should have put in their hands tools to avoid the inevitable.

In this sense, what the film exudes is an elliptical moral condemnation of the military who, above all, had the mission to protect the lives of the Bosnian Muslims, and not to leave them in the hands of the Serbian army. No one knows this more than the Dutch soldiers themselves, many of whom live with lifelong psychological scars in the aftermath of the tragedy. Despite this, the film does not make a political reading of how the tragedy should have been avoided. But, the moral condemnation can be clearly seen.

On the other hand, the film has deep psychoanalytical connotations. It is a punch in the face of those Bosnians who had to live through the terrible events narrated in it. The relationship of the victims of the civil wars is a stormy and conflicted one. No one seems to have time to stop and talk face–to–face about the hardest episodes of the Bosnian war. Let time go by and let the new generations live with their backs turned to what made us suffer so much. But this, it can be bluntly said, is not what the young Bosnian director is willing to do. Her chronicle of the moments leading up to the massacre is an invitation to dwell on it, to look at it, to observe it, to analyse it in microscopic detail. Žbanić makes an exercise of sincerity with herself and with the past of her people. To pretend to look at it face to face. It is an exercise of great moral and existential lucidity. This is where the young Serbian director definitely wins us over. It is not about the complaint who seeks the guilt in order to do justice. Žbanić wants to go further, her existential approach aims at the tortuous labyrinths of the human psyche. Žbanić wants to look trauma in the face. She wants to know it in detail. And she wants to live with it, in order to move on. In this sense, *Quo Vadis Aida?* is a virtuous exercise in personal, moral and social responsibility.

Sometimes the most important issues are not addressed, precisely because they are the most important. This is the case of the Bosnians and the Europeans regarding the Srebrenica massacre. Some, because the event leads them directly to have to face a terrible and painful past. Others, because the issue points to the European Union's own inability to go beyond being a project under permanent construction to become

134

an effective power in its role in international conflicts where the use of violence is needed.

We are experiencing the same uncertainty regarding the invasion of Ukraine. Ukraine, a country that aspires to be part of the European Union in a not distant future, is under an existential pressure unknown in Europe since the Balkan Wars. It is likely that the determination shown by the leaders of the European Union countries has to do with the lack of determination they had in past conflicts and events such as Srebrenica. In any case, the war in Ukraine is a chapter in the history of the Union with unforeseeable consequences.

With the Ukrainian drama, we are once again reliving a similar consternation to that experienced by the founding fathers of the EU and their generation when they laid the foundations of European integration and the same desire: to relegate war to the history of Europe. We do not yet know whether we can win the war for democracy launched in Ukraine by totalitarianism. But, we do know that there is no more democratic, tolerant and inclusive project than that of the young European Union. And that there is no alternative to the duty to defend it at all costs. Solidarity with Ukraine is then, the way to a stronger and more solid European construction.

But in order to defend the European project it is necessary to look back to past, when the tragic events we have discussed in this paper put in check the coercive mechanisms of the European Union, which was still in its formative stage. Almost three decades have passed since the Srebrenica massacre and its profound political, moral and existential implications for Europeans. It is time, therefore, to look at the past with responsibility. There is no better way to prepare for a better future than to assume the collective responsibilities of the European Union. It is not a matter of blaming the Union for its past mistakes, but of ensuring that those mistakes will not be repeated.

The time has come to assimilate Srebrenica and destroy it as a secret. Srebrenica cannot be erased, but we can do away with its secret nature. By doing so, we will overcome the trauma. To assimilate what our civilization failed in, as the only condition for it not to happen again in the future. And the only way to do this is to act in similar situations. In the end, we leap over the criteria of specialisation, or microscopic analysis, only available to a few Scholars, to embrace an axiom of common sense shared by all of us here: that children cannot fix the failures of parents, but we can, at least, prevent our children from falling into the same. It is a film that vindicates memory by shedding light on the darkness. Beyond any other consideration, *Quo Vadis Aida?* is a representation of our most uncomfortable past that at the same time, helps to our healing as a civilization. This is the best legacy we can offer to generations to come.

Bibliography

Arendt, Hannah, 1963: Eichmann in Jerusalem. A Report on the Banality of Evil. London, Penguin.

Bax, Mart. 1995: Medjugorje: Religion, Politics and Violence in Rural Bosnia. Amsterdam, VU University Press.

Casals, Marc, 2021: La piedra permanece. Historias de Bosnia-Herzegovina. Madrid, Libros del K.O.

De Tomás Morales, Susana, 2016: Lecciones identificadas y lecciones aprendidas en conmemoración del 20º aniversario de la masacre de Srebrenica. Madrid, Dykinson.

De Waal, Remko, 2022: Prime Minister Apologies to Dutchbat Soldiers for Lack of Support Over Srebrenica. Dutch News. 19 June 2022. At: https://www.dutchnews.nl/2022/06/prime -minister-apologies-to-dutchbat-soldiers-for-lack-of-support-over-srebrenica/ (Accessed on 28 November 2023).

Goldfarb, Michael, 2015: Srebrenica, 20 Years Later, Politico, 7 July 2015, At: http://www .politico. eu/article/srebrenica-20-years-later/ (Accessed on 28 November 2023).

Groebel, Jo, 1995: The Role of the Mass Media in Modern Wars. In: *Hinde*, Robert A., *Watson*, Helen (eds.), War: A Cruel Necessity? The Bases of Institutionalized Violence. London, New York, Bloomsbury Academic, pp. 143–152.

Gutiérrez Espada, Cesáreo, 2002: Un viaje a Srebrenica. In: *Menéndez Alzamora*, Manuel (ed.), Yugoslavia, el eclipse de la política: Europa ensombrecida. Alicante, Publicaciones Universidad de Alicante, pp. 41–58.

Hayden, Robert M., 1994. Recounting the Dead: The Rediscovery and Redefinition of Wartime Massacres in Late and Post-communist Yugoslavia. In: *Watson*, Rubie S. (ed.), Memory, History and Opposition Under State Socialism. Santa Fe: School of American Research Press, pp. 167–184.

Hasanović, Hasan, 2016: Surviving Srebrenica. Aberdeen, The Lumphanan Press.

Herman, Edward S., 2006: The Approved Narrative of the Srebrenica Massacre. In: International Journal for the Semiotics of Law, 24:4, pp. 409–434.

Hurtes, Sarah, 2020: Interview with Jasmila Žbanić. Eurimages. Council of Europe. June 2020. At: https://rm.coe.int/interview-with-jasmila-zbanic/1680a0c1a5 (Accessed on 22 December 2023).

Klain, Eduard (1998): Intergenerational Aspects of the Conflict in the Former Yugoslavia. In: *Danieli*, Yael (ed.). International Handbook of Multigenerational Legacies of Trauma. New York, Plenum Press, pp. 279–295.

López Jiménez, José Ángel, 2016: In: De *Tomás Morales*, Susana/*Amich Elías*, Cristina/*López Jiménez*, José Ángel/*Martínez Alcañiz*, Abraham (eds.), Lecciones identificadas y lecciones aprendidas en conmemoración del 20º aniversario de la masacre de Srebrenica. Madrid, Dykinson, pp. 119–169.

Malloch–Brown, Mar, 2020: Slow Death or New Direction for the UN? At: https://www.wide r.unu.edu/publication/slow-death-or-new-direction-un (Accessed on 2 April 2023).

Martín Hernández, Rubén, 2008: Consecuencias de la actuación de la ONU en Srebrenica. Instituto Universitario General Gutiérrez Mellado. Boletín de Información. Ministerio de Defensa de España, 306, pp. 25–42.

Moreno Ruiz, Elisa, 2020. Political Violence and Crimes against Humanity in the Second Half of the 20th century in Anthropological Perspective: The Case of Bosnia Herzegovina in the Framework of the War of the Balkans. At: https://repositorio.unican.es/xmlui/bitstream/han dle/10902/19130/MORENORUIZELISA.pdf?sequence=1 (Accessed on 15 October 2023).

Nuhanović, Hasan, 2019: The Last Refuge: A True Story of War, Survival and Life Under Siege in Srebrenica. London, Peter Owen.

Palmberger, Monika, 2016: How Generations Remember: Conflicting Histories and Shared Memories in Post-War Bosnia-Herzegovina. London, Macmillan Publishers.

Ryngaert, Cedryc/*Schrijver*, Nico, 2015: Lessons Learned from Srebrenica Massacre: from UN Peacekeeping Reform to Legal Responsibility. In: Netherlands International Law Review, 62:2, pp. 219–227.

Shaw, Rosalind, 2010: Afterword: Violence and the Generation of Memory. In: *Argenti*, Nicolás, *Schramm*, Katharina (eds.), Remembering Violence. Anthropological Perspectives on Intergenerational Transmission. New York, Berghahn, pp. 251–260.

Simic, Andrei, 2000. Nationalism As a Folk Ideology: The Case of Former Yugoslavia. In: *Halpern*, Joel, *Kideckel*, David (eds.), Neighbours at War: Anthropological Perspectives on Yugoslav Ethnicity, Culture and History. Pittsburgh, Pennsylvania State University Press, pp. 103–115.

Sødtholt, Dag, 2021: Jasmila Žbanić's *Quo Vadis, Aida?* The Weakness of Strangers. September, 16. Montages Magazine. At: https://montagesmagazine.com/2021/09/jasmila-zbanics -quo-vadis-aida-the-weakness-of-strangers/ (Accessed on 10 October 2023).

Sorabji, Cornelia, 1995: A Very Modern War: Terror and Territory in Bosnia-Hercegovina. In: *Hinde*, Robert A., *Watson*, Helen (eds.), War: A Cruel Necessity?: The Bases of Institucionalized Violence. London, New York, Bloomsbury Academic, pp. 80-98.

Sorabji, Cornelia, 2006: Managing Memories in Post-War Sarajevo: Individuals, Bad Memories, and New Wars. In: Journal of the Royal Anthropological Institute, 12(1), pp. 1-18.

Suljacić, Emir, 2001: Srebrenica. No One Beleived Us. In: Observing Memories: The Magazine of the EUROM, European Observatory on Memories, 5.

Tervonen, Taina, 2024. The Bone Whisperers: Two Women Scientists and Their Work to Connect Lost Lives in Bosnia-Herzegovina. Tucson, Arizona, Schaffner.

Tochman, Wojciech, 2009: Like Eating a Stone. Surviving the past in Bosnia. New York, Atlantic Books, Grove Atlantic Ltd.

United Nations Charter. Peace, Dignity and Equality on a Healthy Planet. United Nations. At: https://www.un.org/en/about-us/un-charter (Accessed on 23 December 2023).

United Nations Security Council, 2023: Concluding Major Judicial Cases Mechanism for Criminal Tribunals Prepares for Next Stage of Operations, Its President Tells Security Council. Security Council Press Release SC/15317, 12 June 2023 At: https://press.un.org/e n/2023/sc15317.doc.htm. (Accessed on 22 December 2023).

United Nations, 2024: International Day of Reflection and Commemoration of the 1995 Genocide in Srebrenica. General Assembly. A/78/L.67/Rev.1. 20 May 2024.

Van den Broek, Frans, 2005: Srebrenica y la vergüenza. In: Claves de Razón Práctica, 152, pp. 66–71.

Van der Lijn, Jair/*Dundon*, Jane, 2014: Peacekeepers at Risk: The Lethality of Peace Operations, SIPRI Policy Brief, February 2014. At: https://www.scribd.com/fullscreen/209115745 ?access_key=key1r7p4nhuwyuca9qpt3m2&allow_share=true&escape=false&view_mode =scroll (Accessed on 11 November 2023).

Vitucci, Chiara, 2021: La guerra a la vuelta de la esquina. La mirada del cine a Yugoslavia en llamas. Cine y Derecho. Valencia, Tirant Lo Blanch.

Weber, Max, 1968: Economy and Society, ed. by Guenther *Roth* and Claus *Wittich*. Berkeley, University of California Press.

Peter Robson

Law in War – *The Wind that Shakes the Barley* and the Republican Court Experiment.
Justice in the Time of War in Popular Culture

1. Background: The Justice System in Loach's films

The coverage of the formal justice system is limited in the films of Ken Loach.[1] There is a degree of irony in this absence. Loach studied law and obtained a degree at Oxford and his screenwriting partner for over 25 years since *Carla's Song* (U.K./ Spain/Germany, 1996) is former practicing lawyer, Paul Laverty.[2] The legal system makes few filmic appearances in their work. There is a brief visit to the County Court in the television drama *Cathy Come Home* (U.K., 1966, dir. Ken Loach) where Reg's explanation for his rent arrears is brushed aside as not credible by the judge. The justice system's operation is generally avoided[3] by the Loach/O'Brien/Laverty team responsible for ten "Ken Loach" films from 1998.[4] There are a couple of the later films where we come briefly into contact with the justice system. In *The Angel's Share* (U.K., 2012, dir. Ken Loach) the action starts in Glasgow sheriff court with the sentencing of Robbie (Paul Brannigan) to community service. What we get a glimpse of here in the opening sequence is the unremitting ordinariness of the justice system grinding its way on with not a Horace Rumpole[5] nor Martha Costello[6] in sight. More recently, there is a promise of seeing the lower echelon of the justice

---

1 Like Sidney Lumet before him (Lumet 1995), Ken Loach is always at pains to emphasise that films are a collaborative team effort – Carry on Ken (DVD disc with *The Wind That Shakes the Barley*. The trio, Ken Loach, Rebecca O'Brien and Paul Laverty received a Bafta Scotland award in 2016 for *Outstanding Contribution to Film* through their company Sixteen Films.

2 On whom, it has been suggested the earnest fighter for justice, Dominic Rossi, in the series *The Justice Game* (U.K., 1989, dir. Norman Stone) was based [along with less plausibly Joe Beltrami] – interview with the producer of the series, Peter Brougham March 23, 2006.

3 Although *Ladybird, Ladybird* (U.S.A., 1994, dir. Ken Loach) contains scenes in the Family Court, these are on the specific issue of Court Protection orders for children with its own separate legal test of the best interests of the children. The screenplay was by Scottish writer Rona Munro.

4 *My Name is Joe* (1998); *Bread and Roses* (2000); *Sweet Sixteen* (2002); *Ae Fond Kiss ...* (2004); *The Wind that Shakes the Barley* (2006); *It's a Free World* (2007); *Looking for Eric* (2009); *Route Irish* (2010); *The Angel's Share* (2012); *Jimmy's Hall* (2014); *I, Daniel Blake* (2016); *Sorry We Missed You* (2019).

5 *Rumpole of the Bailey* (long running British TV series 1978-1992).

6 *Silk* (second British TV series 2011-2014 with a woman lawyer as the major protagonist).

system, with the "fitness for work" test appeal of the protagonist in *I, Daniel Blake* (U.K., 2016, dir. Ken Loach) to the First–tier Tribunal. How this body operates, unfortunately, we do not see as Daniel Blake takes badly in the waiting room and dies.[7] The role of the court in *The Wind that Shakes the Barley*[8] is, although limited, rather more significant and sheds light on issues about law in time of war which are largely absent from other "law in war" films.

2. Introduction

"War and civil justice co–exist with some difficulty at the best."[9]

The Courtroom scene in *The Wind that Shakes the Barley* addresses two fundamental and ongoing issues for those involved in revolutionary change concerning the legal order which the Secretary to the Treaty Delegation and prominent anti–Treaty figure Erskine Childers noted.[10] How to win the fight and how to make sure the victory is not simply one on paper. This involves two elements – Law and Order and Law and Justice.

3. Law and Order in Time of War

LILY ROWE:	By whose authority …?
TEDDY O'DONOVAN:	Do you want every merchant and businessman in the county up against us with decisions like that?
LILY:	You're interfering with the court's decisions by your actions Teddy.
TEDDY:	Are you going to throw me in the jail too. Who will fight the war then?[11]

---

7   As a judge in Her Majesty's Courts and Tribunals Service (First Tier Tribunal – Social Entitlement) I was particularly saddened by this omission although I appreciate it made a more compelling drama than most of the hearings I have chaired. He would almost certainly have won on the evidence available. The test applied to Daniel Blake is being abolished in 2023 – as a money-saving option, however, rather than as a recognition of its flaws.

8   The words are from an Irish ballad written by the polymathic Robert Joyce (1936-1883). It is the lament of a young man from Wexford involved in the 1798 rebellion, led by the Society of United Irishmen across Ireland whose sweetheart is killed by a bullet in the conflict. He laments the foreign chains that bind Ireland and envisions his own death. Joyce quit his position as Professor of English at the Catholic University in Dublin and emigrated to the United States following the failure of the Fenian Rising of 1867.

9   Erskine Childers. The Constructive Work of Dáil Éireann, No. 1, Dublin, 1921, p. 30 cited in *Kostonouris* 2020, p. 48.

10 Childers was one of those who rejected the Treaty and was executed on 24 November 1922 by the Free State after the start of the Civil War on 28 June 1922 under the martial law powers introduced in the Dail in September 1922.

11 See Appendix for the full transcript of the courtroom episode.

This exchange in the courtroom in *The Wind that Shakes the Barley* encapsulates a classic dilemma between the social goals of a revolutionary war and the need to win the war of liberation against the immediate oppressors. Which of these priorities will suffer?

4. Law and Justice in Time of War

DAN: So we paint the town Republican green but underneath we're still the same as the English.[12]

If liberation is secured from external oppression, what guarantee is there that in the future there will be greater justice unless the rules and how they are administered are also changed?

This chapter examines how these two themes play out in a major award–winning 21st century film, *The Wind that Shakes the Barley* (2006).[13] The film has a somewhat different focus from most of the other examples of popular cultural representations of law and justice in war with which I am familiar mentioned below.[14]

5. Law and War in Popular Culture

Popular culture has taken the operation of the justice system during war as a theme quite extensively over the years. The focus has been, principally, upon the parallel system of justice operated by the military authorities. In a range of post–World War II films, from the 1950s onwards, the issue of how to maintain military discipline has been a prominent theme. Two noted films look at the issue in terms of disobeying military orders due to alleged cowardice during the Great War 1914–1918. In Stanley Kubrick's *Paths of Glory* (U.S.A., 1957) the refusal of French soldiers to embark on a suicidal attack on a highly fortified German position leads to a "show trial" of three soldiers chosen at random from the Company concerned with the abortive attack.[15] The decision to proceed against these three soldiers and to convict

---

12   Ibid.
13   Cannes Palme d'Or (2006) winner; Irish Film and Television Awards – best film and best Irish film (2006).
14   *de Koster/Leuwers/Luyten/Rousseaux* (eds.) 2012 – *Borgonovo's* chapter on the Republican courts focuses on crime. The Wind that Shakes the Barley is about civil matters.
15   The film also is noteworthy for the erasure of the Jewish subplot in which, in the original screenplay a soldier is removed from the selected scapegoats because this would lead to a recrudescence of allegations of anti-semitism in the French Army – following the infamous Dreyfus Affair which came to a conclusion only a decade earlier. The film was deemed "culturally, historically or aesthetically significant" by the Library of Congress in 1992 and is included in the United States National Film Registry.

is taken on simple grounds of military efficiency. The deaths of the three soldiers is to act as a deterrent to anyone thinking of disobeying orders. In *King and Country* (U.K., 1964, dir. Joseph Losey) the issue is more small scale. It concerns a British soldier, Private Arthur Hamp, who has walked away from the line suffering from what was later recognised as "shell shock".[16] The decision to execute him is taken for the same kind of reason – to stiffen the backbone of anyone else inclined to question the slaughter.

What these films are concerned with is justice in the field where the process is carried out by means of courts martial.[17] Here the rules are laid down by the military authorities and they are outwith the normal criminal and civil justice system. There is also a wealth of material dealing with military/military and military/civilian encounters from major directors such as John Ford (*Sergeant Rutledge,* U.S.A., 1960), Rob Reiner (*A Few Good Men,* U.S.A., 1993), Bruce Bereseford (*Breaker Morant,* Australia, 1996) and William Friedkin (*Rules of Engagement,* U.S.A., 2000). Some have gone beyond issues of refusing to engage the enemy into the more complex territory of the limits of proper military behaviour in relation to civilians. We see this in a film about the Second Boer War 1899–1902, *Breaker Morant.* What is involved here is an attempt to demonstrate, through the means of a court martial, that the British Army would treat any misdemeanours by their forces with the utmost strictness in order to achieve a different "higher" goal – in this instance a peace conference involving German support.

What has *not* been encountered has been the kinds of alternative ways of maintaining law and order and settling disputes, principally between civilians, *during* times of serious conflict where the formal justice system is either under threat or has broken down. This is what we find in *The Wind that Shakes the Barley* with its portrayal of civil business in one of the Republican Courts during the Irish War of Independence. In order to fully appreciate the issues raised in this film it is necessary to explain the nature of the Republican Courts and the novel elements they embodied. These novel elements contributed, as is noted below, to the abandonment of the Republican Courts in the compromised Irish Free State which emerged from the Irish Civil War. The Civil War, in fact, could be said to have played out the conflict between the parties we see in the courtroom scene – one side focusing on the struggle in terms of national identity, the other on the socio–political future at stake.

---

16 Tom Courtenay received the award for the Best Actor for his role as the ill-fated Private Hamp at the 1964 Venice Film Festival.

17 See the essays in this volume on *Paths of Glory* and *Mangal Pandey: The Rising.*

6. The Republican Court in Context

The relationship between England (later Britain) and Ireland extends back to invasion by the Normans from 1169 through various later attempts to impose control over the island by Henry VIII and later Cromwell. These interventions were seriously resisted and control was always limited. A later feature in the 16th and 17th centuries involved the "plantation" of Protestants from Scotland especially in the Province of Ulster. Resistance took various forms including the rebellion of the United Irishmen in 1798 as well as an abortive 1867 Fenian Rising. The latter half of the 19th century found Anglo–Irish politics dominated by policies centred around some form of power devolution described as "home rule". This culminated in Irish Home Rule legislation – the Government of Ireland Act 1914. It would have provided self–government within the United Kingdom. Many in Ulster sought to be excluded from this process and indicated armed resistance would ensue. Whether it might have enjoyed success was rendered moot by the outbreak of the Great War in August 1914.

At the time when *The Wind that Shakes the Barley* starts, the war between Britain and Germany from 1914 to 1918 was over. The unsuccessful Easter 1916 Rising by Irish nationalists seeking to leave the British Empire, had been crushed and the heavy–handed treatment of the rebel leaders had transformed support for full independence. Home Rule – the dominating theme of in 19th century and Edwardian Irish politics – no longer seemed a workable option. The General Election of December 1918 had returned 73 nationalist Sinn Féin members out of a total of 105 MPs. Refusing to take their seats in Westminster, they sat in the Mansion House in Dublin as Dáil Éireann and proclaimed an Irish Republic on the 21st of January 1919.[18] The Irish Republican Brotherhood and Irish Volunteers had, more or less, fused into the Irish Republican Army and were fighting for the withdrawal of Britain from Ireland. Along with regular British military forces and the armed Royal Irish Constabulary, a group of ex–soldiers and others were paid by Britain to conduct a campaign against the Republican forces. From the mixed colours of their hastily assembled police and army clothing some of these Auxiliaries acquired the name "Black and Tans". There were some 10,000 British troops consisting of the Black and Tans, the Auxiliaries, police and various British army regiments. The rebels had around 3,500 rifles and around 300 combatants.[19] Given the imbalance of forces, the Irish revolutionaries opted for guerrilla tactics employing Flying Columns to harass the British authorities. This involved attacks on police barracks and tax offices as well as the military along with the destruction and seizure of property and land. Many of the landowners were absentee landlords. The conflict involved

---

18 *Kautt* 1999; *Coleman* 2013.
19 *Laverty/Loach* 2006, p. 12.

civilians and the deaths between January 1919 and the ceasefire/Truce in July 1921 of over 1,000 people. During this time the provinces of Munster and Leinster were under martial law including the southwest county of Cork where *The Wind that Shakes the Barley* is set.[20] During this time Dáil Éireann sought to create State institutions as an alternative to the existing structures including local Government and courts.

> "Although the Dáil had decreed as early as August 1919 that a scheme of national arbitration courts was to be set up and a committee appointed to devise schemes to put the decree into effect, it was left to individual constituencies to make their own arrangements. The committee did not meet regularly, and progress in bringing forward a definite plan was slow."[21]

There had been plans for alternative types of dispute resolution canvassed from 1905 onwards. The proposal by founder of Sinn Féin, Arthur Griffith, at a National Convention of groups on 6 December 1905, for "national arbitration courts" has been described by Mary Kotsonouris not as a policy but as "rather part of the vision of a new Ireland that was in a state of constant flux."[22] She points out that there was no evidence to suggest that any particular thought was given to what national arbitration courts would entail and whether they could be extended beyond the conciliation of civil disputes, as the term suggests.[23] The issue, however, was given a little more clarity when in 1912 Sinn Féin included in their constitution an item about the courts which clearly stated that their task would be "the speedy and satisfactory adjustment of disputes".[24]

Along with this new system, during the War of Independence, there was a boycott of the British court system as reported in the *Irish Law Times*:

> "[T]he Sinn Féin policy of organising a parallel State had obvious legal implications and attracted significant public participation. Lawyers, juries and the general public were persuaded or intimidated to boycott the British Crown courts in order to entrench the position of the rival Dáil courts. Legal business before the established courts began to slow down."[25]

There were, at the same time, spontaneous actions by people in rural areas to set up their own justice mechanisms.[26] As Fitzpatrick noted, these actions against the existing legal order had a double effect as they

20 *Campbell* 1994, map D at p. 31.
21 *Casey* 1973.
22 *Kotsonouris* 2020, p. 7.
23 Ibid.
24 *Kotsonouris* 2020, p. 8.
25 (1920) *I.L.T.* vol. 54, no. 2,802, p. 247; (1921) *I.L.T.* vol. 55, no. 2,836, p. 139; no. 2,839, p. 156 (cited in *Mohr* 2018, p. 36).
26 *Maguire* 2013, p. 9.

"[A]lso threatened to destroy not only the remaining great landlords but also prosperous Irish nationalist farmers. Sinn Féin activist Kevin O'Shiel described the unrest as a 'prairie fire over Connaught', 'sparing neither ranch nor medium farm'. The Volunteers as a result issued a directive forbidding their men from engaging in cattle drives or land grabs."[27]

Many Sinn Féin branches in the more radical areas of the south and west set up arbitration courts to settle land disputes. In May 1920, the Republic formally adopted the Courts, and they were put under the Dáil's Department of Agriculture; an indication of their initial function as a means of resolving land disputes. Kevin O'Shiel was put in charge of the Dáil Éireann Land Commission, an arbitration body set up in mid–1920 to deal with land disputes which proved quite successful at clamping down on cattle driving and land occupations.[28]

Criminal matters were also covered initially by *Dáil Eireann i*n June 1920, organised by the Republican Government's Department of Home Affairs. When *Dáil Eireann* appointed Ministers, Arthur Griffith who, as noted, had raised the notion of "national arbitration courts" back in 1905, was given the Home Affairs portfolio.

"These 'Republican Courts' (as they became to be known) mirrored the tiered British system, establishing benches at the parish, district, circuit, and Supreme Court levels. Decisions were made by judges rather than juries; judges were elected at conventions, held by the major groups in the independence front: the local Labour council, the IRA, Sinn Féin and the women's organisation *Cumann na mBan.*"[29]

Women held office in these courts with one woman recorded in June 1920 by the Cork Examiner sitting in Cork as well as across other parts of Ireland. In that month of 1920, the Republican authorities transferred the authority over the Courts to their Ministry for Home Affairs under Austin Stack. The Dáil Courts were now to be regarded as criminal and civil courts, with the right to administer law in place of the British courts. This went beyond the more modest goals of the arbitration courts and is described by Ó Dubhir as "a direct challenge to the legitimacy of British rule in Ireland."[30] The Dáil Courts were formally established by a decree of Dáil Eireann on June 29, 1920, and directed to apply the law as it existed on January 21 1919 – the day the *Dáil* declared independence from Britain.[31]

Although the Dáil itself may have been slow to implement their August 1919 declaration, the impact on the ground appears to have been perceived by the British as significant.

---

27 *Fitzpatrick* 1998, p. 132.
28 This support for the existing small property owners against the landless poor is an issue which is raised in the Court scene in *The Wind that Shakes the Barley.*
29 *Borgonovo* 2012, p. 54.
30 *Ó Dubhir* 2005, pp. 134-135.
31 Ibid.

"In July 1920 Alfred Cope, who was Assistant Under–Secretary in Dublin Castle, warned a cabinet conference in London that the Sinn Féin Courts were doing more harm to the prestige of the government than the assassinations."[32]

Lord Dunraven, an Irish unionist, wrote in July 1920 to The Times:

"[A]n illegal Government has become the *de facto* Government. Its jurisdiction is recognised. It administers justice promptly and equably and we are in this curious dilemma that the civil administration of the country is carried on under a system the existence of which the *de jure* Government does not and cannot acknowledge and is carried on very well. The logical deduction is that profound dissatisfaction with the origin of the law, not with law and order, is the cause of the trouble."[33]

As Borgonovo notes, the parallel system followed a familiar hierarchical structure. At the bottom of the three tiers below the Supreme Court, Circuit and District Courts were the Parish Courts. He draws attention to their innovative and inclusive elements:

"Parish judges were elected by local bodies including the Sinn Féin branch, the militant organisations the IRA and *Cumann na mBan*, the local trades council and farmers' groups and local clergy. The profile of Republican judges was quite egalitarian; many were young men, some were trade unionists and some were even women, but also many were also Catholic priests."[34]

Ó Dubhir suggests that the Dáil Courts were "a curious mixture of the revolutionary and the conservative "since the law used was almost exclusively British Common Law and the right to private property rigorously upheld.[35] There is also the suggestion that the ancient Irish Brehon idea of keeping peace between neighbours and compensation was a feature in the early work in County Limerick.[36] Ó Dubhir also notes that the spread of the courts all over the country was also paralleled by a campaign in which the IRA burned various existing British court houses.[37]

The Dáil Courts received a boost to their operation after the Truce of 11 July 1921 and business expanded considerably in the six months between this date and the acceptance of the Treaty with Britain by the Dáil on 7 January 1922. Litigants took advantage of the cessation of hostilities to resort in greater numbers to the Dáil or Republican Courts, and counsel and solicitors appeared more frequently. There was uninterrupted communication between the District Court Registrars in the country and Ministry for Home Affairs; the arrangement of Circuit Sittings presented

---

32 *O'Broin* 1989, p. 86.
33 *Kostonouris* 2004, p. 12.
34 *Borgonovo* 2012, p. 54.
35 *Ó Dubhir* 2005, pp. 145-148.
36 *Maguire* 2013, p. 17.
37 *Ó Dubhir* 2005, pp. 145-148; see also *O'Riordan, Burns* and *O'Connor* 2019 for those that survived including the French Gothic style Sligo courthouse from 1878 and several in the larger towns. There had been a wave of impressive courtroom building in the 1870s.

no difficulty. The result was a great expansion of business at Circuit Sittings. As later Supreme Court judge Cahir Davitt recalled, these covered cases involving the administration of estates, declarations as to the ownership of land and other property, enforcement of obligations, setting aside and rectifying deeds, actions for breach of promise of marriage and for judicial separation, actions for assault, slander, trespass, trover and conversion, detinue, breach of contract, breach of warranty, eviction and rent disputes.[38]

7. The Republican Court in The Wind that Shakes the Barley

The film centres on the journey of two County Cork brothers, medical graduate, Damien O'Donovan (Cillian Murphy) and committed Republican Volunteer, Teddy O'Donovan (Pádraic Delaney) during the War of Independence and the Civil War.[39] The central dynamic is how it is that the two brothers end up fighting successfully together for liberation from Britain in the War of Independence but then find themselves on opposite sides in the ensuing Civil War.

It is the action during the War of Independence which brings into play the new justice system. Whilst the fighting is going on with varying degrees of intensity across the whole country we see how the War of Independence is played out in one small rural location in the west of Ireland where martial law was in operation.[40] We see the operation of one of the Flying Columns conducting the guerrilla war including the training of volunteers and the carrying out of an ambush on the British military along with assassination squad business. The narrative also includes the exacting of the death penalty on a local landowner and a Volunteer who betrays the location of a "safe house". The Flying Column Volunteers are finally seen returning from a campaign. They discuss the kinds of actions on which they have been working such as attacks on police barracks and tax offices, but it is mentioned that there have been setbacks with the loss of comrades.

The group enter a court where a hearing is taking place involving a loan due to be repaid by an Irish Gaelic speaking woman, Mrs Rafferty, to a local businessman,

---

38 *Kotsonouris* 2020, p. 48 citing Davitt. Cahir Davitt (15 August 1894 – 1 March 1986) was an Irish judge who served as a Judge of the Supreme Court from 1966 to 1976, President of the High Court from 1945 to 1966, a Judge of the High Court from 1951 to 1966 and a Judge of the Circuit Court from 1926 to 1951.

39 It has been noted in Wikipedia that there are "a small number of parallels" between the film and the book *The Scorching Wind* (1964) by Walter Macken (1915-1967) – These are limited to the narrative element of two brothers opting for different sides in the Civil War. The screenwriter has revealed that he has not read the Macken book – interview with the author April 3rd, 2023.

40 *Campbell* 1994, p. 31.

Mr Sweeney.[41] The court inquires into the circumstances of the loan and whether the debtor indicated she would have difficulties repaying the debt. Instead of finding for the businessman the court orders him to pay a sum to Mrs Rafferty within a week. This is in recognition of the leonine nature of the contract and its rapaciousness. Sweeney refuses and is then taken into custody for disrespecting the court and its decision. He is freed by Teddy O'Donovan, the leader of the local Volunteers and they repair to a local pub, we assume, to discuss his financial support for the Volunteers. The chair of the judicial panel, Mrs Lily Rowe, goes out into the street and demands that Teddy return to the court to give an account of his behaviour. He returns and there ensues a short but impassioned debate about the authority of the court, the need for confidence by the populace in the nascent Republic's tools of government and the kind of post–revolutionary society they are fighting for in the war.

8. The Courtroom Encounter

Two principal themes are played out in the Courtroom scene. They both centre on what is the actual goal of the struggle? Ending British rule or a just society. There appears to be not so much a conflict between ending British colonial rule and achieving a fairer society as a need by one side to proceed in stages from one to the other. First a free Ireland. Then a just Ireland. That is the perspective of Teddy O'Donovan. The reverse is not possible. There can be no just Ireland unless British rule is ended. That involves armed struggle since the British are clearly not leaving voluntarily. The British reaction to the 1918 General Election results, the subsequent convening of *Dáil Éireann* and Declaration of Independence shows this clearly.[42] Martial law is in operation across great swathes of Ireland including Cork. In the meantime anything that assists the likely success of the freedom struggle has to be accepted. In the short term those with money need to be accommodated. If this means that their pursuit of debts from poor struggling citizens has to be approved in the new courts, then so be it. That is the first area of dispute between Lily Rowe and Damien on the one hand and Teddy and his adjutant, Rory O'Shea, on the other.

---

41 She speaks English in the published screenplay – *Laverty/Loach* 2006, p. 90 – bemoaning the level of interest being charged on her loan.
42 The results of the 1918 Westminster Election and the dominance of the Independence Party are mentioned by Damien when he explains that Sinn Féin won 73 out of 105 seats. The failure of Redmond's Home Rule approach and Sinn Féin's refusal to take the seats in Westminster and instead set up an Irish Assembly in Dublin and the subsequent Declaration of Independence are not laid out in any detail. The script avoids the "potted history" in a character aside found in many films such as *Nicholas and Alexandra* (U.K., 1971, dir. Franklin J. Schaffner). In this film there is a scene where we see Lenin conversing with Trotsky and identifying an ambitious fellow in the room as Stalin – Lenin warns Trotsky to be careful of him.

Teddy makes clear the primacy of the armed struggle and of the superior role of men, as opposed to women, in this and demeans the whole court process. After Lily has ordered Sweeney to be detained in the cells below the Court for contempt of court he asks, "are you going to put me in the jail too. Who will fight the war then? You?"

Allied to the question of getting arms, though, is the question of community support and how the trust of the people is to be maintained, and, by inference, their crucial assistance in providing food and shelter in the resistance to the British forces. Lily states that the trust of the people is at risk if the new rule of law and the courts are ignored. Teddy responds suggesting that trust can be earned in different ways. "We'll maintain the trust of people with weapons in our hands. We have men on the four corners of this town defending ourselves ... We took it from the British by force..."

Damien O'Donovan, Teddy's brother, however, points out that what Teddy is doing is to undermine the very first judgment of the new Republican Court by deciding to settle matters on the grounds of simple short–term expediency. Teddy reiterates the need for arms for the ongoing revolutionary struggle and his adjutant, Rory expresses the choice in simple terms: "There's a war on right. We have one objective – to get the British out of Ireland and the Sweeneys of this world give us rifles."

After Rory O'Shea has stormed out of the court, Teddy and Damien remain along with Trade Unionist, Dan, to argue about what kind of Ireland they are fighting for. Is it simply a new green Irish capitalist order or something that will redress the disparities of wealth? Dan professes loyalty to the armed struggle but asks why the IRA are backing the landlords, crushing the little people and backing "local bigwigs".[43] He concludes with an impassioned plea about the importance of the Republican courts: "But you sure as hell better respect this court. This is our Government, it is our Government." The encounter ends with Teddy promising to provide Mrs Rafferty with financial assistance and then leaving. This pragmatic solution does not, however, address the fundamental issue of what kind of society is being created to replace British colonial rule.

Despite Teddy's assurance that they will tear up the Treaty once the country is strong enough, the rejection by Damien and others of Dominion status within the British Empire leads to the Civil War in which Teddy opts to support the limited gains of day–to–day autonomy delivered by the Treaty. This seems to be driven also by the fear of the threat by Britain to wage "immediate and terrible war".

---

43 An oblique reference to the Ballinrobe case where the IRA reinstated the landowners by removing the sons of the impoverished squatters to enforce the first decree of a Dáil court in favour of the landowners. http://www.historicalballinrobe.com/page/the_first_dail_court?path= 0p4p (Accessed on 22 December 2023).

It is a Treaty which was forced on the combatants, though, rather than a product of a victory. The stakes were high given the implications for Britain's other colonies if independence could be achieved after a relatively short armed struggle. As Dualta, one of the warring brothers expresses it in Walter Macken's 1964 tale of the struggle for independence and the civil war, *The Scorching Wind*: "We didn't defeat them. We made it impossible for them to rule."[44]

The perspective of those who signed and supported the Treaty was that it would provide a stepping stone to a fully independent Ireland. Those who rejected the Treaty saw it as a betrayal of the Republic they had been fighting for. As Dominic, the other brother in Macken's book suggests, behind the headlines about Free State of Ireland, Historic Agreement and Irish Provisional Government there lurked the loss of the goals of the Republic. "It was only when you read on that you realised the Irish Republic was lost in the small print."[45]

According to director Ken Loach, the film attempts to explore the extent to which the Irish revolution was a social revolution as opposed to a nationalist revolution. Loach commented on this theme in an interview for the DVD release of the film:

> "Every time a colony wants independence, the questions on the agenda are: a) how do you get the imperialists out, and b) what kind of society do you build? There are usually the bourgeois nationalists who say, 'Let's just change the flag and keep everything as it was.' Then there are the revolutionaries who say, 'Let's change the property laws.' It's always a critical moment."[46]

Although, this is not what is happening in the first part of the courtroom scene, it is the issue which Dan raises with the young men in the courtroom after the disposal of the Sweeney/Rafferty case.

9. The Republican Courts and the Armed Struggle

The conflict which we see in the first part of the Court sequence was reflected at the national political level. The need for the enforcement of the court edicts was a problem:

> "When Griffith sent the neophyte O'Shiel to Cathal Brugha, Minister for Defence, to ask for IRA assistance in the impasse after Ballinrobe,[47] Brugha heard him out in silence before saying with absolute finality that he had no time for courts, police or their ilk.

---

44 *Macken* 1964, p. 290. This tale of two brothers fighting on different sides in the Civil War is the final part of Macken's trilogy of Irish history – *Seek the Fair Land* (1959) – Cromwell in Ireland; *The Silent People* (1962) – the famine of the 1840s.

45 *Macken* 1964, p. 276.

46 Toronto's *Eye Weekly*, 15 March 2007.

47 A dispute between two small landowners and those who had made claims on their land which was the first dispute dealt with in the Dail court in May 1920.

Nothing should be allowed to deflect attention from the paramount importance of the war: the rest were refinements that could be considered once the enemy had been forced out."[48]

Kotsonouris suggests that this was an issue which was to remain unresolved: "The tension between what came to be seen as the two parts of the national struggle never eased and each thought the other had the secondary role."[49]

The "putative" army of *Dáil Éireann* had duties to the Army Council and the Courts to the Home Affairs Ministry.

What the Court scene in *The Wind that Shakes the Barley* highlights is people seeking another way of administering the rules of the system. Not only are the Court actors more inclusive with significant female participation but the rules are tempered with mercy. The Court deals in justice as well as applying legal rules. This is a theme which has many resonances with debates down through the ages about the nature of law. These debates have usually been expressed in terms of the relationship between human law and "natural law" between scholars from St Thomas Aquinas[50] through to Fuller[51] and Finnis[52] and their positivist antagonists.[53] It is not just scholars who have confronted these issues. They have also figured in the construction of the English Common Law. The tempering of rules with equity has been part of the emergence of the system that exist there today.[54] The notion of infusing judicial decision–making with community values has suffered as a concept through its association with the courts and tribunals of Nazi Germany[55] and Stalin's Russia[56]. It is, however, a recognised practice in contemporary British courts in which changes in society's views on such issues as extra–marital relationships,[57] marital rape[58] and gay rights[59] have all been recognised as changing the meaning and application of well–established rules.

There is, however, a clear indication in *The Wind that Shakes the Barley* that, in seeking to adopt a new future for justice in the Republican Courts, it will not be enough to adopt the pre–existing order. The second part of the Court scene lays bare this conflict. If the Republican Courts are going to do what the British courts would have done, all that would have changed is the colour of the flag from the red,

---

48 *O'Shiel* 1966.
49 *Kotsonouris* 2020, p. 16.
50 *Aquinas* 1485.
51 *Fuller* 1960.
52 *Finnis* 1980.
53 *Kelsen* 2009; *Hart* 1961; *Raz* 1970.
54 *Jackson* 2015.
55 *Muller* 1991.
56 *Solomon* 1997.
57 *Fitzpatrick v Sterling Housing Association* (1999) 4 All ER 705.
58 *Stallard v HM Advocate* 1989 S.C.C.R. 248.
59 *Fitzpatrick v Sterling Housing Association* (1999) 4 All ER 705.

white and blue of the Butcher's Apron[60] to the green flag of Sinn Féin. The Trade Unionist, Dan expresses it forcefully in the Courtroom scene after the merchant Sweeney is released from custody: "So we paint the town Republican green but underneath we're still the same as the English." He points out that whether the British are in charge or not, the society is significantly unequal. What is to be done about this is left hanging. As Dan points out those who had nothing under colonial rule have nothing guaranteed after achieving independence.[61]

10. The Republican Courts, Society and the Treaty

The action moves on to the news that a truce has been agreed to end the fighting. The joy at the news of the cessation of hostilities and the celebratory dance is followed by the details. The limited gains on offer are shown in the picture house when the newsreel is played with the Treaty and its broad terms revealed. There will be an Irish Free State. It will have full control over customs, tariffs and economic policy. Ireland will, however, remain a Dominion within the British Empire with an oath of allegiance to the King by Members of the Parliament. The response of the audience to this information is not positive. "Is this what we fought for?" asks Damien. The reaction in more detail is revealed in a debate between the opposing factions. We see the conflict of views between Freestaters and the Anti–Treaty IRA: on the one hand "immediate and terrible war" promised by the British as noted by Teddy and on the other full "freedom within our grasp." Again the contrast is laid out between refusing and continuing the struggle with the limited arms available and the threat to Britain's Empire which granting full independence would entail. Dan again makes the point that the fundamental structural inequality will remain with formal independence. More can be achieved in the revolution which has the British withdrawing. "If we ratify this Treaty all we're changing is the accents of the powerful and the colour of the flag." The contrast between the desire for peace and the IRA's radical programme of social justice is also seen in the denunciation by the priest of those rejecting the Treaty. The "Anti–Treaty Irregulars" are excommunica-

---

60 The Butcher's Apron is a pejorative term for the Union flag, common among Irish republicans, referring to the blood-streaked appearance of the flag and referring to atrocities committed in Ireland and other countries under British colonial rule.

61 This theme of long-term goals and short-term expediency in settings of revolution and war is one which is raised in other films: *This Above All* (U.S.A., 1942) in which war hero Clive Briggs (Tyrone Power) deserts because he is convinced that the war against Germany will leave the rotten class system intact. His girlfriend, upper-class Prudence Cathaway (Joan Fontaine) puts forward the need to defeat the enemy of all first before curing society's inequalities. She also stresses the things that bind all classes together. In *Land and Freedom* (U.K., Spain, Italy, Germany, France, 1995), an earlier Ken Loach film scripted by Jim Allen, the conflict is between the need to collectivise for the benefit of the landless peasantry set against the need to defeat Franco's forces before engaging in radical social change.

ted. The legitimacy of the results of the June 1922 election leading to the acceptance of the Treaty is disputed by Damien pointing out that the threat of war by the British was hanging over the heads of the electorate. They walk out of the chapel.

The shift into fraternal conflict is portrayed and the setting of former Volunteers against each other. The film ends shortly after the death of Damien at the hands of a Free State firing squad commanded by his brother, Teddy. The latter delivers Damien's farewell letter to his sweetheart Sinead. He also hands over the locket of Micheal O' Sullibeean, the first casualty in the film at the hands of the Black and Tans which Damien had kept. Sinead tells Teddy to get off her land and that she never wants to see him again. With that the film fades to black over the strains of Pádraig Pearse's[62] *Oró, Sé Do Bheatha 'Bhaile* (Oh–ro, you are welcome home) – the song sung by the Volunteers when returning from their actions against the British. How the dispute between the Free State forces and the Irish Republican Army will play out is not made clear. We do not know how the experiment of the Republican Courts will fare with the introduction of elected judges from the community, women judges involved and community values informing decisions. *The Wind that Shakes the Barley*, however, gives us a glimpse into these possibilities over a century ago. It is consistent with the dominant theme from the films of Loach, Laverty and O'Brien that there are different and better ways of ordering civil society.

11. The fate of the Republican Courts

What we do not have with the Republican Court scene and the film itself as a whole is a clear indication of what kind of social arrangements and justice system will emerge from the struggles of the War of Independence or the Civil War. We know that Teddy is prepared to temper the rule of law with expediency. It is not entirely fanciful to imagine him 5 years on from the commencement of the Free State in December 1922 holding some kind of position within the justice system. What would have changed? What would have happened to the Republican Courts instituted in parallel to the British–based court system operating before the War of Independence. With the Truce putting a halt to hostilities between the proclaimed Republic and Britain, as noted above, the new approach of the Republican Courts was embraced. Initially, the Minister in charge, Austin Stack, made the expansion of the Courts during the Truce a point of honour. Stack, in his ministerial report of 16 August 1921, was able to write that the Courts were operating again in every part of

---

62　Teacher, barrister, poet, IRB militant and 1916 Easter Rising Proclamation signatory – executed 3 May 1916.

the country.[63] The Republican Courts which were operating expanded their business extensively between the Truce and the Treaty as noted above.

The Provisional Government announced in the public press on 17 January 1922 that the law courts and all public bodies, which had acted under the authority of the British government, were to continue in operation until the establishment of the Free State.[64] The Dáil courts established by the decree of the First Dáil in 1920 entered into an era of uninterrupted expansion. The Circuit List prepared for the spring sittings in the towns of Munster, Leinster and Connacht required extra judges such as Lavery, Flood, Wyse Power and Goff who were given temporary commissions in order to deal with the pressure of cases waiting to be heard.[65] The original imperial Court houses were taken over for use in the process.

Their operations were, however, short lived. With the acceptance of the Treaty by 64 votes to 57 in the Dàil on 7 January 1922 and the outbreak of the Civil War hostilities on 26 June 2022 the Provisional Government determined to close the Republican Courts, since there was no further reason to preserve the visible structures of separatist policy.[66] They were declared henceforth to be of no status. The following notice appeared in the official journal of the Irish Government, Iris Oifigiúil, on 1 August 2022. The Minister for Home Affairs (Aire um Gnothai Duitche) decreed with the concurrence of the Cabinet of Dáil Eireann

> "that the decree of the Aire um Gnothaí Duitche (Minister for Home Affairs) purporting to establish courts of law and equity and criminal jurisdiction as part of the government of the Irish Republic be and the same is hereby rescinded and declared to be of no effect as from this date save to the extent to which the said decree was or may have been effective to establish Parish Courts and District Courts outside the city of Dublin."[67]

The Dáil Courts were decried by the Minister for Home Affairs, Kevin O'Higgins as having been "channels of corruption and abuse".[68] Despite, apparently, having done some good work in providing a rough and unlearned settlement of minor disputes, they were incapable of administering anything in the nature of strict law.[69] Their fate appeared sealed. This proved to be a tortuous process.

In a slightly bizarre way, the Dáil Courts were formally "disappeared" by decree of the Minister of Home Affairs declaring that they had, in effect, never existed. The rationale was that the Dáil Courts were originally established to provide an acceptable alternative to those which were functioning under the British government,

---

63 *Kotsonouris* 2020, p. 44 citing NA, DE 25/1.
64 NA, S1 Proclamation 16 January 2022 published in *Iris Oifigiuil* No 5, 14 February 2022 (cited in *Kotsonouris* 2020, p. 50).
65 *Kotsonouris* 2004, p. 56.
66 Ibid., p. 67.
67 *Kotsonouris* 2020, p 72.
68 *Kotsonouris* 2004, p. 57.
69 *Kotsonouris* 2020, p. 88.

but these were now in Irish hands and there was no longer any need to have two systems. It was a waste of money paying for a complete judicial system which was not being utilised and which had criminal, licensing, lunacy and other jurisdictional powers which the other courts lacked. As Kotsonouris puts it, "the tone was brisk and practical, with no hint of nostalgia for the fairly recent days when the same courts were being extolled as the showpiece of Irish self–sufficiency."[70] Even more striking is the absence of reference to a characteristic which was being heavily promoted elsewhere – their essential "illegality" which Kevin O'Higgins had earlier stressed.[71]

For a range of reasons, then, it was decided to wind up the Republican Courts and effectively return to the pre–War court system.[72] This, however, proved to be somewhat complicated. In essence, a sleight of hand was employed by which, at one and the same time, the Republican Courts were wound up, and their work was incorporated into the revived Imperial court system. This was done through the work of the Dáil Courts Winding–up Commission.[73] The cases which had been before the Republican Courts were completed within the umbrella of the Free State courts. This process turned out to be highly protracted mainly due to the personnel in charge. It is covered in extensive detail by Kotsonouris.[74]

What is important, however, was that the novel aspects of the Republican Dáil Courts which were noted above were abandoned. There was no election element in the judicial realm. The concerns of community justice were subsumed within the notion of legalism. Nor were there any female judges in Ireland until 1964.[75] What we see in *The Wind that Shakes the Barley* was an experiment ahead of its time which briefly flourished and was then done away with. Its principal features, however, are to varying degrees found in modern court systems with the gender and community values issues most prominent, and in some jurisdictions, election is a feature.

Bibliography

Amez, Benoît, 2012: Maintenir ou éloigner du front?: le dilemme des autorités militaires belges face aux déliquants militaires au cours de la guerre 14–18: le cas des compagnies spéciales. In: *de Koster,* Margo/*Leuwers,* Hervé/*Luyten,* Dirk/*Rousseaux*, Xavier, (eds.): Justice in Wartime and Revolutions: Europe, 1795–1950. Brussels, Algemeen Rijksarchief, pp. 107–124.

---

70 *Kostonouris* 2004, p. 73.
71 Ibid.
72 Ibid.
73 Ibid.
74 Ibid.
75 *The Irish Times*. 13 October 1983 (obituary of District Court Justice Eileen Kennedy).

Amez, Benoît/*Rousseaux*, Xavier, 2012: L'affaire Ferfaille en "Belgique libre" (27 octobre 1917–26 mars 1918): excès de la justice militaire, laboratoire de la justice scientifique ou instrument de l'affirmation nationale? In: *de Koster,* Margo/*Leuwers,* Hervé/*Luyten,* Dirk/*Rousseaux*, Xavier, (eds.): Justice in Wartime and Revolutions: Europe, 1795–1950. Brussels, Algemeen Rijksarchief, pp. 125–152.

Aquinas, St Thomas, 1485: Summa Theologiae (Treatise on Law) (current edition NovAntiqua available at: https://novantiqua.com/author/novantiqua/ (Accessed on 5 January 2023).

Boldorf, Marcel, 2012: Judicial Prosecution of Business Elites in the Soviet Occupation Zone and the Early GDR. In: *de Koster*, Margo/*Leuwers*, Hervé/*Luyten*, Dirk/*Rousseaux*, Xavier, (eds.): Justice in Wartime and Revolutions: Europe, 1795–1950. Brussels, Algemeen Rijksarchief, pp. 215–228.

Borgonovo, John, 2012: Republican Courts, Ordinary Crime, and the Irish Revolution, 1919–1921. In: *de Koster,* Margo/*Leuwers,* Hervé/*Luyten,* Dirk/*Rousseaux*, Xavier (eds.): Justice in Wartime and Revolutions: Europe, 1795–1950. Brussels, Algemeen Rijksarchief, pp. 39–56.

Campbell, Colm, 1994: Emergency Law in Ireland 1918–1925. Oxford, Clarendon Press.

Casey, James P., 1973: The Genesis of the Dáil Courts. 9 Irish Jurist (n.s.) 326–338.

Coleman, Marie, 2013: The Irish Revolution, 1916–1923. London, Routledge.

Davitt, Cahir, 1968: The Civil Jurisdiction of the Courts of Justice in the Irish Republic 1920–1922. 3 Irish Jurist (n.s.) 121–122.

Debruyne, Emmanuel, 2012: "Mon recours est rejeté: je dois mourir": les condamnés à mort des conseils de guerre allemands en France et an Belgique occupées, 1914–1918. In: *de Koster*, Margo/*Leuwers*, Hervé/*Luyten*, Dirk/*Rousseaux*, Xavier, (eds.): Justice in Wartime and Revolutions: Europe, 1795–1950. Brussels, Algemeen Rijksarchief, pp. 89–106.

Dempsey, Pauric, 2009: Diarmuid Crowley Dictionary of Irish Biography. At: https://www.dib.ie/index.php/biography/crowley-o-cruadhlaoich-diarmuid-a2253) (Accessed on 20 December 2022).

de Koster, Margo/*Leuwers*, Hervé/*Luyten*, Dirk/*Rousseaux*, Xavier (eds.), 2012: Justice in Wartime and Revolutions: Europe, 1795–1950. Brussels: Algemeen Rijksarchief.

Dorney, John, 2013: 'Peace After the Final Battle': The Story of the Irish Revolution 1912–1924. Dublin, New Island Books.

Dorney, John, 2019: The Rise and Fall of the Dáil Courts, 1919–1922. At: https://www.theirishstory.com/2019/07/25/the-rise-and-fall-of-the-dail-courts-1919-1922/#.Y_iY0XbP3IU) (Accessed on 24 February 2023).

Finnis, John, 1980: Natural Law and Natural Rights. Oxford, Clarendon.

Fitzpatrick, David, 1998: Politics and Irish Life, 1913–1921: Provincial Experiences of War and Revolution. Cork, Cork University Press.

Fuller, Lon, 1964: The Morality of Law. New Haven, Yale UP.

Greenfield, Steve/*Osborn*, Guy/*Robson,* Peter, 2001: Film and the Law. London, Cavendish.

Greenfield, Steve/*Osborn,* Guy/*Robson,* Peter, 2010: Film and the Law: The Cinema of Justice. Oxford, Hart.

Grillère–Lacroix, Diane, 2012: Justice et occupation italienne en France (1940–1943): l'organisation judiciaire au cœur des enjeux de souveraineté. In: *de Koster*, Margo/*Leuwers*, Hervé/*Luyten*, Dirk/*Rousseaux*, Xavier (eds.): Justice in Wartime and Revolutions: Europe, 1795–1950. Brussels, Algemeen Rijksarchief, pp. 153–172.

Hart, Herbert Lionel Adolphus, 2012 (1961): The Concept of Law. 3rd edition, Oxford, Clarendon.

Jackson, R. M., 2015: The Machinery of Justice in England. Cambridge, Cambridge UP.

Kautt, William H., 1999: The Anglo–Irish War, 1916–21: A People's War. Westport CT, Praeger Publishers.

Kekkonen, Jukka, 2012: Judicial Repression During and After the Finnish (1918) and Spanish (1936–1939) Civil Wars: a Comparative Analysis. In: *de Koster*, Margo/*Leuwers*, Hervé /*Luyten*, Dirk/*Rousseaux*, Xavier, (eds.): Justice in Wartime and Revolutions: Europe, 1795–1950. Brussels, Algemeen Rijksarchief, pp. 57–72.

Kelsen, Hans, 2009: Pure Theory of Law. 2nd edition, Singapore, Landmark.

Kotsonouris, Mary, 2004: The Winding Up of the Dáil Courts, 1922–25: An Obvious Duty. Dublin, Four Courts Press.

Kotsonouris, Mary, 2020: Retreat from Revolution: The Dáil Courts, 1920–24. Dublin, Irish Academic Press.

Ledesma, José L, 2012: Popular Justice, Revolution and Political Contention in the Spanish Civil War (1936–1939 In: *de Koster*, Margo/*Leuwers*, Hervé/*Luyten*, Dirk/*Rousseaux*, Xavier, (eds.): Justice in Wartime and Revolutions: Europe, 1795–1950. Brussels, Algemeen Rijksarchief, pp. 73–88.

Lignereux, Aurélien, 2012: Les cadres indigènes des policies impériales dans la France des départements annexés (1796–1814). In: *de Koster*, Margo/*Leuwer*s, Hervé/*Luyten*, Dirk/*Rousseaux*, Xavier, (eds.): Justice in Wartime and Revolutions: Europe, 1795–1950. Brussels, Algemeen Rijksarchief, pp. 5–22.

Laverty, Paul/*Loach*, Ken, 2006: The Wind that Shakes the Barley. Cork, Galley Head Press.

Lumet, Sidney, 1995: Making Movies. London, Bloomsbury.

Macken, Walter, 1964: The Scorching Wind. London, Pan Macmillan.

Maguire, Roderick, 2013: The People's Courts: Ireland's Dáil Courts, 1920–24. Saint Colmans, Claremorris Credit Union et al., transcript of a radio programme.

Mohr, Thomas, 2018: Irish Law Journals and the Emergence of the Irish State, 1916–1922. In: Journal of European Periodical Studies, 3:1, pp. 29–48. doi: https://doi.org/1 0.21825/jeps.v3i1.8093.

*Mulle*r, Ingo, 1991: Hitler's Justice: The Courts of the Third Reich. Cambridge, Harvard UP.

O'Broin, Leon, 1989: W. E. Wylie and the Irish Revolution 1916–1921. Dublin, Gill and Macmillan.

Ó Dubhir, Liam, 2005: The Donegal Awakening: Donegal in the War of Independence. Cork, Mercier Press.

O'Riordan, Colum/*Burns*, Paul/*O'Connor*, Ciaran (eds.), 2019: Ireland's Court Houses. Dublin, Irish Architectural Archive.

O'Shiel, Kevin, 1966: 'Memories of My Lifetime', a Series of Twelve Articles. In: The Irish Times, November 1966.

Raz, J, 1970: The Concept of a Legal System. Oxford, Clarendon.

Renglet, Antoine, 2012: Antwerp and Namur under "States of Siege" during the French Directory: Policing Practices and the Authorities' Relationships in Maintaining Order. In: *de Koster*, Margo/*Leuwers*, Hervé/*Luyten*, Dirk/*Rousseaux*, Xavier, (eds.): Justice in Wartime and Revolutions: Europe, 1795–1950. Brussels, Algemeen Rijksarchief, pp. 23–38.

Simoens, Tom, 2012: Belgian Military Justice in the First World War: a Difficult Expansion In: *de Koster*, Margo/*Leuwers*, Hervé/*Luyten*, Dirk/*Rousseaux*, Xavier, (eds.): Justice in Wartime and Revolutions: Europe, 1795–1950. Brussels, Algemeen Rijksarchief, pp. 173–192.

Solomon, Peter H., 1997: Soviet Criminal Justice Under Stalin. Cambridge, Cambridge University Press.

Venema, Derk, 2012: The Judge, the Occupier, his Laws, and their Validity: Judicial Review by the Supreme Courts of Occupied Belgium, Norway, and the Netherlands 1940–1945. In: *de Koster*, Margo/*Leuwers*, Hervé/*Luyten*, Dirk/*Rousseaux*, Xavier, (eds.): Justice in Wartime and Revolutions: Europe, 1795–1950. Brussels, Algemeen Rijksarchief, pp. 342–352.

Wikipedia, n.d.: The Wind That Shakes the Barley. At: https://en.wikipedia.org/wiki/The_Wind_That_Shakes_the_Barley_(film) (Accessed on 2 June 2024).

Appendix: The Courtroom Scene[76]

LILY:	Did you agree the terms on the loan and make it clear to Mr Sweeney but you wouldn't be able to repay him for quite some time?
MRS RAFFERTY:	(*Speaks Gaelic*)
MR SWEENEY:	She knows exactly what she's talking about. She agreed the terms and said she'd start repayments straight away.
LILY:	You'll be given time to ….
SWEENEY:	She has a huge backlog.
LILY:	Thank you, that's enough, Mrs Rafferty.
	Mrs Rafferty you agreed on this loan, but did you let Mr Sweeney know that you wouldn't be able to repay it immediately?
SWEENEY:	You do know exactly what it was.
	She said she'd be able to start paying right away at the rate agreed.
LILY:	She will be given time.
	I'm only filling in what she said.

---

76 The following version from the film differs slightly from the script in *Laverty/Loach* 2006, pp. 90-96. This stems from Loach's desire, when using non-professional as well as professional actors, not to inhibit the players from delivering the sense of their contribution as opposed to their precise "lines" – interview with the screenwriter, Paul Laverty, 3 April 2023. Reprinted with kind permission of Paul Laverty to Peter Robson.

(*Sweeney mumbles*)

LILY: Sinead, do you have those figures for me?
SINEAD: The accumulated interest, Mr Sweeney, it's over 500%.
SWEENEY: Interest is bound to accumulate if you're not making repayments.
That's normal commercial practice.
FROM BACK OF THE COURT: Come off it now, Sweeney, 500? Come off it.
SWEENEY: It's standard normal practice. What am I supposed to do? Offer charity?
LILY: This is a recognised court under the authority of Dáil Éireann, and a bit of decorum is required.
Mr Sweeney, frankly, my sympathies lie with Mrs Rafferty in this matter.
SWEENEY: That's very clear, Mrs Rowe.
LILY: Those are extortionate interest rates to be charging. It's abuse of your position in the community to be charging that. This is a Republican court, not an English court. I hereby order you to repay Mrs Rafferty, 10 shillings and sixpence. You have seven days in which to do so. That is this day next week. Thank you.
SWEENEY: Me repay her? Are you joking me? There's no way I'm paying money to Mrs Rafferty. She's the one who owes me money! I am the aggrieved party here.
LILY: Sit down please.
SWEENEY: You're asking me to forget, to waive my interest. I am the one who is owed money and do you call that justice.
LILY: Sit down!
SWEENEY: You got the result that you wanted.
A kangaroo court is what it is. Me pay her? No way! Let me go! What do you think you're doing? Get your hands off me! Get your hands off me! There's no way...
Let go of me! For God sake.

He is hustled off out of the court and down into the cells below.

TEDDY: (from the top of the stairs) Bring him back here. Bring him back. Bring him back hee.

Sweeney leaves the Court building with Teddy and his group.

COURT OFFICER: Teddy O'Donovan's after taking Mr Sweeney off us. He's taken him out the front door of the court.
LILY: [*out in the street*]
Teddy O'Donovan! Teddy O'Donovan, come back into this courthouse immediately! Teddy O'Donovan, I'm not standing here all day for you! Teddy O'Donovan, come back here, please.

LILY:	Who the hell do you think you are to interfere with a court decision?
TEDDY:	Lily calm down for a second.
LILY:	By whose authority…
TEDDY:	You answer my question,
	By whose authority?
	Do you want every merchant and businessman in the county up against us with decisions like that?
SINEAD:	You're interfering with the court's decisions by your actions Teddy.
TEDDY:	Are you going to throw me in the jail too. Who will fight the war then? You?
LILY:	What Mr Sweeney did to Mrs Rafferty is wrong Teddy and you can't have one…
TEDDY:	It was wrong but I need the man's money to buy weapons. What are we going to do without weapons. We can't fight a war like that. Are you going to buy them with a hurl? [sporting stick for the Gaelic game of Hurling]
LILY:	How are we supposed to maintain the trust of the people if you undermine the court's decisions?
TEDDY:	We'll maintain the trust of people with weapons in our hands because we have men on the four corners of this town defending this town at this very moment. We took it from the British by force.
DAMIEN:	And the first judgment of this, an independent court, you have undermined by deciding to settle it in a pub.
TEDDY:	He provides us with money to buy weapons. There is a consignment coming in from Glasgow in the next few weeks. You tell me how I'm going to pay for that, if he's sitting down in the cells sulking.
DAN:	We should enforce the court's decision. I am volunteering. Anyone else?
RORY:	Hold on a minute, hold on. There's a war on right. We have one objective to get the British out of Ireland and the Sweeney's of this world give us rifles. That's more important than a box of fucking groceries. A little clarity now in the name of God.
TEDDY:	Well said, Rory boy, well said.
DAN:	So, we paint the town Republican green but underneath we're still the same as the English.
RORY:	We're not the same as the English.
	Better than painting it fuckin' red anyway.
	Justice and equality for all. Take a copy of the Proclamation.
	They not paying their fucking rent anyway.
	(Leaves)
DAN:	Are you boys finding this funny? Turn out your pockets lads. Come on how much money have you got in your pockets? Be quiet, be quiet. how much money have you got?
TIM:	What are you talking about?
NED:	Be careful now, Daniel
DAN:	Be quiet, be quiet.
NED:	Answer him Tim.
DAN:	Answer a civil question – how much money have you got? how much?
TIM:	I've a shilling alright.

DAN:	Ned how much land do you own? Answer me come on. Have you a blade of grass to your name?
NED:	No, not a blade no.
TERENCE:	These boys are fine.
DAN:	Let me finish? You're paupers just like me. Take a look up and down this country and see the amount of volunteers that are involved in land seizures and cattle drives. Do you want to know why that is happening do you?
LEO:	That's enough of that.
DAN:	It's not enough of it. The IRA are backing the landlords and crushing people like you and me.
TEDDY:	You sat down with the IRA last night.
DAN:	I'm talking here.
TEDDY:	You want madness up and down the countryside.
DAN:	You saw it here two minutes ago. You saw it here backing the local bigwigs and selling out a mother who hasn't got penny in her pocket. Just like yours. Now Teddy, I have no problem taking any order from you, any order you want to give me. I'll jump off a cliff if you want. But you sure as hell better respect this court. This is our Government, it is our Government.
TEDDY:	I understand what you're saying. I will pay for the woman's groceries out of my own pocket.
DAN:	It's not about that.

Note: Ned, Tim and Leo are bystanders in the Court.

Part 3

Crime and Law in Music and Bollywood Drama

Stefan Machura and John Cunningham

Law and War in the Opera

1. Introduction

Opera is one of the most highly respected, and emblematic, forms of art in Western culture. It remains also, with variation between countries, a popular form of entertainment and still sometimes comes with the notion of providing moral edification. Recorded opera music and performances, streamed on the internet or on DVD, have increased the genre's reach and accessibility significantly.[1] Especially when as a reaction to closures during the Covid crisis, opera houses had to find alternative channels to stay relevant to audiences.[2]

Opera excels in the portrayal of deep emotions experienced by the characters. The necessities of singing and acting simultaneously, normally on a theatre stage, trigger stories ripe with profound, existential challenges, stories that allow the exaggeration required by the operatic form.[3] No wonder that strong legal conflict and heinous crimes are a major part of the opera repertoire.[4] Audiences find themselves attracted to the stories involving law and crime. Indeed, operas often present legal conflicts of varying nature. They are "often dense with legal issues".[5] Like no other art form the opera with its confluence of music, theatre, and numerous other stage crafts, allows the expression of emotions involved in and triggered by law–breaking.[6] It also lets the audience experience situations of grave injustice and the struggle against it.[7]

Law and crime alone can raise strong feelings.[8] Of the many authors making this point, Émile Durkheim and Eugen Ehrlich must be the most prominent. According to Durkheim, people have an interest in the basic norms of society. They want to see them upheld and wrongdoers punished. This enforces the reassuring feeling that society is functioning.[9] Law can be defined and backed up by the state but also arise from the rules by which people organise their daily lives.[10] Law is recognisable,

---

1 *Abbate/Parker* 2015, p. xv.
2 *Annunziata/Annunziata* 2020.
3 *Abbate/Parker* 2015, p. 15.
4 *Tritter* 2004; *Annunziata/Colombo* 2018; *Brunt* 2021; *Machura* et al. 2023.
5 *Annunziata/Colombo* 2021, p. 145.
6 *Machura* et al. 2023, pp. 92–93.
7 *Lacerda* 2017.
8 *Hogan/Emler* 1981; *Tyler* et al. 1997.
9 *Durkheim* 1982.
10 *Ehrlich* 2022.

according to Ehrlich, by the strength of disapproval provoked by law–breaking.[11] The difference between "law" and "morals" is gradual for Ehrlich. In opera, law and morals are typically not strictly distinguished.[12] Often, a simple model of "good" and "bad" applies in opera. The law violations and crimes are of a kind that is universally rejected, such as homicide, robbery or sexual assault, and thus timeless.

As a genre, opera thrives off depictions of characters exposed to death and danger.[13] Lodewijk Brunt emphasises that they "are part of violent situations" and are shaped by them.[14] In opera, crime is "personalised"; it "clings to certain characters".[15] According to Brunt, opera "approaches the true emotional connotations of death, terror, and debauchery. (…) opera reveals something about crime that cannot be found anywhere else in such a concentrated form".[16] A key vehicle is the aria in which a character's inner feelings are laid bare for several minutes, much like a dramatic soliloquy (speaking thoughts aloud). A character might contemplate committing an outrageous act, then is visited by scruples and second thoughts, but finally announce her determination to follow the plan to the end. Or, following a different pattern, in the aria "Mi si affaccia un pugnal" from Verdi's *Macbeth* (towards the end of Act 1), the title character is now encouraged to kill the king (but he has second thoughts in the middle part of the aria). The operatic form engages the audience in terms of right and wrong.

Not much work has been done so far on law or crime in the opera[17] and also on war in the opera.[18] The combination of the two, law and war in opera seems to have been even more neglected by academics. As opera is increasingly consumed in its recorded form, we have suggested applying methods developed for the study of law in film to the depiction of law in opera.[19] In this article, we are drawing on recorded operas combining issues of law and war. A strand in current musicology emphasises that opera is a performance and that its meaning can be studied by comparing different stagings of opera.[20] Operagoers themselves relate one performance of an opera to other performances.[21] They may also draw on parallels and differences between the presentation in an opera and the content of a literary source which inspired the composer, or compare an opera performance with a film on the same

---

11 Ibid., p. 197.
12 *Ferreri* 2017, p. 116.
13 *Conrad* 1987, p. 11; *Brunt* 2021, p. 72.
14 *Brunt* 2021, p. 86.
15 Ibid., pp. 82, 85.
16 Ibid., p. 86.
17 *Brunt* 2013, p. 78; *Annunziata/Colombo* 2021, p. 149; *Machura* et al. 2023.
18 As exemptions e.g.: *Gossett* 2007; *Roth* 2017; *Risi* 2018; *Siopsi* 2020; *Walton* 2021.
19 *Machura* et al. 2023.
20 *Champion* 2016; *Risi* 2022.
21 *Risi* 2022, p. 93.

story. We are therefore also discussing one opera's treatment of law and war in its context with the original novel and later film versions.

The following starts by exploring the centrality of war as a theme in opera, and then examines the relation between audience and opera. We continue investigating how war is portrayed in selected examples of opera, chosen for their coverage of key elements recurring in popular culture's stories of armed conflict. These include the use of law as a tool of power in war and its aftermath, the depiction of the horrors of war, lawlessness, and the breakdown of authority in defeat as well as brutal occupation. The penultimate part offers an intertextual reading of a staging of Prokofiev's *War and Peace* to demonstrate how the meaning of a story can be changed for reasons of political propaganda. The conclusion emphasises the potential of opera and of an analysis of opera when it comes to the confluence of law and war.

2. War as Backcloth or as Main Topic for Opera Plots

War is often used as a backcloth for opera plots, against which personal tragedy or comedy is played out. For example, in Verdi's *Aida* (1871) the war between Egypt and Ethiopia frames the tragedy of the titular character and Radamès both of whom are torn between loyalty to their respective nations and their love for each other, a conflict resolved only by their death. While in Mozart's *Così fan tutte* (1790) Ferrando and Guglielmo pretend to be called off to war so that they can return in disguise to test the fidelity of their fiancées. Few operas before the 20th century, however, deal with the topic of war itself (and not as background to e.g., a love story). Mieczysław Weinberg's *The Passenger* (1968) is a powerful example of opera's potential to challenge audiences and confront human nature and the very depths of tragedy. The work is set on a cruise ship after World War Two. On the upper deck a German couple, Lisa and Walter, are sailing to Brazil. Unknown to Walter, Lisa was a guard at Auschwitz. She thinks she recognises one of the other passengers as a former inmate, Marta. The opera juxtaposes Lisa's remembering of Auschwitz with the present day. Lisa is convinced that Marta died in Auschwitz; Marta's fate is left ambiguous as the opera ends in darkness. Born in Poland, Weinberg had sought refuge in the Soviet Union in the aftermath of World War Two. Despite support from the Union of Soviet Composers, Weinberg was unable to get the opera staged. *The Passenger* was finally premiered in 2006 in a semi–staged production.[22] More recently, Kevin Puts' Pulitzer–Prize–winning opera *Silent Night* (2011) is set in the trenches of World War One around the spontaneous and fleeting 1914 Christmas truce. The work explores the

---

22   The first full staging took place in July 2010 at the Bregenzer Festspiele.

futility of war and the disconnect between leaders making decisions from afar and the individual soldiers suffering the tragic consequences.

War puts lives and property in danger, evokes terror and fear, but also acts of heroism. If the audience accepts a non–realistic portrayal, and it does when it sets foot into the opera house or turns to a recording, these are all aspects which can be shown to great effect in opera with its penchant for extreme emotional upheaval. The combination of war, law and crime can be even more appealing to the operagoer — and be more rewarding for the artists and the opera industry.

As Clemens Risi writes, opera can not only be used to express emotions of grief about the losses and victims of war. But it can also motivate enthusiasm for war. At minimum, opera "rhythmically overwhelms the bodies of spectators with sounds musically firing up actions of war".[23]

Pictures 1 and 2: Stills from Combattimento di Tancredi e Clorinda, performed by the ASKO Ensemble, De Nederlandse Opera (1993, dir. Pierre Audi).

---

23 *Risi* 2018, p. 125.

In Claudio Monteverdi's short operatic scena *Il Combattimento di Tancredi e Clorinda* (1624), we find the core constellation of war and law. Published in his eighth book of madrigals (1638), the piece is set during the first Crusade and uses "an extended passage from Torquato Tasso's epic poem *Gerusaleme liberata*".[24] The poem is a fictionalised telling of Goffredo of Bouillon's battle with Muslims to take Jerusalem. In Monteverdi's scena, the Christian knight Tancredi follows an enemy knight, not recognising that it is his love, Clorinda. Asked what he is bringing, Tancredi tells her "War and death". In a long and bloody fight, he mortally wounds her (Pictures 1 and 2). Only when Tancredi lifts the dying opponent's helmet, he recognises and baptises Clorinda. War allows actions which otherwise constitute capital crimes and it even pits people who are otherwise close against each other in furious hate. Yet, the opera also shows that the warriors may follow a code of rules. When Tancredi realises that the enemy is on foot, he dismounts. A knightly law of honour governs his actions.[25]

With its mixture of heroism, religious conflict, romantic sub–plots and magic, *Gerusaleme liberate* became widely used for opera plots into the 19th century, inspiring almost 100 operas and ballets. These works – such as Handel's, first major success, *Rinaldo* (1711) – tend to focus on Rinaldo, a knight betrothed to Goffredo's daughter Almirena, and the Saracen sorceress Armida. Armida is also Queen of Damascus, wife of Argante. The latter falls in love with the captured Almirena, much to the chagrin of Armida. The two reconcile by the end of the opera as they lead the Saracen army. They are defeated and convert to Christianity with the fall of Jerusalem (in the 1731 version they remain unrepentant); Almirena and Rinaldo are reunited. In *Rinaldo* the kidnapping of Almirena by Armida is central. It provides the main thrust of the action. The context of war also allows for honour to shine through, as at the end of the opera Goffredo forgives his vanquished enemies and gives them their freedom. Handel's librettist, Aaron Hill, invented the character of Almirena; he "was responsible for the absurd conversion to Christianity, no doubt a concession to English taste".[26]

Other operas based on *Gerusaleme liberate* tend to focus on the relationship between Armida and Rinaldo, and his abandonment of her. Armida is sent to murder Rinaldo but instead falls in love with him and keeps him under her spell in an enchanted garden; Rinaldo is eventually convinced to go back to his Christian duties and abandons Armida. Written against the backdrop of the Iraq War, in Judith Weir's *Armida* (2005) the story was transported to the contemporary Middle East. Rinaldo

24 *Siopsi* 2020, p. 26.
25 Staging by the ASKO Ensemble, De Nederlandse Opera, 1993, dir. Pierre Audi, https://bangor-naxosvideolibrary-com.bangor.idm.oclc.org/title/OA0975D (Accessed on 21 July 2023).
26 *Dean/Knapp* 1995, p. 172.

is a soldier torn between his duty and a desire for peace.[27] Armida is a television journalist for Metropolis News who interviews the soldiers but falls in love with Rinaldo; she takes him to her apartment. His fellow soldiers come to his rescue but instead of being convinced to return to his duties: love triumphs, the war ends. Weir's *Armida* evokes operatic history and the long tradition of Tasso's story to suggest that the crusades are ongoing but also to make a poignant call for peace.

Law is not only what follows from court rulings, what is passed in parliament, or what is set in force as secondary legislation by administrations. Especially in times before the full blossoming of the modern state, laws are also the rules that people follow to organise their lives.[28] As in Tancredi's example, warriors may keep to the patterns of behaviour which are honourable and as decent as it can get in an armed conflict. This includes the protection of civilians where at all possible, and the merciful and respectful treatment of captured enemies, as in Handel's *Rinaldo*. As will be demonstrated, these grounds make rich pickings for opera. In unique ways, opera can show moral reasoning, the reigning in of temptations, the overpowering force of hate as well as feelings of brotherhood in the wake of mortal danger, the triumph of victory, or the bitterness accompanying loss of lives and sheer survival.

3. Relation of Opera and Audience

Opera must be understandable and digestible if it wants to appeal to a mass audience. This has both commercial and ideological aspects. After emerging from its rarefied origins in the early 17th century, opera has primarily relied upon paying audiences, and so it remains. Modern opera companies spend considerable time and resources engaging new audiences through a variety of outreach projects. Indeed, the war on opera in Britain in recent years is ostensibly about making it more accessible to a greater number of people, as evidenced by the chief executive of the Arts Council, Darren Henley, who has suggested that the future of opera lies in "car parks, pubs and on tablets",[29] though this also reflects a neo–Marxist ideology that problematises traditional Western high culture. While there are thousands and thousands of operas, and new ones are composed and premiered constantly, the repertoire tends to be dominated by a limited number of "canonic" works by composers such as Mozart, Verdi and Wagner, with the 19th century being particularly well represented.[30]

---

27 It was commissioned by Channel 4 and broadcast on 25 December 2005. Wise Music Classical n.d.
28 *Ehrlich* 2022.
29 *Sherwood* 2022.
30 According to Operabase (2024), the top ten opera composers by number of performances are: Verdi, Mozart, Puccini, Rossini, Wagner, Donizetti, Tchaikovsky, Handel and Beethoven; the librettist Francesco Maria Piave was also included.

These works are often set in far–distant periods of time and reflect sentiments and worldviews of when they were composed and premiered. Naturally, the experience of opera is a fluid one. What contemporary audiences may have understood from these works may not be what may appeal to modern audiences. The earliest opera plots were largely drawn from Greek or Roman mythology or were about noble characters: monarchs, gods, or heroes. This remained the case with the rise of *opera seria* in the early 18th century; through the reforms of Zeno, Metastasio, Rameau and Gluck *opera seria* remained based on stories from antiquity. With the development of *opera buffa* (comic opera) plots began to reflect the concerns and interest of the bourgeoisie and lower social classes, and thus began to challenge the traditional modes of high culture. At the culmination of Mozart's *Don Giovanni* (1788), one of the high points of the opera repertoire, the arrogant and promiscuous titular character is dragged down to hell ensuring that the powerful aristocrat receives his just deserts while his servants endure. Similarly, in *Le nozze di Figaro* (1786) it is the servants who triumph over their master.

Towards the end of the 18th century, there developed a dissatisfaction with the rationalism of the Enlightenment and with centralised aristocratic control culminating in the American and French Revolutions. With it, the arts, including opera, "turned from classical to national historical subjects".[31] It was not until the mid–19th century that operas began to be centred on realistic characters in ordinary situations, such as Verdi's *La Traviata* (1853). While around the same time, inspired by German Romanticism and fuelled in part by antisemitism, Richard Wagner was reconceptualising opera through what he termed "Gesamtkunstwerk" (total artwork) in which music, drama, poetry and staging were synthesised – believing opera to have become debased and shallow. Wagner outlined his ideal opera in *Opera und Drama* (1852),[32] arguing that Greek mythology was best suited for his *Gesamtkunstwerk*. Against a backdrop of German nationalism and the struggle for Germany to achieve nationhood, for his *Ring* cycle of four music dramas (written between 1848 and 1874; first performed in 1876) Wagner turned to Germanic mythology.[33]

Inevitably, the majority of operas have plots rooted in the past, often the distant past, and are set in locations far removed from the experiences of today's audiences. Making operas relatable to the audience of the present has always been a challenge for producers reviving popular works. Productions often rely on the universal appeal of many of the works' themes. For modern producers, the musical score is the least flexible element, notwithstanding the need in particular cases to reconcile performing traditions (e.g. replacing the castrati of Baroque operas or traditions of cutting or adding numbers), the challenges of establishing "authentic" texts or

---

31 *Cannon* 2012, p. 107.
32 *Wagner* 1995.
33 *Grey* 2008 provides a good introduction.

choosing between versions of the same opera. Thus, when recreating operas, the staging is most subject to change, and indeed is generally considered to be a blank canvas. Opera is, of course, a multi–sensory experience requiring acting and action as well as the music. Staging and costumes are vital aspects of translating operas to modern audiences, helping them to navigate the often complex and convoluted plots (and sub–plots), sung in a language that is often not vernacular.

Robert Cannon describes three essential approaches in the production of historical operas, each informed by contemporary taste (and budget): "recreation of the original"; "modern equivalent of an original"; "interpretations".[34] Attempting to recreate the original opera can be difficult and sometimes impossible, as we often know so little about staging etc.; often at least partly speculative, such productions can, however, be informative in terms of reconstructing how historical operas worked. However, it is the last two approaches that tend to be most often encountered today, arguably helping to keep opera invigorated by bringing works to new audiences (though not always successfully: Claus Guth's 2017 production of *La Bohème* at the Opéra National de Paris rendered in outer space). In modernising the setting, an opera originally taking place in a mythical medieval city–state can be transformed into a modern 21st–century setting. The duke becomes a president. The longing girl of a 19th–century story now is a prostitute.[35] In another opera staging, knightly armour is replaced with 19th–century or even modern military uniforms. Interpretations can also be more abstract, though. The human drama at the heart of the plots stays recognisable. Such interpretations can help modern audiences to relate to the plot and the characters using a more recognisable and easily decoded series of signs, though they too can be heavily imbued with political leanings and ideologies not originally intended. Modern producers and directors also need to increasingly be aware of audience sensitivities.[36]

The requirement of understandability to the audience is one of the dimensions making a study of law and crime in popular culture and here: in the opera, worthwhile.[37] It demonstrates what is possible to articulate about war and law, it allows to gauge what appears believable to consumers of opera. The argument may be raised that friends of opera are but a small segment of society.[38] Indeed, today's audiences are typically older and more middle–class and educated than the average

---

34 *Cannon* 2012, p. 99.
35 At the Mariinsky Theatre in St. Petersburg director Graham Vick presented Natasha in a staging of Prokofiev's *War and Peace* as a prostitute (*Holm* 2021).
36 A good example is the 2015 production of Rossini's *Guillaume Tell* at the Royal Opera House: see *Walton* 2021, pp. 211–213.
37 *Machura/Litvinova* 2021; *Machura* et al. 2023.
38 One survey concluded that 3.7% of adults in England attended an opera/operetta in 2016/17; annual surveys were conducted between 2005 and 2016, showing a decline from 4.4% at the start of the period: *Statista* 2018.

citizen but exactly with these characteristics, they form an influential section of society. Studying their media and art consumption is therefore important.

On a basic level, law is a tool of power. Opera tells stories of the use of law in war or in the aftermath of war. In the following, selected operas are used to exemplify how different messages can be suggested to the opera audience.

Picture 3: Promotion picture for Simon Boccanegra at the Royal Opera. The writing in the background points at the shady past of the Doge – he has been a pirate. Source: https://www .opera-online.com/en/items/productions/simon-boccanegra-royal-opera-house2018-1991 (Accessed on 23 July 2023).

War is in fact a recurring theme in Verdi's works, where he is often concerned with the abuse of power.[39] As such they are reflections of the period in which they were composed and first performed. Italy underwent a radical socio–political transformation during Verdi's lifetime. His early operas coincided with the rise of the Risorgimento movement, which agitated for the unification of Italy. Most famously the chorus "Va, pensiero" ("Go, thoughts") from *Nabucco* (1842), Verdi's first major success, became associated with the movement. As Philip Gossett has noted, "there are many pages in the earlier operas of Verdi (…) where arias or choruses convey a message of hope and the conviction that armed struggle would be necessary to give birth to a new country."[40] That ambition was realised in 1861. Before this Verdi had to contend with official censorship – as did most opera composers into

---

39 *Gossett* 2007.
40 Ibid., p. 21.

the 20th century; the choice of text or subject could have significant consequences. As Gossett concluded, Verdi "knew the dangers of accepting the idea of a 'just' war, but he was also willing to risk much to change the political system under which Italy suffered before 1860."[41] War and conflict were, of course, part of the human experience then as now. Indeed, looking more broadly at the connection between opera and war, Benjamin Walton has recently argued convincingly that "the world of opera (…) might be best understood through the prism of wartime".[42]

Pictures 4 and 5: Scenes from Attila staged at the Teatro Regio di Parma: the brutality of his reign and the resistance it ignites.

---

41   Ibid., p. 25.
42   *Walton* 2021, p. 213.

"Grant him peace" are the last words in Verdi's opera *Simon Boccanegra* (1857). The title character is a former pirate and folk hero, made Doge, ruler of Genua (Picture 3). Two dimensions of the story can be distinguished. On a macro level, there is the seemingly endless civil war in Genua, and it is the hope of one of the main characters, Grabrielle Adorno, that it will eventually be superseded by "Italian brotherhood". Adorno will be the new Doge as the opera ends. On the micro level of the opera characters, lust for power, love and jealousy involve the protagonists in an epic struggle with another. In Verdi's piece, law is not mythologised but appears as a tool of power, which remains in the hands of Boccanegra, the Doge. Only, at his life's end, he understands to temper it with forgiveness. In other words, not the law and power but a benign spirit will improve society and people's relations.[43]

Crime as an integral part of war is portrayed in Verdi's *Attila* (1846). Not only this, but Attila's soldiers also wholly embrace committing crime as a part of their craft that they fully enjoy. *Attila* starts with a chorus of Huns:

> "Shouts, pillage, groans, blood,
> rape, devastation, massacre and fire are Attila's sport,
> O lavish table which provides us with such rich fare!
> Odin does not disappoint us. This is Valhalla here!
> You open to heroes, blessed land, you are ours,
> Long live Attila! He discovered it."[44]

The men are under strict orders to kill. Attila reprimands them when he sees a group of female prisoners (Picture 4): "Who dared, against my interdict, to save them?" Devastation is an original aim for him: "my hardy courser will speed over mountains of dust and bones, l will scatter to the winds the guilty ashes of your proud cities."

Revenge and resistance are topics often repeated in opera. In *Attila*, the captured Roman heroine Odabella swears to kill the Hun's leader, following the example of Judith in the Bible (Picture 5). Finally, she stabs him.

In addition, high treason as a form of crime is in evidence in Verdi's *Attila*. Rome's ambassador Ezio suggests to Attila that they share power: Attila is to rule the world with the exemption of Rome, which shall be Ezio's realm. Ezio is a "disturbing character",[45] as he is ready to bargain with the enemy. However, in the opera, he is rejected by Attila and returns to Rome having learnt a lesson.

---

43 *Simon Boccanegra*, staged at the Teatro Regio di Parma, 2010, dir. Daniele Callegari, https://bangor-naxosvideolibrary-com.bangor.idm.oclc.org/title/A00008884 (Accessed on 20 July 2023).
44 All direct quotes cited from *Attila* played at the Teatro Regio di Parma, 2010, dir. Pier Francesco Maestrini, https://bangor-naxosvideolibrary-com.bangor.idm.oclc.org/title/721608 (Accessed on 22 July 2023).
45 *Rindo* 1984, p. 251.

The horrors of war are part of many operas and the depiction can be similar as in *Attila*. Among the dangers of war are lawlessness and the breakdown of authority in defeat. Lawlessness as a consequence of military defeat is depicted in one of the key Russian "national" operas, Alexander Borodin's *Prince Igor* (first performed 1890).[46] It long forms part of the cultural canon in Russia and is commonly interpreted as a warning that Russia needs to be united to survive. According to this myth, power must be concentrated in the strong hands of a towering figure who subjugates external enemies and suppresses internal disorder and rule breaking.

Picture 6: Still from Prince Igor performed at the Metropolitan Opera: Galitsky expressing his political objectives to the acclaim of his followers.

In the opera, the prince of one of the medieval Russian states, Igor, decides to go to war against a mighty (barbaric) neighbour. For the time of his absence, he leaves the administration of his principality in the hands of his brother–in–law, Prince Galitsky. The war goes horribly wrong, and Igor finds himself a captive of the enemy's Khan. His inability to return creates a power vacuum back home which is cruelly filled by Galitsky and his marauding men. In a particularly poignant scene, women turn to Igor's wife, Galitsky's sister, to seek justice and secure the release of an abducted maiden. As their last hope, Princess Yaroslawna is asked to protect their "honour". Galinsky and his thugs would be worse than the enemy, fearless now that Prince Igor is absent. The Princess overcomes her state of numbed grief for her absent husband and decides to take action. But when she confronts her brother, she is horribly mocked and humiliated by him. Even her fidelity is called into question, surely, she

---

46 A modern interpretation of *Prince Igor* for a Western audience was staged at the Metropolitan Opera in 2014, dir. Dmitri Tcherniakov and Gianandrea Noseda, Deutsche Grammophon DVD 073 5146 and a patriotic version for a domestic Russian audience at the Mariinski Theatre St. Petersburgh in 1998, dir. Yevgeny Sokovnin and Irkin Sabitov, Decca Music Group DVD 074 173-9.

must share her brother's uninhibited lust. Departing, Galitsky declares he will free the girl — and take another instead.

Later, among his drunken men (Picture 6), Galitsky unveils his future plans: he wants to become elected as ruler and will seize the treasury among other things — "what else is power for?" The Galitsky figure reminds of Bermbach's book title, "Where Power is Completely Based on Crime. Politics and Society in the Opera".[47] It is solely the promise of the otherwise forbidden, of plunder, which attracts Galitsky's followers.

Therefore, Igor and his principality face three threats: isolated from other Russian states, and especially if governed by a selfish and corrupt ruler like Galitsky, they are too weak to defend themselves against the threat of external enemies. But there is also the presence of an unreliable element among the Russian people, which as the opera suggests, needs a firm hand to be suppressed. The latter are personified in the two storytellers,[48] Skula and Yeroshka, who dodge fighting in Igor's army and then join in with Galitsky for the wine and the excessive fun. When Prince Igor eventually returns, they decide to support him to avoid punishment, and announce his comeback. Yet, the city lies in ruins, having been weakened by lawlessness, it has been destroyed by the enemy. All this is presented to at least a Russian audience as a timeless warning. The simplicity of the political concept lends itself well to theatrical treatment which requires the personalisation of ideas in characters.

The aftermath of war, with a violent and brutal occupation by foreign forces, is depicted in the version of Verdi's *I vespri siciliani* (1855) staged at the Teatro Regio di Parma in 2010.[49] Here, the medieval story is transplanted to 19th–century Palermo with French occupiers in period blue uniforms and Sicilian population. Early on, a French soldier comments that their leader, Monforte, used "excessive cruelty" to kill the former ruler of Palermo. Later, at the Sicilian vesper, when brides and grooms are dancing, French soldiers imagine raping the women and proceed to do so. The Sicilians start to feel the "fury of a lion", want revenge and there is a call to arms. Indeed, in a previous scene, a local resistance leader plotted a classic strategy to provoke the French into becoming so oppressive and brutal that the people will rise against them.

---

47 Translated book title of *Bermbach* 1997.
48 To be precise, they are *Gudok* players, who in old Russia told stories and news accompanied by their instrument (the guitar-like *Gudok*). They were the journalists of the day.
49 Dir.: Pier Luigi Pizzi, https://bangor-naxosvideolibrary-com.bangor.idm.oclc.org/title/A000089 58 (Accessed on 28 July 2023). All direct quotes are from the accompanying libretto.

PLOTTER: The people still lack strength and confidence.
LEADER: No matter! In spite of that we must risk
an audacious, desperate coup!
And may the day come at last
when the French perpetrate such brutality
that the people are forced
to rise and take up arms!

With these all too familiar dynamics between invading forces and local opposition, the opera covers a timeless constellation. The crimes of one side can be utilised by the other, with the population trapped in the middle. Verdi's opera also includes the character of Arrigo, a Sicilian patriot and released prisoner of war, who, upon learning that the French governor Monforte is his father, betrays plotters trying to assassinate this man. Patriotic duty, honour and a father–and–son drama are interwoven in the operatic drama. As the curtain falls, the grand finale culminates with the rallying cry "Revenge! Revenge! Revenge!".

Similar themes emerge in Vincenzo Bellini's *Norma* (1831). The opera takes place in the first century BC during the Roman occupation of Gaul. The Gallic high priestess Norma is abandoned by her lover Roman proconsul of Gaul, Pollione, with whom she has had two children. Pollione has, however, fallen in love with another priestess, Adalgisa. She in turn is horrified to learn that Pollione intends to abandon the mother of his children. Norma's relationship with Pollione has not only led her to break her sacred chastity vows but also sees her in bed with the enemy, literally and figuratively. The abandonment and betrayal drive her to consider murdering her two sons as they sleep ("Can I kill them? What guilt have they? They are the children of Pollione: That is their crime!"),[50] but she instead entrusts them to Adalgisa, who swears never to love Pollione again and to persuade him to return to Norma. When Adalgisa fails to change Pollione's stance, Norma summons the Gauls to "War, plunder and death." However, a human sacrifice is first needed. Pollione is captured but Norma cannot bring herself to kill him and instead retires to question him: "What insidious priestess, spurred this infidel to the worst of crimes". She demands that he renounces Adalgisa, but he refuses. The enraged Norma threatens to kill their children, as well as all Romans and Adalgisa. Pollione pleads with Norma to kill him instead ("Oh! Kill me, kill me, But on her have pity …"). In the finale, Norma decides to take his place on the sacrificial pyre: "a perjured Priestess has broken her holy vows, has betrayed her nation and our fathers' gods." To which the gathered crowd responds: "a crime! Oh, what wrath! Tell us all." Norma's selflessness reignites Pollione's love for her and he follows Norma into the flames, watched by her father, Oroveso, and the crowd of Gallic warriors. As with many operas, the plot of *Norma* creates tension between duty and desire,

---

50 English translations taken from *Operas, Arias, Composers, Singers*, n.d.

highlighting the consequences of betrayal. Amidst the chaos of impending war and her internal conflicts, Norma can even consider – and threaten – infanticide, murder, and genocide. The laws of her morality ultimately prevent her from carrying out these acts; the crime of treason and of breaking sacred vows can only be assuaged through self–sacrifice.

Having shown basic patterns of how law and war are depicted in opera, we now turn to an intertextual analysis of a historically significant opera, comparing it with the earlier novel and two film versions. The results of political context and censorship forms part of the analysis. Likewise, audiences may compare the treatment of a story in different versions.

5. Intertextual Analysis of War and Peace

How opera becomes a tool of propaganda and self–assurance is illustrated by Sergei Prokofiev's *War and Peace*. Francesca Zambello, responsible for the *mise en scène* of a staging at the Opéra National de Paris in 2000, characterised the opera as a "glorification of war".[51] Prokofiev started composing the opera in 1941 and continued to work on it for several years, responding to but never fully satisfying the demands of Stalin's culture apparatus.[52] The mammoth opera reflects the climate of the Second World War and the influence of censorship. It had to wait until 1991 before it was staged in an unabridged form at the Mariinsky Theatre in St. Petersburg.[53]

A contextual analysis comparing the opera staged in Paris with Tolstoy's novel and two of its film versions[54] shows how the depiction of war crimes in Prokofiev's opera changed in the overall attempt to create a Russian ultra-nationalistic version of the original novel. In the final scene of jubilation about the victory over Napoleon and his invading army, the opera's focus becomes abundantly clear. The mass chorus sings: "We've defended Russia" and "our great land". "Right was on our side." Francesca Zambello subverted the ending in the recording of the Paris staging. Visually, the final focus is on the reunited characters Natasha and Pierre. Yet, the colossal choir and orchestral music stays the same.

In contrast to the opera, Tolstoy's novel is much less militaristic but still deeply political. The novel's main character Count Pierre Besuchov devotes himself to starting a family and re–building Russia after the war. The end alone is different from the opera, focus on what a man can contribute in civilian live here, and

---

51 *La Guerre et la Paix*, TDK, 2003, DVD DV-OPWP, supplement *A propos de 'La Guerre e la Paix'*. In the following, the discussion is mainly based on this Paris version which in the second part "War" has only a few omitted scenes compared to the original.
52 *Seinen* 2009.
53 *War and Piece*, dir. Graham Vick, Arthouse Music, 2015, Blue-Ray 109093.
54 About the novel and the US-Italian and soviet films: *Litvinova/Machura* 2005.

nationalist pathos there. The American–Italian film version of *War and Peace* (1956, dir. King Vidor) is truer to Tolstoy's ideas: as Pierre and his future wife Natasha step out of the family's ruined palace into a garden, a text is shown speaking of the need to value life. Life is God and to love life means to love God. This contrasts with the blunt words "love for everyone is love for no one", in the opera formulated by one of its patriotic heroes, the Russian officer Prince Andrey Bolkonsky. The message of the opera contrasts with the message of Tolstoy: benign philosophy is replaced with rampant nationalism.

In 1812, right was on the Russian side to defend themselves. In the opera, the kind of rule and law the French would bring is depicted very negatively. Napoleon sings of his plans, of mercy to the conquered and decreeing fair laws. Yet, the behaviour of his troops looting Moscow and shooting suspected arsonists without a proper trial reveals a different reality. One of the opera's main characters, Count Pierre Besukhov, is arrested when trying to defend a woman and only just evades to be executed as a spy.

The burning of Moscow marks a major difference between novel and opera. Tolstoy writes that the fires started without human intention. Fires self–ignited in wooden buildings abandoned by fleeing Muscovites, setting them aflame here and there, then everywhere.[55] The opera, however, depicts the locals as either deciding to torch their own city to defeat Napoleon or as egging on others to do so. A scorched–earth policy that takes away food and shelter from the civilian population may constitute a war crime. In the opera, any thought of this is evaded: the people themselves want it! On the larger scale, the devastation of Russia is blamed exclusively on the French in the opera. But it was also a Russian defence policy. Patriotism is rampant among Russians in the opera, where Tolstoy delicately deals with the fact that some peasants saw advantages in parting from the Russian aristocrats and taking their lives in their own hands.[56] Historically, there were even uprisings.[57]

The Russian Field Marshal Kutuzov, portrayed as the decisive leader, similarly to how Stalin's image was painted in soviet propaganda, was given the central part in the opera *War and Peace*, marking a difference to both, Tolstoy's book and Prokofiev's original concept.[58] The core of Tolstoy's philosophy, underlying the novelist's work, is expressed in the figure of the peasant soldier Platon Karatáev met by the book's main protagonist, Count Pierre Besukhov, in French captivity. He has a deeply religious worldview. Describing qualities of political leaders in the aftermath of World War One, the sociologist Max Weber cited Platon Karatáev as an

---

55 *Tolstoy* n.d., book 11, ch. XXVI.
56 Ibid. n.d., book 10, ch. XI.
57 *Schklovskij* 1928, pp. 76–77.
58 *Seinen* 2009, p. 425.

example of an all–encompassing ethic of love which goes to the point of giving up self–interest.[59] Tolstoy characterises Platon as follows:

> "Karatáev had no attachments, friendships, or love, as Pierre understood them, but loved and lived affectionately with everything life brought him in contact with, particularly with man — not any particular man, but those with whom he happened to be."[60]

In the soviet opera, the Platon Karatáev figure is not given the lines to explain his philosophy of love, which would be not easily reconcilable with the intended epos of national resistance. Pierre sings in the Paris staging of Prokofiev's opera:

> "In knowing hardship, the horror of death, pain and suffering, I've found peace. The struggle within me is over. And I made a friend in prison, with a man by the name of Platon. He was Russian to the marrow, a kind and well–rounded man. He lives in dear memory." (Quoted after the English subtitles.)

This is clearly an ideologically sanitised version of Platon Karatáev. Gone is what made the figure stand out for Weber and Tolstoy himself. The execution of prisoners by the French, shakes Pierre to the core, Platon comments the horrors in the novel with: "ah, what a sin... what a sin! (…) Where there's law there's injustice".[61] Again, he makes a wider point and is not expressing opposition against the French.

In Prokofiev's opera, the killing of prisoners is exclusively committed by the French. Again, it sanitises Tolstoy's novel: in his text, a Russian officer's order "we won't take them!", seals the fate of French prisoners.[62] However, in the American–Italian film, the painful episode is not omitted. The commanding Russian officer instructs his men that they know what to do. Shots ring out and death screams are heard. Kill or be killed, that is the war, the officer tells Pierre, ignoring the difference when the enemy is captured, unarmed and helpless.[63] The opera transports a myth that made sense to Russians in the Second World War to keep up morale — Russians do not commit war crimes — into our times. The colossal soviet film *Wojna i mir* (UdSSR, 1965–1967, dir. Sergei Bondarchuk) similarly does not touch this sore point. Instead, Russian soldiers feed their exhausted French prisoners in a gesture of human solidarity. Tolstoy has both, the shooting of prisoners, but also the scene in which Russian soldiers assisted starving and freezing French: "'They are men too,' said one of them".[64]

---

59 *Weber* 1971, p. 575.
60 *Tolstoy* n.d., book 12, ch. 13.
61 Ibid., book 12, ch. XII.
62 Ibid., book 14, ch. XI.
63 Similar words are spoken by Andrey at the eve of the battle of Borodino when he suggests that not taking prisoners would make wars more unlikely (*Tolstoy* n.d., book 10, ch. XXV). But as it is written, the reader is not invited to share this view but rather to understand Andrey's hate of the military and war.
64 *Tolstoy*, n.d., book 15, ch. IX.

6. Conclusion

The discussion of law and war as depicted in opera confirms the music theatre's ability to clearly depict, draw on and produce deep emotions. This makes opera attractive to audiences seeking an immersive experience of singing, orchestral music, acting, and other stage crafts. The emotional power of opera makes it an effective tool of propaganda, with depictions of war likely to create a common patriotic feeling among the audience, to ignite resistance to or dislike of an enemy. Opera may also be used to warn of the dangers of a feeble government that invites foreign invaders, as in the example of *Prince Igor*. The soviet opera *War and Peace* demonstrates how an original, more sombre literary source can be subverted to produce a rousing call to become patriots rallying behind an all–powerful leader. Yet, other political sentiments expressed in opera may include a more peaceful message, one of warning against the horrors of war as in *The Passenger*, *Armida*, *Simon Boccanegra* or *Il Combattimento di Tancredi e Clorinda*. Depictions of law and crime form one of the means at the disposal of opera to tell stories, to attract, fascinate and influence audiences.

Opera needs to be understandable to a wide audience. It may therefore show what can be grasped by the public: understandings of law, of war and of war crime. Our analysis has shown that a wide range of themes can be and is depicted in the opera. Some of them are going into the very detail of war strategies. In *I vespri siciliani*, this goes so far as to include a ruthless way to incite an insurgency. Thus, opera is able to combine elements at an abstract level of conducting state affairs and organising war with elements of on–the–ground experience of the defeated, oppressed and abused.

Bibliography

Abbate, Carolyn/*Parker*, Roger, 2015: A History of the Opera: The Last Four Hundred Years. London, Penguin.

Annunziata, Filippo/*Annunziata*, Clarissa, 2020: Dove sono i bei momenti…? Opera Production and Aesthetics in the Age of Covid–19. In: Rivista di diretto delle arti e dello spettacolo, No. 2, pp. 5–11.

Annunziata, Filippo/*Colombo*, Giorgio Fabio (eds.), 2018: Law and Opera. Cham, Springer.

Annunziata, Filippo/*Colombo*, Giorgio Fabio, 2021: Opera and Law: Critical Notes. In: Law and Literature, 33:1, 141–157.

Bermbach, Udo, 1997: Wo Macht ganz auf Verbrechen ruht. Politik und Gesellschaft in der Oper. Hamburg, Europäische Verlagsanstalt.

Brunt, Lodewijk, 2013: Wie ik liefheb, moet ik doden. Misdaad in het muziektheater. In: Tijdschrift over Cultuur en Criminaliteit, No. 3, 78–89.

Brunt, Lodewijk, 2021: Crime at the Opera House. In: *Siegel*, Dina/*Bovenkerk*, Frank (eds.), Crime and Music. Cham, Springer, pp. 73–86.

Cannon, Robert, 2012: Opera. Cambridge, Cambridge University Press.

Champion, Holly, 2016: Dramaturgical Analysis of Opera Performance: Four Recent Productions of Dido and Aeneas. PhD dissertation, University of New South Wales.

Conrad, Peter, 1987: A Song of Love and Death: The Meaning of Opera. London, Chatton and Windus.

Dean, Winton/*Knapp*, John Merrill, 1995: Handel's Operas, 1704–1726. Oxford, Oxford University Press.

Durkheim, Émile, 1982: The Division of Labour in Society, translated by George Simpson. New York: The Free Press.

Ehrlich, Eugen, 2022: Grundlegung der Soziologie des Rechts. 5th edition, Berlin, Duncker und Humblot.

Gossett, Philip, 2007: War and Peace in the Operas of Giuseppe Verdi. In: Bulletin of the America Academy of Arts and Sciences, 60:3, 20–25.

Gossett, Philip, 2012: Giuseppe Verdi and the Italian Risorgimento. In: Proceedings of the American Philosophical Society, 156:3, 271–282.

Grey, Thomas (ed.), 2008: The Cambridge Companion to Wagner. Cambridge, Cambridge University Press.

Ferreri, Silvia, 2018: Legal Issues in Italian Opera. In: *Annunziata*, Filippo/*Colombo*, Giorgio Fabio (eds.), Law and Opera. Cham, Springer, pp. 103–117.

Hogan, Robert/*Emler*, Nicholas, P., 1981: Retributive Justice. In: *Lerner*, Melvin J./*Lerner*, Sally C. (eds.), The Justice Motive in Social Behavior. New York, Plenum Press, pp. 125–143.

Holm, Kerstin, 2021: Verdammte Modernisierer. In: Frankfurter Allgemeine Zeitung, 3. August, p. 11.

Lacerda, Gabriel, 2017: Law and Opera. Stimuli to a Sensible Perception of Law. In: Journal of the Oxford Centre for Socio–Legal Studies, 2, 90–106.

Litvinova, Olga/*Machura*, Stefan, 2005: Krieg und Gesellschaft: Mehrebenenanalyse der amerikanischen und sowjetischen Verfilmungen von Tolstojs Roman "Krieg und Frieden". In: *Machura*, Stefan/*Voigt*, Rüdiger (eds.), Krieg im Film. Münster, Lit, pp. 103–132.

Machura, Stefan/*Litvinova*, Olga, 2021: Reflections of Legal Culture in Television Comedy: Social Critique and Schadenfreude in the US Series "Frasier". In: International Journal for the Semiotics of Law, 34:1, pp. 89–108.

Machura, Stefan/*Litvinova*, Olga/*Cunningham*, John, 2023: Analysing Law in Opera. In: Law and Humanities, 17:1, pp. 90–111.

Operabase, 2024: 10 Most Played Composers. https://www.operabase.com/statistics/en (Accessed on 18 February 2024).

Operas, Arias, Composers, Singers, n.d.: Norma Libretto English Translation. https://www.opera-arias.com/bellini/norma/libretto/english/ (Accessed on 18 February 2024).

Rindo, John Patrick, 1984: A Structural Analysis of Giuseppe Verdi's Early Operas and their Influence on the Italian Risorgimento. PhD dissertation, University of Oregon.

Risi, Clemens, 2018: Die ästhetische Gewalt des Kriegs in der Oper. In: *Bosch*, Aida/*Pfütze*, Hermann (eds.), Ästhetischer Widerstand gegen Zerstörung und Selbstzerstörung. Wiesbaden, Springer VS, pp. 119–129.

Risi, Clemens, 2022: Opera in Performance: Analyzing the Performative Dimension of Opera Productions, translated by Anthony A. Mahler. London, Routledge.

Roth, Dennis, 2017: Krieg in der Oper. Freiburg, Rombach.

Schklovskij, Viktor, 1928: Materiali i stil w romane Lva Tolstogo "wojna i mir". Moscow, Federazija.

Seinen, Nathan, 2009: Kutuzov's Victory, Prokofiev's Defeat: The Revisions of "War and Peace". In: Music and Letters, 90:3, pp. 399–431.

Siopsi, Anastasia, 2020: Images of War in Opera. In: Open Journal for Studies in History, 3:2, pp. 25–34.

Statista, 2018: Share of Adults Who Attended an Opera or Operetta in the Last Year in England from 2005/06 to 2016/17. https://www.statista.com/statistics/556334/adults-opera-attendance-uk-england/ (Accessed on 18 February 2024).

Tolstoy, Leo, n.d.: War and Peace. Translated by Louise and Aylmer Maude. https://www.gutenberg.org/files/2600/2600-h/2600-h.htm#link2HCH0055 (Accessed on 27 July 2023).

Tritter, Daniel F., 2004: Opera and the Law: Dramma Giocosa. In: The Opera Quarterly, No. 1, 7–25.

Tyler, Tom R./*Boeckmann*, Robert J./*Smith*, Heather J./*Huo*, Yuen J., 1997: Social Justice in a Diverse Society. Boulder/Colorado, Westview Press.

Wagner, Richard, 1995: Opera and Drama. Translated by William Ashton Ellis. Nebraska, University of Nebraska Press.

Walton, Benjamin, 2021: Operatic Encounters in a Time of War. In: Journal of War and Culture Studies, 14:2, 211–229.

Wise Music Classical, n.d.: Judith Weir. Armida (2005). https://www.wisemusicclassical.com/work/34840/Armida--Judith-Weir/ (Accessed on 10 March 2024).

Weber, Max, 1971: Politik als Beruf. In: *Weber*, Max, Gesammelte Politische Schriften. 3rd edition, Tübingen, Mohr, pp. 505–560.

John Cunningham

That's When I Reach for My Revolver.
War Crime and Popular Music

Popular music reflects the culture from which it emerges; it has the power to shape that culture. This is particularly true in terms of attitudes to armed conflict. There is a long tradition of popular music songs about war; those written in the 1960s in response to the Vietnam War have enjoyed the most lasting cultural legacy. The rise of the countercultural hippie movement positioned many artists in opposition to the war in Vietnam. Protest songs fuelled the antiwar movement in America and gave voice to the generation facing conscription.[1] Music also became an important way for soldiers to cope with the impact of the war, as Douglas Bradley and Craig Werner have documented.[2] In times of war – and, indeed, peace – songs about conflict and its aftermath can be consoling and cathartic or antagonising and provocative, or perhaps all these things. Depending on perspective, they can be a call to arms or a tool of propaganda. Popular music has also been used as a weapon of torture in the War on Terror, with prisoners in Guantanamo Bay being subjected to endless repetitions of songs by Queen, Metallica, and Barney the Dinosaur, among others.[3] Within the repertoire of songs about war, artists have also sought to address transgressions of the laws of war: war crimes.

A war crime is a violation of the laws of armed conflict. The concept originates in the late 19th century with the Hague Conventions and has expanded to incorporate various other treaties such as the 1949 Geneva Conventions (which protects those not or no longer involved in armed conflicts). However, as the United Nations (UN) notes "there is no one single document in international law that codifies all war crimes."[4] Under Article 8 of the Rome Statute of the International Criminal Court, the UN's definition of war crimes encompasses a great deal of actions, including (but not limited to) the wilful killing of civilians or prisoners of war, torture, unnecessary destruction of property, unlawful deportation, and the taking of hostages. At the time of writing (Spring of 2024) the Global Conflict Tracker website lists over thirty

---

1 Examples are numerous, such as: *Eve of Destruction* (Barry McGuire, U.S.A. 1965); *7 O'clock News/Silent Night* (Simon and Garfunkel, U.K. 1966); *Draft Morning* (The Byrds, U.S.A. 1968); *Fortunate Son* (Creedence Clearwater Revival, U.S.A. 1969); *War* (Edwin Starr, U.S.A. 1969); *Ohio* (Crosby, Stills, Nash and Young, U.S.A. 1970).
2 *Bradley/Werner* 2015.
3 *Hintjens/Ubaldo* 2019.
4 United Nations n.d.

armed conflicts across the globe.[5] However, only two currently dominate media in the West: the war in Ukraine and the Israel–Gaza conflict – though the latter has largely displaced the former in terms of media coverage. Accusations of war crimes have been levelled against both Russia and Israel and have fed into mainstream media narratives that are not easily allowed to be challenged. Popular music has the power to subvert narratives and offer a direct and sometimes visceral response to these events.

When examining songs that deal with aspects of armed conflicts referring to, or discussing, transgressions of the laws of war, one must bear in mind that there is often a disparity between the popular usage of a term and its legal definition, especially in popular cultural discourse. The primary focus in any such study will typically be the lyrics; the ways in which they are conveyed, and the musical context undoubtedly contribute to the meaning, though is largely beyond the scope of this chapter.[6] One must also be cognizant of perspectives in any conflict and the positionality of associated discourse. If one man's terrorist is another man's freedom fighter, then one country's "special military operation" is another's war crime. The following discussion takes a broad view of war crimes to include examples that fit the definitions offered by the UN, but which may not necessarily be legally defined as such. On one hand, a song such as *Belsen Was a Gas* (U.K. 1979) by the Sex Pistols unambiguously refers to a recognised war crime, the Holocaust. On the other, the events referenced in U2's *Sunday, Bloody Sunday* (Ireland 1983) are certainly criminal – and have been investigated as such – but do not count as a war crime *per se* despite bearing all the hallmarks of it. Bloody Sunday (or the Bogside Massacre) took place in Derry on 30 January 1972, when occupying British soldiers shot 26 unarmed civilian, civil rights protesters, of which fourteen died; it remains the worst mass shooting in Northern Ireland.[7] In December 2023 it was ruled that only one of the soldiers would face trial for murder. These two examples also demonstrate the complexities of popular music as a function of socio–political discourse, and the two broad categories into which such songs tend to fall: cathartic universalism and transgressive specificity. Written at the height of The Troubles in Northern Ireland by a band from Dublin geographically and physically but not culturally removed from the conflict, *Sunday, Bloody Sunday* positions itself as a serious antiwar song, which reflects on the futility of armed conflict and expresses a desire for unity

---

5 Global Conflict Tracker n.d.
6 The complexities of copyright and cost of reproducing song lyrics are prohibitive. All of the songs and music videos discussed in this chapter are freely available on legal streaming services such as Spotify and on YouTube. The lyrics for English language songs discussed can be found on sites such as AZ Lyrics; sources for translations of Hebrew songs are given below at appropriate points.
7 See, for example, *Walsh* 2000. The events also inspired other songs such as, Paul McCartney's *Give Ireland Back to the Irish* (U.K. 1973); Black Sabbath's *Sabbath Bloody Sabbath* (U.K. 1973).

and peace. Its title is specific, but the universal themes and non–confrontational questioning have allowed it to become a transferrable anthem decades since the Good Friday Agreement. *Belsen Was a Gas* by contrast is a deliberately antagonistic, specific, and yet, historically inaccurate portrayal of life/death in one of the most notorious Nazi concentration camps, Bergen–Belsen. Two versions of the song were included on *The Great Rock 'n' Roll Swindle* (U.K. 1979), the soundtrack album to the mockumentary film of the same name (U.K. 1980, dir. Julien Temple). The version with Johnny Rotten was taken from the band's final concert in January 1978. The version with the infamous Great Train Robber, Ronnie Biggs was recorded shortly afterwards by remaining members, Steve Jones (guitar) and Paul Cook (drums), during their stay in Rio de Janeiro visiting Biggs; he had fled there in 1970 to avoid extradition. For different reasons, whether delivered by Rotten or Biggs *Belsen Was a Gas* makes for uncomfortable listening.[8] But arguably it is a discomfort that resonates authentically with the stark reality of the war crimes to which it refers. To dismiss the song as glorifying Nazi atrocities or mocking victims of the Shoah misses the point, though it is easier than confronting the darkness it embodies (see also below). Fundamentally these songs thus also embody questions about the limits of free speech and free expression, the essential tenets of any liberal democratic society.

This chapter offers a preliminary enquiry into popular music responses to war crimes, not just in terms of the songs themselves but through the actions of the artists and states. Popular music is a broad term used here as a shorthand for various genres including pop, rhythm and blues, rock, metal, hip–hop and rap. The music examples are necessarily selective. Much of the repertoire discussed is of the Anglo-phone tradition, and as such offer perspectives that are often geographically outside the direct sphere of conflict; they can also be distanced temporally. It is not possible in a relatively short essay to offer a detailed critique or an exhaustive account of war crimes in popular music; however, some broad trends are identifiable, such as the use of war crimes as modes of cultural transgression, defiance and catharsis – directly or indirectly. The first part of the essay looks at Naziism and the Holocaust: these songs were almost exclusively written decades after the atrocities occurred, especially from the 1960s onwards and reached a peak in the 1980s and 1990s. The punk movement of the late 1970s saw the absorption of Nazi symbology as a means of generational transgression, which extended to confrontational songs about the Holocaust, such as *Belsen Was a Gas* (even down to the use of, grammatically incorrect, German versions of the song titles given in Gothic script on pressings of the album: *Einmal Belsen war vortrefflich* and *Einmal Belsen war wirklich vortreff-lich*). The second section moves from historical atrocities to contemporary ones, first

---

8 A live version sung by Sid Vicious was released on the posthumous album *Sid Sings* (U.K. 1979).

in Ukraine. When Russia invaded Ukraine in February 2022 many commentators drew parallels between Vladimir Putin and Hitler. The War in Ukraine shows how contemporary popular musicians have engaged in political activism through their engagement with Putin's alleged war crimes. This typically comes from legacy artists who have a strong commercial platform from which to align themselves to causes, often repurposing existing songs to make a contemporary comment but also by releasing new material. Historically, this has been a relatively straightforward moral question for artists, but today, in the censorious gaze of highly divisive and increasingly illiberal social media, artists must weigh the consequences of their support or silence carefully. On state levels too, freedom of speech is increasingly limited by left–wing authoritarianism, where new hate crime laws are enacted with disturbingly ambiguous and vague criteria. The Incitement to Hatred and Hate Offences Bill recently passed in the Irish Republic and Scotland's Hate Crime and Public Order Act are two glaring examples of the erosion of democratic values by an elite political class, ushering in de facto blasphemy laws. In the final section, we look at examples of how music is used within the context of the ongoing war in the Middle East, to see how songs can be implicated in war crimes or indeed give comment on the mood of a beleaguered nation and form the soundtrack to war – or war crime, depending on the perspective taken. Songs that respond to conflict and war crimes can be – and are – exploited as a means of soft power to coerce and censor through the prism of war crimes.

1. Prologue to History

The establishment of the modern State of Israel in 1948 was effectively built on the Holocaust, the most infamous genocide and war crime in history. Popular music has not been a significant part of Holocaust studies.[9] There is, however, a sizable body of songs that address the Holocaust, directly or indirectly.[10] It is perhaps

---

9 There is no comparable text, for example, to *Wlodarski* 2015, which deals with the art music tradition.

10 *For example (chronological; not intended to be exhaustive):* Woody Guthrie, *Ilsa Koch* (U.S.A. 1948); Bob Dylan, *With God on our Side* (U.S.A. 1964); Captain Beefheart and His Magic Band, *Dachau Blues* (U.S.A. 1969); Kinky Friedman and the Texas Jewboys, *Ride 'em Easy* (U.S.A. 1973); Pink Floyd, *Waiting for the Worms* (U.K./U.S.A. 1979); Sex Pistols/Sid Vicious, *Belsen Was a Gas / Belsen Vos a Gassa* (U.K. 1979); Red Rider, *Lunatic Fringe* (U.S.A. 1981); Leonard Cohen, *Dance Me to the End of Love* (U.S.A. 1984); Rush, *Red Sector A* (Canada 1984); The Style Council, *Ghosts of Dachau* (Germany/U.K. 1984); Anthrax, *The Enemy* (U.S.A./Jamacia 1985); Amy Grant, *Lead Me On* (U.S.A. 1988); Anthrax, *Belly Of The Beast* (U.S.A./Jamacia 1990); Peter Himmelman, *Untitled* (Jamacia 1992); Janis Ian, *Tattoo* (U.S.A. 1993); The Indigo Girls, *This Train Reversed* (U.K. 1994); Martin Page, *The Door* (U.S.A. 1995); Jill Sobule, *Attic* (U.S.A. 1997); Slayer, *SS-3* (U.S.A. 1997); Remedy, *Never Again* (U.K. 1998); Dan Bern and the International Jewish Banking Conspiracy, *Lithuania*

unsurprising that most of these songs date from before the turn of the millennium. As D. X. Ferris notes, "For a generation whose parents who remembered World Ward II, Nazi imagery was an easy card to play when you wanted to be transgressive."[11] Not all these songs are, of course, transgressive. Many embody a desire for healing and remembrance. However, some have proved highly controversial. Arguably the best example of this is *Angel of Death* by (the now retired) Slayer. Released as the first song on their third album, *Reign in Blood* (U.S.A. 1986),[12] *Angel of Death* was written by guitarist Jeff Hanneman (1964–2013). Hanneman came from a military family – his brothers fought in Vietnam, and his father fought in World War II – and had a keen interest in military history. Slayer were one of the pioneers of thrash metal, which originated in San Francisco in the early 1980s. A sub–genre of heavy metal, thrash is characterised by fast tempos, heavy guitar riffs and virtuosic guitar solos; the genre is dominated commercially by the so–called "Big Four" of Metallica, Megadeth, Slayer and Anthrax. Embodying much of the transgressive ethos of punk, lyrically thrash songs often tend to engage in politics, especially anti–establishment ideas, including opposition to armed conflicts. *Angel of Death* became Slayer's signature song, closing almost all of their concerts since 1988. It courted much controversy, especially around the time of its release, which coincided with the establishment of the Parents Music Resource Centre.[13] *Reign in Blood* was released on Rick Rubin's label Def Jam Records, but their distributor, Columbia Records, refused to issue the album because of the artwork on the cover and because of the lyrics in *Angel of Death*: the album was ultimately distributed by Geffen Records.[14] The lyrics of *Angel of Death* describe the sadistic experiments of Josef Mengele, one of the physicians at the Auschwitz concentration camp where an estimated 1.1 million prisoners were murdered, most of whom were Jewish.[15] The song opens with a high–pitched scream and uses a variety of musical, sonic and textual techniques to evoke a relentless sense of claustrophobia. The lyrics alternate between first and third–person narratives and neither endorse nor explicitly condemn the abuses of Mengele. Media reception of the song was largely negative, underpinned by accusations of Nazi–sympathising and racism. For example, Paul Elliott posed the question of whether the band were either "Nazi apologists or naive dickheads". Describing Slayer as "the foulest, most provocative and probably the

---

(U.S.A./U.K. 2002); Matisyahu, *Jerusalem (Out of Darkness Comes Light)* (U.S.A. 2006); Say Anything, *Alive With The Glory Of Love* (U.S.A. 2006); Anarchy Club, *Get Clean* (2009); Disturbed, *Never Again* (U.S.A. 2010). The album *Atrocities* (U.K. 1986), by Christian Death, deals almost exclusively with the Holocaust.

11 *Ferris* 2008, p. 115.
12 For the album, see *Ferris* 2008.
13 For the PMRC, see *Chastagner* 1999. A prescient musical response to the movement's censorship is Megadeth's *Hook in Mouth* (U.S.A. 1988).
14 *Ferris* 2008, pp. 89–94.
15 Auschwitz-Birkenau Memorial and Museum n.d.

best speed metal band yet", he asked, "have they gone too far this time?"[16] The song certainly proved controversial. Inter alia, it led to the album's release being delayed in the U.K. and generated much (negative) publicity for the band. In the interview with Elliott, singer and bassist Tom Araya noted: "people think we're pro–Nazi, but that song has nothing to do with whether you're for or against it, it's just a song that tells what happened. What's the big deal?".[17] The issue, according to Elliott and many other journalists, was that the song doesn't openly condemn Mengele's actions. History is not enough. The band (here and in other interviews) retreated to a position of essentially allowing the song to speak for itself. Elliott concluded that Slayer were at best naïve, arguably not aided by the somewhat glib responses from some members of the band:

> "They've chosen a subject which invites controversy and haven't even taken the precaution of making their sympathies entirely clear. ... The subject hasn't been treated with even a fraction of the respect and sensitivity which it demands and, for that Slayer deserve all the flak that's directed their way."[18]

And flak they got. But controversy is, or at least was, hard currency among music–buying youth: to date, *Reign in Blood* has sold over 500,000 copies in the U.S. alone. Songwriter Hanneman often offered the defence of *Angel of Death* that it was simply obvious from the song that Mengele was bad, emphasising the importance of freedom of speech in art. For example, speaking in 1987, he contested:

> "I feel you should be able to write about whatever you want. 'Angel of Death' is like a history lesson, but as soon as we released it everybody was calling us Nazis. Our singer's a dark–skinned Chilean, there's no way we're fascists. I'd read a lot about the Third Reich and was absolutely fascinated by the extremity of it all, the way Hitler had been able to hypnotise a nation and do whatever he wanted, a situation where Mengele could evolve from being a doctor to being a butcher."[19]

One explanation for the reception of *Angel of Death* is that it challenged prevailing popular culture notions of the Holocaust and how it should be approached. And it did so in a highly transgressive musical style. It did so at a time when the Holocaust was increasingly depicted in media and art. Sophia Marshman has argued that popular representations of the Holocaust in novels and films such as *Sophie's Choice* (U.S.A., 1982, dir., Alan J. Pakula) or *Schindler's List* (U.S.A., 1993, dir. Steven Spielberg) tend to "affirm life rather than death, survival rather than destruction", which has been underpinned by "the marginalization of survivor testimony. ... instead of the Holocaust being edged to the margin of consciousness as a 'historical event', a sanitised popular image of the Holocaust has come to dominate the public

---

16 *Elliott* 1987.
17 Ibid.
18 *Elliott* 1987.
19 *Witter* 1987.

imagination".[20] Against such a popular cultural backdrop the seemingly impartial and highly descriptive lyrics of *Angel of Death*, which unflinchingly recount war crimes at Auschwitz, jarred. The lyrics and musical style – message and medium – created a cultural dissonance. Moreover, *Angel of Death* foregrounded, if not the voices of the victims, their experiences in a visceral way. Indeed, the song epitomises what Matthew Boswell has described as "Holocaust impiety".

In his 2012 book, *Holocaust Impiety in Literature, Popular Music and Film*, Boswell explores representations of the Holocaust across various media that transgress the idea of "Holocaust piety" as argued by Gillian Rose. Using Spielberg's *Schindler's List* (1993) as a primary example, Rose argued that popular culture works dealing with the Holocaust offered "particularly sentimental or sanctimonious approaches to the genocide".[21] In contrast Boswell defines Holocaust impiety as referring to "Works that reject redemptory interpretations of genocide and the claims of historical ineffability ... can be similarly defined as those that deliberately engineer a sense of crisis in readers, viewers or listeners by attacking the cognitive and cultural mechanisms that keep our understanding of the Holocaust at a safe distance from our own understanding", challenging those of later generations.[22] Taking punk and post–punk rock as his starting point, Boswell uses four artists to exemplify the concept of "Holocaust impiety" in popular music, from the mid–1970s to mid–1990s: the Ramones, the Sex Pistols, Joy Division and the Manic Street Preachers. On both sides of the Atlantic, punk bands regularly used Nazi imagery such as the swastika and made references to the Holocaust in song lyrics, but Boswell argues that this was not about supporting or glorifying the genocide but rather it was another facet of the movement's challenge to authority and conservative values: they were instead mocking Naziism. The Holocaust was, however, central to the punk movement, which itself left a lasting legacy on popular music. For example, Boswell suggests that the Sex Pistols were:

> "generally happy to use the swastika as an instrument of boorishness and to profess total ignorance about the events and political movements referenced by their clothing; at the same time, they made direct, impassioned, provocative statements about the Holocaust in songs that betrayed the degree to which genocide had impacted on its members and, more broadly, on the youth culture of the 1970s."[23]

Boswell discusses two Sex Pistols songs in particular, *Belsen Was a Gas* and *Holidays in the Sun*. The former, credited to Sid Vicious, Paul Cook, Steve Jones and John Lydon (Johnny Rotten), though written by Vicious before he joined the Sex Pistols, particularly captures the essence of Holocaust impiety: "[W]ith its

---

20 *Marshman* 2005.
21 *Boswell* 2012, p. 1; see also *Rose* 1996.
22 *Boswell* 2012, p. 3.
23 Ibid., p. 105.

brattish tone and near–total disregard for historical specificity, the song provides ample ammunition for those who regard it as a straightforward abuse of the Holocaust";[24] it was especially jarring for older generations given that the liberation of Bergen–Belsen in 1945 had been caught on film and shown in British cinemas. As Boswell notes, there were no gas chambers at Bergen–Belsen; however, he suggests that "giving the lie to the title, the song is in fact historically literate, referencing the fact that, for the purposes of Nazi propaganda, concentration camp prisoners *were* compelled to write letters that portrayed their conditions in an unfeasibly favourably light".[25]

Jones and Cook rerecorded *Belsen Was a Gas* with Ronnie Biggs in early 1978, with a different musical arrangement and an additional verse written by Biggs. They also recorded *No–one is Innocent*, not discussed by Boswell. Included on the album *The Great Rock 'n' Roll Swindle* (U.K. 1979), the song epitomises not just Holocaust impiety but a wider cultural impiety through flouting social norms and niceties. The lyrics, written by Biggs, invoke the Sex Pistol's own irreverent – and heavily censored hit – *God Save the Queen* (U.K. 1977). Sung in Biggs' broad cockney accent and replete with a rousing singalong chorus and saxophone solo, God is now implored to save (inter alios) Idi Amin (the brutal Ugandan despot), Ian Brady and Myra Hindley (the Moors Murderers), the Sex Pistols and Biggs himself. Arguably most offensive, however, was the call to save Martin Bormann and other Nazi's fleeing justice, observing that their war crimes weren't the result of wickedness but rather was what they perceived as "fun". In Biggs' own words: "The message of the song is simply this: if God is going to save the Queen, then he should save Myra Hindley, and Martin Boorman [sic] and Ian Brady. He has to save everybody or nobody. Because, no–one, absolutely no one [sic], is innocent."[26] Bormann, Hitler's private secretary, apparently died by suicide in 1945 but his body was only recovered in 1972 and not conclusively identified until the late 1990s, leading to various rumours; he was thought to have fled to Brazil. Bormann was tried *in absentia* in Nuremburg: in 1946 he was convicted of war crimes and crimes against humanity. *No–one is Innocent* was released as a single reaching no. 7 in the U.K. charts, the B–side was Sid Vicious' iconoclastic cover of *My Way*: nothing was sacred. The cover of the 12" single (titled *The Biggest Blow: A Punk Prayer*, a reference to Biggs' role in the Great Train Robbery) depicts Jones, Cook and Biggs playing atop the roof of a boat, with an actor as Bormann in Nazi uniform playing bass; the image is from the Sex Pistols' mockumentary film *The Great Rock 'n' Roll Swindle*, in which the fictionalised Bormann appears wandering around Rio de Janeiro during the band's visit. The use of such imagery – lyrically and visually –

---

24   Ibid., p. 106.
25   Ibid., p. 107.
26   *Lott* 1978.

naturally had shock value. The Sex Pistols' disdain for cultural norms meant that they cavorted not only with real criminals but with (fictionalised) war criminals. As the band's manager Malcolm McClaren advised in the film, "cultivate hatred, it is your greatest asset. Force the public to hate you." Crass, boorish and offensive *No–one is Innocent* forces us, through the lens of crime and war crime to confront the limits of freedom of speech and expression.

If the Sex Pistols' impious appropriation of war crimes (and war criminals) was reflective of the transgressiveness of the punk movement, for the Manic Street Preachers Holocaust impiety was an opportunity to demonstrate their intellectualism. The band's third album, *The Holy Bible* (U.K. 1994), saw them move away from the heavily produced American rock–inspired style of their first two albums. *The Holy Bible* lyrically centres around human suffering, with songs dealing with freedom of speech, anorexia, serial killers, suicide, dictatorships, the penal system, and the Holocaust. Most of the lyrics were written by Richey Edwards, who, suffering with severe depression, went missing on 1 February 1995. The band's visit to Dachau and Bergen–Belsen in 1993 inspired *The Intense Humming of Evil*, which opens with the sound of industrial machinery leading to a lengthy sample taken from a 1946 report on the Nuremberg Trials, underscored by a death march. Lyrically and musically much more complex than *Belsen Was a Gas*, the song is thematically similar to *Angel of Death* and also shifts between perspectives, though *The Intense Humming of Evil* is less ambiguous in its moral judgement; even allowing for the equivalising of Naziism and Winston Churchill. Singer and guitarist, James Dean Bradfield, asked for a rewrite of the initial draft of the lyrics, noting "you can't be ambivalent about a subject like that [the Holocaust]".[27] It represents a very different sort of Holocaust impiety. Boswell concludes that the song "finds little value in traditional forms of artistic commemoration or even punk aggression .... and [can be read as] an implicit attack on the idea that the Holocaust can provide the foundation for aesthetic or artistic innovation".[28]

It is hardly surprising that songs that deal with war crimes so specifically and graphically form a relatively small part of the wider genre of popular songs about war. The use of Nazi symbolism, however, can also be understood as part of a wider cultural comment on the war crimes with which it is intrinsically bound. This is particularly true of the post–war generation who had spearheaded the cultural revolution of the 1960s, themselves shaped by the Second World War and its aftermath. A powerful example can be found in Pink Floyd's 1979 rock opera *The Wall* and the film based on it, *Pink Floyd The Wall* (U.K., 1982, dir. Alan Parker), centred around a depressed rock star, Pink (played in the film by Bob Geldof),

---

27 Quoted in *Price* 1999, p. 147.
28 *Boswell* 2012, p. 129.

who builds a psychological wall to help him deal with his emotional trauma.[29] Released shortly after the Falklands War ended, the film begins with Pink staring at a television screen remembering his father, who was killed at Anzio in 1944. The scene is underscored by one of the most powerful war songs in the popular repertoire, *When the Tigers Broke Free*, an account by Roger Waters of his father's death; the song was deemed too personal by the rest of the band and wasn't included on the studio album. The War is a recurring feature in *The Wall*, the central driving force behind Pink's decline. Towards the end of the film under the influence of drugs Pink imagines himself as a dictator (*In the Flesh*), with his concert as a neo–Nazi rally; he is now the personification of what his father died fighting against. Pink's hallucination builds to a crescendo over the next two songs, *Run Like Hell* and *Waiting for the Worms* before he finally breaks down (*Stop*) and is put on trial (*The Trial*). Inspired by the Falkland's War, Pink Floyd's next album – the last to feature Waters – *The Final Cut* (U.K. 1983) became another concept album, in opposition to war.

2. Civil War

The lack of specificity in many antiwar songs means that their meaning is malleable and can shift over time. While the Cold War thawed the Vietnam War continued to cast a shadow on American culture. Guns n' Roses were singing of the war memorial in Washington, D.C. and the assassination of JFK and Martin Luther King Jr in *Civil War*, a song first released in 1990 on the charity album *Nobody's Child: Romanian Angel Appeal* and later included on the band's 1991 album *Use Your Illusion II*. Typical of the protest song genre *Civil War* is a criticism of war in general, with all conflicts rendered as civil wars on a global scale. The song opens with a sample from the movie *Cool Hand Luke* (U.S., 1967, dir. Stuart Rosenberg): the famous speech delivered by the Captain (played by Strother Martin) after beating the titular Luke (Paul Newman) to the ground: "what we've got here is ... failure to communicate. Some men you just can't reach. So you get what we had here last week, which is the way he wants it ... well, he gets it. I don't like it any more than you men." After which the song begins with Axl Rose whistling the American Civil War song *When Johnny Comes Marching Home* (also whistled at the end of the song); the song, which looks forward to the safe return of soldiers, was popular among both sides of the American Civil War. Towards the end of the song, *Civil War* also quotes a speech by a guerrilla from the Peruvian Shining Path party, recited by Rose: "we practice selective annihilation of mayors and government officials, for example, to create a vacuum, then we fill that vacuum. As popular war advances,

---

29   See *Mabbett* 1995; *Blake* 2008; *Guesdon/Margotin* 2017.

peace is closer".[30] Written in the late 1980s, the release of *Civil War* coincided with the First Gulf War (17 January 1991), thus taking on a new resonance. It was regularly played by the band during their *Use Your Illusion* world tour of the early 1990s, where lead singer Axl Rose would often wear clothing with the American flag during the song. After a performance of the song at Noblesville, Indiana in May 1991, Rose used the song to comment on the antiwar movement then gathering pace in America, reducing it to easily identifiable sides representing good and evil, telling the crowd:

> "We'll dedicate that to all the military people that were here tonight. I think anybody in their right mind, anybody that has a brain at all, wasn't too excited with the concept of goin' to war. But once we were in it, I think you're a fuckin' asshole not to fuckin' root for our side. I mean, I met all these people [saying] 'We shouldn't be having a fucking war': well, it's too late, *asshole!*".[31]

Civil War has been a staple of the band's reunion tours (2016–present). In the wake of the Russian invasion of Ukraine, the song has been regularly performed against the backdrop of a video of a distressed Ukrainian flag and images of devastated buildings and bombings. The band typically has Ukraine flags flying at the side of the stage; Rose sometimes performs in a t–shirt bearing the flag. In several concerts, Rose has dedicated the song to the victims of the war in Ukraine.[32] He has been a vocal critic of Vladimir Putin, from the stage and on social media. Rose was among those to tweet the Ukrainian flag in the wake of the invasion,[33] and ended a tweet in July 2022 by thanking their fans,

> "for showing such love and support during the tour for the people of Ukraine and their noble and horrifying fight for freedom against an increasingly totalitarian regime ran by a callous, lying, murderous, little man with outdated ambitions and no regard for human life."[34]

Rose's rededication of *Civil War* – and his public statements of support – demonstrates how the war in Ukraine has generally proved morally straightforward for Western mainstream artists, who have found it easy to pick sides, especially amidst the UN–backed International Criminal Court's issuing of an arrest warrant on 17 March 2023 for Putin in connection with the alleged war crime of unlawful deportation and transfer of children.[35] Examples of support for Ukraine have been almost unanimous amongst popular music figures; 2022 saw a flurry of songs released,

---

30 The CD liner notes attribute the quote to a "Peruvian Guerrilla General"; its origins appear to be an interview with "Jorge": Chicago Tribune 1989.
31 Noblesville, Indiana (29 May 1991). Various unofficial recordings are available on YouTube.
32 For example, during a June 2023 performance in Tel Aviv: see *Steinberg* 2023.
33 *Rose* 2023.
34 *Rose* 2022.
35 United Nations 2023.

rereleased and performed in support for Ukraine. A *Concert for Ukraine* was held in Birmingham's Resorts World Arena on 29 March 2022, featuring performances by Ed Sheeran, Snow Patrol, Manic Street Preachers, Billie Eilish, Gregory Porter and others. The concert was broadcast live on ITV and raised over £13 million for humanitarian relief, underscoring the cathartic effect of such events.[36] Ukrainian president Volodymyr Zelensky appeared (via pre–recorded) message at the 2022 Grammy Awards, noting that "our musicians wear body armour instead of tuxedos" and imploring the audience to "tell the truth about this war on your social networks, on TV".[37] On the year anniversary of the Russian invasion, American country star Brad Paisley released *Same Here*, a newly written song featuring Zelensky.

Roger Waters – the co–founder of Pink Floyd, who left the band acrimoniously in the mid–1980s – is one of few well–known artists to offer another perspective on the war. His position on Ukraine runs counter to the mainstream political and media narratives of the conflict. Waters posted an open letter on Facebook to Ukraine, in response to a letter by a Ukrainian fan, Alina Mitrofanova, in which he called for "an immediate ceasefire. … [because] if all our leaders don't turn down the rhetoric and engage in diplomatic negotiations there will be precious little of Ukraine left when the fighting is over", noting that "I will do anything I can to help effect the end of this awful war in your country, anything that is except wave a flag to encourage the slaughter. That is what the gangsters [i.e. political leaders/governments] want, they want us to wave flags."[38] At the request of Russia, Waters addressed the UN Security Council on 9 February 2023. In calling for an immediate ceasefire, he denounced the invasion as "illegal" and condemned it "in the strongest possible terms" but noted that Russian aggression was "not unprovoked".[39] Waters' stance sparked backlash from the Ukrainian ambassador who, accusing him of being a tool of Russian propaganda; he dismissed Waters telling him to "Keep strumming the guitar. … It suits you more than lecturing the security council on how to do its job."[40] In a subsequent *Rolling Stone* interview, Waters (inter alia) described "the American Empire" as "the most evil of all" and instead blamed NATO for provoking Russia's invasion; he further suggested that accounts of Russian war crimes in Ukraine were fabricated: "You've seen it on what I've just described to you as Western propaganda. … It's exactly the obverse of saying Russian propaganda; Russians interfered with our election; Russians did that. It's all lies, lies, lies, lies."[41] Such comments came at a cost. In January 2024 Waters was dropped by German

---

36 ITV News 2022.
37 Recordings of the speech can be freely found on YouTube.
38 *Waters* 2022.
39 The speech is transcribed in *Waters* 2023. A recording of the full speech is available on YouTube: The Human Exploring Society 2023.
40 *Borger* 2023.
41 *Ball* 2022.

record label BMG in January 2024 over comments about Ukraine, and Israel (see also below).[42]

Waters' presentation of a counter–narrative has been unparalleled among mainstream artists, including his erstwhile bandmates. Pink Floyd (without Waters) reformed to record their first new material since 1994's *The Division Bell* in a protest song, *Hey, Hey, Rise Up!*, based on the Ukrainian song *The Red Viburnum in the Meadow* with vocals (in Ukrainian) by Andriy Khlyvnyuk. Guitarist and vocalist, David Gilmour – whose daughter–in–law is Ukrainian – described the song as a show of "anger at a superpower invading a peaceful nation".[43] The accompanying video of the song (dir. Mat Whitecross) opens with the sound and images of tanks and shelling accompanied by text explaining that the band had been inspired by a video of Khlyvnyuk singing *The Red Viburnum in the Meadow* on Instagram three days after the invasion had begun on 24 February 2022. The rest of the video shows similar scenes of war and those affected by it, interspliced scenes of Pink Floyd performing the song (bathed in the colours of the Ukrainian flag) with Khlyvnyuk in military uniform projected on a screen singing. The artwork of the single release featured the band's name in blue and yellow, atop a sunflower – the national flower of Ukraine. This was also a reference to the video widely shared on X of a Ukrainian woman early in the invasion challenging Russian soldiers, telling them to carry sunflower seeds in their pockets so that the flowers could grow from their dead bodies;[44] a brief clip from the video was included in the music video (at 2.18–2.20). Pink Floyd also removed their post–1987 music as well as Gilmour's solo work from digital music sites in Russia and Belarus. The band's most famous works – with Waters – were not taken down, leading to suggestions that Waters had blocked them from doing so. Gilmour wouldn't confirm or deny: "Let's just say I was disappointed and let's move on. Read into that what you will."[45]

Other Western artists released songs and statements in support of Ukraine. For example, U2 released the newly written acoustic track *Walk on Ukraine*. The accompanying black and white video is a single shot of Bono and the Edge performing the song. Others re–packaged pre–existing songs in support for Ukraine. In March 2022 Sting recorded an acoustic version of his 1985 song *Russians*, prefacing the song as follows:

> "I've only rarely sung this song in the many years since it was written because I never thought it would be relevant again. But, in the light of one man's bloody and woefully misguided decision to invade a peaceful, unthreatening neighbour, the song is, once again, a plea for our common humanity. For the brave Ukrainians fighting against this

---

42 *Madarang* 2024.
43 *Savage* 2022.
44 *Khan* 2022.
45 *Petridis* 2022.

brutal tyranny and also the many Russians who are protesting this outrage despite the threat of arrest and imprisonment. We, all of us, love our children. Stop the war."[46]

The recourse to acoustic instruments seeks to underscore the authenticity of the message by embracing a quasi–folksong veneer. Similarly, Bon Jovi repurposed *We Don't Run* as a song in support for Ukraine. The song – a typically anthemic rock song – was originally released on their 2015 album *Burning Bridges* and performed acoustically for the social action platform Global Citizen in support for Ukraine and refugees from the war. The song was originally written about the band's relationship with their former record label, Universal, and the departure of founding guitarist Richie Sambora. As lead singer Jon Bon Jovi explained,

> "I think that the lyrics and the recording of it captured that sentiment. It was a defiant song in the face of adversity whether it was with the record company situation that I had to go through, or the future of the band being called into question. 'We Don't Run' is a battle cry for anyone who feels their back against the wall."[47]

The song had been previously dedicated, demonstrating the flexibility of wartime allegiance. On 3 October 2015, Bon Jovi played in Israel for the first time; Jon Bon Jovi prefaced a performance of *We Don't Run* noting that "I think this should be the fight song for Tel Aviv",[48] a sentiment he reiterated when the band next played in Tel Aviv in July 2019.

3. Holy Wars … The Punishment Due

The very act of performing in Israel has proved controversial for Western popular music artists for decades. To do so – or to refuse to do so – has been understood as a political act, often framed in the context of alleged war crimes perpetrated by the Israel Defence Forces (IDF). Such allegations have been made since the foundation of the State of Israel in 1948 but calls for boycotts by popular music artists have been particularly strong since the turn of the twenty–first century. The Palestinian Campaign for the Academic and Cultural Boycott of Israel was established in 2004,[49] and was instrumental in the foundation of the (also) Palestinian–led Boycott, Divestment and Sanctions (BDS) movement (founded 2005), which in its own words "works to end international support for Israel's oppression of Palestinians and pressure Israel to comply with international law".[50] Ahead of their 2015 concert

---

46 *Sting* 2022.
47 iHeartRadio 2016.
48 There is no official video of the performance but at the time of writing fan footage is available on YouTube.
49 Boycott, Divestment, Sanctions n.d.
50 Boycott, Divestment, Sanctions: Official website n.d.

the BDS unsuccessfully lobbied Bon Jovi to boycott. Other artists capitulated under such pressure. Elvis Costello cancelled concerts in 2010, as did Lauryn Hill in 2015. However, other acts including Santana, Guns n' Roses, Metallica, Elton John, Radiohead and Madonna all defied calls to boycott and performed in Israel in the mid–2010s. In 2014 several musicians including Brian Eno and Roger Waters supported the BDS movement through the Artists for Palestine U.K.'s lobbying of artists to boycott Israel. Nick Cave refused to sign an open letter and went ahead with his tour of Israel, which prompted a backlash and public attacks from Eno and Waters.[51] In May 2021 over 600 musicians signed a petition ("Musicians for Palestine") on (then) Twitter calling for artists to boycott performing in Israel, in the framing of colonial oppression the letter noted that,

> "As musicians, we cannot be silent. Today it is essential that we stand with Palestine. We are calling on our peers to publicly assert their solidarity with the Palestinian people. Complicity with Israeli war crimes is found in silence, and today silence is not an option."[52]

Signatories included members of Rage Against the Machine, Roger Waters, Serj Tankian (System of a Down), Patti Smith and Julian Casablancas (The Strokes).

On 7 October 2023 war crime and popular music met in the most visceral way imaginable. As part of the day's atrocities Hamas–led terrorists attacked, raped and murdered civilians gathered for the Supernova Sukkot Gathering, an open–air festival of trance music. In the Supernova attack 364 civilians were murdered, with many more wounded and at least 40 taken hostage. Across the 7 October attacks over 1200 were murdered in total, and 253 were taken hostage. The atrocities of 7 October saw the biggest single loss of Jewish life since the Holocaust. The horrific attacks have led to popular music artists in Israel directly addressing the attacks and the ensuing war in Gaza. As the war has developed it has proved increasingly divisive in the West. Perhaps sensing the potential for commercial consequences many A–list music celebrities have opted for a strategy of public silence. Billionaire pop icon Taylor Swift has been called upon by both sides of the conflict, showing the importance of such soft power and where it lies. In November 2023 the State of Israel account on X asked the singer to call for the return of one of the hostages, Roni Eshel, a nineteen–year–old Swift fan. Other (non–captive) Swift fans have been using the hashtag #SwiftiesForPalestine to call for their idol to speak out against Israel.[53] Swift released her latest album in April 2024, titled (without even the merest hint of irony) *The Tortured Poets Department*, but has been tight–lipped on the conflict, as has fellow cultural (and commercial) megastar Beyoncé.

---

51 Artists for Palestine 2017.
52 Posted 27 May 2021 by @Musicians4PS.
53 *Young/Bachman* 2023.

In the months that followed October 7 with Israel's military incursions into Gaza; music became bound up with international politics as Israel's entry to the Eurovision Song Contest was subjected to censorship amidst calls for a boycott of the competition should they even be allowed to participate. Musicians for Palestine posted another open letter in late 2023, which garnered over 6.000 signatures, calling for a ceasefire, noting that:

> "The unfolding human catastrophe for 2.3 million Palestinians in Gaza, half of them children, is 'a textbook case of genocide', in the words of both the prominent US–based Israeli scholar of genocide Raz Segal and leading former UN human rights official Craig Mokhiber. … As musicians, we uplift the voice of the oppressed. We un-flinchingly condemn oppression in all forms, just as we condemn harming civilians, without hesitation, no matter their identity."[54]

In the wake of the terror attacks, there has been "a veritable avalanche of new music solely focussed on October 7 and its aftermath. It's hard to think of a single musical artist in Israel who hasn't made new music to meet the moment".[55] Sung in Hebrew, among the most controversial of these songs is Ness and Stilla's *Harbu Darbu* (typically translated as "Swords and Strikes"; also Hebrew slang for destroying Israel's enemies). Released in November 2023 the song conveys support for the IDF while also condemning the Hamas attacks as well as those who support Palestine, including calling for the death of Western celebrities Bella Hadid, Dua Lipa and Mia Khalifa: "All IDF units are coming to do Harbu Darbu on their heads".[56] Former porn actress, Khalifa, responded to the song on X unironically accusing Ness and Stilla of cultural appropriation: "Y'all that song calling for the IDF to kill me, Bella, and Dua is over a DRILL beat, they can't even call for genocide in their own culture, they had to colonize something to get it to #1."[57] Drill originated in Chicago in the early 2010s and is prominent in Palestinian rap (in postmodern terms only perceived oppressors can be guilty of appropriation[58]); stylistically drill is characterised by aggressive, violent, provocative and often nihilistic lyrics. *Harbu Darbu* also refers to Palestinians as descendants of Amalek, the tribe regarded in the Torah as the eternal enemy of Israel and referred to in post–October 7 speeches by Benjamin Netanyahu – something used as part of South Africa's submission to the International Court of Justice as evidence of "Expressions of Genocidal Intent against the Palestinian People by Israeli State Officials and Others" as part of an allegation of genocide and collective punishment "intended to bring about the destruction of a

---

54 Musicians for Palestine 2023.
55 *Zaltzman* 2024.
56 Translations are taken from the version of the official music video posted by the YouTube account Israeli Songs with English Subtitles.
57 2 December 2023 (@miakhalifa). At the time of writing the post has garnered over 2 million views.
58 See *Pluckrose/Lindsay* 2022, pp. 223–227 and passim.

substantial part of the Palestinian national, racial and ethnical group".[59] The music video shows Ness and Stilla in several locations using shooting gestures in the chorus. Reaching no. 1 on the Israel Singles Chart, the song marks a shift in the tone of Israeli popular music, which according to Shayna Weiss previously has tended to be more reflective and melancholic.[60] The recourse to drill music reflects the anger and desire for retribution among many Israelis (again, transgressively aligned message and medium). At the time of writing, *Harbu Darbu* has been streamed and viewed over 30 million times (over 23 million views on YouTube; almost 7 million plays on Spotify, for example) on various platforms and has also been part of a TikTok trend to show support for Israel.

Outside Israel the song has received strong criticism in some quarters as part of a wider cultural discourse of violence, for example, as Diana Abbany has noted:

"In this disturbing environment, music video clips use music, lyrics, visuals, and cultural symbols to disseminate ideas that either endorse or incite mass murder. ... [*Harbu Darbu*] employs derogatory terms, calling Palestinians 'rats and sons of Amalek'. This reference to an ancient tribe, portrayed in the Torah as the eternal enemy of the Jewish people that needs to be annihilated, echoes the words of the Israeli Prime Minister Benjamin Netanyahu at the start of the ground invasion of Gaza. It reflects how political statements can circulate, infiltrate the mind and reappear in popular culture. This biblical reference has long been used by the Israeli far right to justify violence against Palestinians. In this war, it serves to justify the brutal assault on Gazans and add a religious connotation to the war."[61]

Abbany went on to argue that "songs do more than convey hate and violent messages; they also facilitate crafting historical narratives and promote shaping extreme nationalist identities, especially in times of war, as exemplified by the 'Friendship song 2023'".[62] The video of the controversial song, created by The Civil Front, was performed against a backdrop of militaristic and patriotic images by a group of Israeli children the song declares how in a year Gaza will be annihilated. The Gazans are described as "Swastika–bearers", evoking parallels with the Holocaust. Thus, Abbany argues, "the song not only legitimizes the killing and elimination of the eternal enemy, but also shapes extreme nationalist sentiments and deforms historical realities."[63]

Asfa Sultan has argued that "Songs like 'Harbu Darbu' and 'Zeh Aleinu' are not 'soundtracks of resistance' – they're celebrations of death". Describing *Harbu*

---

59   International Court of Justice, Press release (unofficial) 2023. The report of the Special Rapporteur concluded in March 2024 "that there are reasonable grounds to believe that the threshold indicating Israel's commission of genocide is met": United Nations: The Question of Palestine 2024.
60   *Zaltzman* 2024. See also *Weiss* 2021.
61   *Abbany* 2024.
62   Ibid.
63   Ibid.; see also *Sultan* 2024.

Darbu as one "of Israel's many genocide anthems", Sultan has argued that such songs are "pop propaganda", including Odiah and Izi's *Horef '23* ("Winter of '23") and *Zeh Aleinu* ("It's On Us") by Subliminal, Hatzel and Raviv Kaner. The latter song is militaristic and defiant in the rapped verses, equating the October 7 attackers with Nazis and boasting of the moral and military strength of Israel in the face of the atrocities. The sung refrains look to the future but warn that the actions of Hamas will be neither forgiven nor forgotten:[64]

The music video begins with a brief shot of a baby awakening before turning to scenes of the aftermath of the October 7 attacks; the rest of the video intersperses the three singers with scenes of the IDF and the war. Sultan has, however, argued that such songs "released by Israeli artists 'in response' to October 7 have done more than just convey hatred – they are facilitating shaping extreme nationalist identities and dehumanising an entire people".[65] These songs that seek to embody a call for revenge have been described by Shahla Omar as "Israel's military–pop complex", arguing (unironically) that "Emboldened by far–right rhetoric, a new music genre has emerged in Israel, one that celebrates the death of Palestinians and the destruction of Gaza."[66]

Other examples have been less controversial but no less powerful. For example, Maor Ashkenazi and Noam Choen's *Shir Shel Noam 2* ("Noam's Song 2"), which features Noam Cohen, a survivor of the Supernova massacre. The song, and music video, recreates and recounts events of 7 October at the festival as experienced by Cohen.[67] Outside Israel, there have been songs penned calling for a ceasefire and promoting the "free Palestine" agenda, with its calls for the eradication of the State of Israel in the "From the river to the sea" chant. As one report notes,

> "The rise in popularity of songs that sympathise with the Palestinians or encourage Hamas – including by artists who generally avoid politics – reflects anger over Israel's bombardment of Gaza, its occupation of Palestinian territory and U.S. and European support for its military campaign."[68]

Ahead of the 68th edition of the Eurovision Song Contest in Malmö in May 2024 popular music and allegations of war crimes again came into sharp focus. Accused of war crimes and genocide Israel was subject to calls for their exclusion from Eurovision 2024, with critics arguing that Russia had been expelled in the wake of the invasion of Ukraine. In January 2024 calls for a boycott of the event should

---

64 English translations of the lyrics are available on the official Subliminal account on YouTube, accompanying the music video.
65 *Sultan* 2024.
66 *Omar* 2023.
67 English translations for several of these songs can be found at on the *Unpacked for Educators* website, which provides and creates resources for teaching students aged 10 and up enabling educators to 'bring the best of Judaism and Israel'.
68 *Saafan/Madi/Shakhshir* 2024.

Israel be allowed to participate came from The Association of Composers and Lyricists of Iceland. (The runner–up in Iceland's competition to select the country's entry was the Palestinian singer Bashar Murad; the video for his song *Wild West* includes footage of an interview with a Palestinian woman speaking about the importance of music in the refugee camps.) This was echoed by a petition signed by over 1.400 Finnish self–identified music industry professionals, calling for Israel to be banned because of alleged "war crimes".[69] By the end of the month, the Irish state broadcaster, RTÉ, similarly received over 1.000 emails calling for a boycott.[70] The pro–Palestinian Irish entry, Bambie Thug (a self–described non–binary, queer witch), also called for Israel to be barred from competing but lacking the courage of such convictions resisted calls to boycott the event. In the same vein of performative virtue, in March the U.K.'s entrant, Olly Alexander (who was a signatory of another open letter in which Israel was described as an "apartheid regime"[71]), was pressured by over 450 activists (under the moniker Queers for Palestine[72]) to boycott Eurovision over Israel's participation, noting:

> "There can be no party with a state committing apartheid and genocide. ... At a time when accountability is so urgently needed, Israel's inclusion in Eurovision would enable and cover up its war crimes and crimes against humanity. Understanding the propaganda value of its participation in the contest to artwash its ongoing genocide, Israel's President, Isaac Herzog, stated 'it's important for Israel to appear in Eurovision'".[73]

When Alexander refused to withdraw Queers for Palestine doubled down on their stance, writing on Instagram about "genocidal, apartheid Israel" accusing those such as Alexander who refused to boycott the Eurovision of a "misuse of power" by choosing to "downplay the genocide in Gaza by vaguely calling it a mere 'situa-

---

69 *Bryant* 2024.
70 *Blake Knox* 2024.
71 *Sky News* 2023.
72 For a recent critique of the performative irony of this Neo-Marxist activist group in the cultural and socio-political context of the Middle East, see *Navabi* 2023. It is worth noting, though, that Navabi (and other commentators) conflates queerness with sexual identity. This is a baited trap, which means that any form of criticism or critique can be disingenuously labelled as "hate" or "oppression" etc. In postmodern terms, however, "queer" – as defined by David Halperin – is not something one is (noun), but rather something one does (verb); it is, in fact, distinctly and overtly a political activity. And it is a political project, which largely resists definition or categorisation. In Halperin's own words (*Halperin* 1995, p. 62, but also *passim*; emphasis is original): "Unlike gay identity ... queer identity need not be grounded in any positive truth or in any stable reality. As the very word implies, 'queer' does not name some natural kind or refer to some determinate object; it acquires its meaning from its oppositional relation to the norm. Queer is by definition *whatever* is at odds with the normal, the legitimate, the dominant. *There is nothing in particular to which it necessarily refers.* It is an identity without an essence." For a detailed and insightful analysis of this concept, its history and relation to "Queer Theory", see *Pluckrose/Lindsay* 2020, pp. 89–110.
73 Queers for Palestine 2024.

tion'", while also accusing organisers of perceived double–standards given that they "were quick to ban Russia after the invasion of Ukraine".[74]

In response to calls to expel Israel from Eurovision, in February over 400 "celebrities" and entertainment figures signed an open letter of support of the country's "continued inclusion":

> "We have been shocked and disappointed to see some members of the entertainment community calling for Israel to be banished from the Contest for responding to the greatest massacre of Jews since the Holocaust. October 7 was a day in which a music festival meant to celebrate life was attacked by Hamas and saw 364 innocent civilians killed, hundreds maimed and brutalized, over 40 festivalgoers taken hostage, and many raped. Israel is fighting a war against a European Union–designated terrorist group that once again broke a ceasefire that day, and then went on to slaughter over 1,200 people. This current round of fighting is not a war that Israel wanted or started. To punish Israel would be an inversion of justice. Israel also has a long and storied history in Eurovision. … Furthermore, we believe that unifying events such as singing competitions are crucial to help bridge our cultural divides and unite people of all backgrounds through their shared love of music. The annual Eurovision Song Contest embodies this unifying spirit. Every year, millions of people across Europe and around the world join in a massive display of cultural exchange and celebration of music. Those who are calling for Israel's exclusion are subverting the spirit of the Contest and turning it from a celebration of unity into a tool of politics. We support all of this year's contestants as well as your decision to reject the calls to expel Israel from the Contest. We are looking forward to a successful and exciting Eurovision 2024."[75]

Objections to Israel's participation extended to the official song itself. Performed by Eden Golan, the song was originally titled *October Rain*. Written by Keren Peles, Avi Ohayon and Stav Berger, the song allegedly referred to the 7 October attacks and the war in Gaza. In February 2024 Eurovision Song Contest (ESC) organisers, the European Broadcasting Union (EBU) accused the song of having an overtly political message and requested that it be rewritten. The rules of the contest state that it is "a non–political event. All Participating Broadcasters … shall be responsible … to make sure that the ESC shall in no case be politicized and/or instrumentalized and/or otherwise brought into disrepute in any way".[76] Indeed, several songs have fallen foul of this and have been banned from the contest. Most recently, in 2021 the Belarusian entry by Galasy ZMesta, *I Will Teach You* was seen as potentially legitimising President Lukashenko's suppression of anti–government protestors; the band were asked to resubmit the song, though the resubmission was also rejected and they were excluded from the contest.

---

74 Alexander posted his reply to Queers for Palestine on Instagram: *Alexander* 2024.
75 Creative Community for Peace 2024.
76 Eurovision n.d.

Under pressure from Israel's president, Isaac Herzog, the nation's broadcaster, Kan, which is responsible for selecting the country's song made changes to the lyrics – after an initial and short–lived show of defiance. In a speech on 25 February Herzog declared the importance of Israel's participation in Eurovision, given its global reach. The final revised version – titled *Hurricane* – removed what were considered to be references to the attacks, such as the song's title.[77] Yoav Tzafir, director and producer of Israel's Eurovision delegation, supported the compromise to allow their participation but noted that "We were not willing to send a shallow pop song. We changed the lyrics, but the song remains a powerful and moving ballad that speaks of heartache. Personal heartache, but a song that Israelis can also relate to this year."[78] The comprise was not greeted with universal approval. For example, Einav Schiff accused Kan of folding "like a deck of cards", offering the following conclusion:

> "[T]he game of Chicken led by the corporation exposed the bluff: more than what pushes us to be right – and we are – we're afraid to discover the truth. The political credit for war still somehow continues, but the cultural credit is dwindling before our eyes. The illusion that we can be a small country at war that has inflicted tens of thousands of casualties, including innocent men and women, and even children who are always innocent, and still behave as if it's 1999, has exploded because they thought they could act with vigilance and not wisdom. It's a shame they came out looking, well, especially foolish."[79]

Indeed, not only this but the song was also criticised for not addressing the realities of the 7 October massacre more directly. In an opinion piece, Noa Limone accused Israel of being most afraid of "being rejected from the European milieux", arguing that the song's references to 7 October were not only oblique but simply poor quality:

> "'October Rain' is an arbitrary collection of words and sentences that do not cohere into any significant statement. It looks more like the product of a word generator. Even AI has more soul than this gibberish. … What important message are we fighting for by insisting not to change the words? After all, in practice, there is no statement here. In this sense, it would have been better to send a song like 'Harbu Darbu', because at least it has something to say. Something warlike, vengeful, some say racist, but at least clear. Alternatively, if we enter the world of fantasy, we could send an anti–war protest song, maybe a song about peace. We had them once, no? But no, we've created the musical version of the political center; i.e. meaningless drivel."[80]

---

77 *Lahav* 2024.
78 *Stern* 2024.
79 *Schiff* 2024.
80 *Limone* 2024.

The accompanying music video has also been interpreted on social media platforms as containing symbolic references to the 7 October attacks.[81] Much of the video shows Golan in several outfits surrounded by a group of dancers dressed in white and later in black. Several of the scenes are shot in a field below an uprooted tree. At various points Golan and the dancers look to the sky – perhaps a reference to the powered paragliders used in the attacks. She also wears in some scenes a crop top with a small opening, seen by some as a symbolic bullet hole.

4. Conclusions

War crimes and popular music are unlikely bedfellows. There is, nevertheless, a sizable body of songs that deal with or reference war crimes to various extents. One could argue that popular music, however, is ill–equipped to deal with such weighty and complex subjects. The typically short format and reductive, partisan positionality of popular music lyrics make the unpicking of complex geo–political situations challenging at best; they have "limited scope for reaching serious insight or meaning".[82] Nevertheless, popular music (and social media) can encapsulate – and manipulate – in sometimes quite visceral fashion general feelings in a way that is reflective and persuasive, regardless of the objective veracity of the message.[83] Popular music is populist, designed to appeal to mass audiences, especially the young. As David Jones and M. L. R. Smith point out in their study of musical responses to the War on Terror:

> "If [popular music] aspires to any higher cultural ambition it is to express mass opinion, and in particular to be the voice of youth, that is to say, usually the least culturally sophisticated social demographic. Therefore … the medium is attuned to capture the popular mood of the moment."[84]

Moreover, they add, in the current technological age, popular music can be created quickly with relatively little cost and disseminated quickly through streaming, video hosting sites and social media.

Musical responses to war crimes, and war in general, are inevitably political statements. Today's artists are expected to make such statements as much with their words on social media as through their lyrics; in such contexts, their actions too also come under scrutiny. Musical responses to the ongoing conflicts in the Middle East and Ukraine offer a window into the ways in which popular music – and artists themselves through silence/words and non–/actions – can be used, typically in the

---

81 Summarised in *Yaakov* 2024.
82 *Jones/Smith* 2023, p. 2455.
83 *Brown/Volgsten* 2006.
84 *Jones/Smith* 2023, p. 2455.

vernacular, to represent and subvert narrative discourse. They also demonstrate how only particular conflicts – and alleged atrocities – receive attention. A privileged few of today's forever wars are extensively covered by (legacy and social) media, in real time; a consequence of the commercialisation of the news industry. Despite the extent of knowledge available, however, conflicts tend to be represented reductively, often split along lines of political affiliation or national perspective; something that appears to be accelerating in the age of social media. Current conflicts are bound up with reports and accusations of war crimes and other atrocities. We have seen how popular music has become a mode of defiance and resistance in Israel, not just in the hip–hop songs but writ large in the guise of the Eurovision – in times of war even the most vapid, kitschy entertainment takes on potential significance and cultural value. However, the most impious songs – if we may more broadly borrow Boswell's concept – are intricately bound with freedom of speech, an increasingly fragile concept in Western purportedly liberal democracies. Popular music responses to the Holocaust serve to demonstrate how such songs can be culturally cathartic, even when they are transgressive and challenging. It is arguably these songs that require greatest protection.

Bibliography

Abbany, Diana, 2024: Soundscape of Hate. The Music of Genocide Amidst the War on Gaza. Untold Mag, February 7. At: https://untoldmag.org/soundscape-of-hate-the-music-of-geno cide-amidst-the-war-on-gaza/ (Accessed on 3 April 2024).

Alexander, Olly, 2024: Instagram post, March 29. At: https://www.instagram.com/p/C5GSC5 -tkCA/?igsh=Mmp4c3R4NDB6dnd3 (Accessed on 13 April 2024).

Artists for Palestine, 2017: Artists Respond to Nick Cave's Comments. November 20. At: https://artistsforpalestine.org.uk/2017/11/20/artists-respond-to-nick-caves-comments/ (Accessed on 12 February 2024).

Auschwitz-Birkenau Memorial and Museum, n.d. At: https://www.auschwitz.org/en/ (Accessed on 13 November 2023).

Ball, James, 2022: Roger Waters. I'm on a Ukrainian "Kill List". Rolling Stone, October 4. At: https://www.rollingstone.com/music/music-features/roger-waters-ukrainian-kill-list-12 34604081/ (Accessed on 3 April 2024).

Blake Knox, Kirsty, 2024: RTÉ Flooded with Emails Urging Boycott of Eurovision Song Contest over Israel Taking Part. Irish Independent, March 6. At: https://www.independent.i e/irish-news/rte-flooded-with-emails-urging-boycott-of-eurovision-song-contest-over-israe l-taking-part/a1788311642.html (Accessed on 13 April 2024).

Blake, Mark, 2008: Comfortably Numb. The Inside Story of Pink Floyd. London, Da Capo Press.

Borger, Julian, 2023: Ukraine Denounces Roger Waters as "Another Brick in the Wall" of Moscow Propaganda. The Guardian, February 8. At: https://www.theguardian.com/world/2023/feb/08/roger-waters-pink-floyd-un-security-council-ukraine-russia (Accessed on 23 March 2024).

Boswell, Matthew, 2012: Holocaust Impiety in Literature, Popular Music and Film. London, Palgrave Macmillan.

Boycott, Divestment, Sanctions: Official website, n.d. At: https://bdsmovement.net/ (Accessed on 13 March 2024).

Boycott, Divestment, Sanctions, n.d.: The Palestinian Campaign for the Academic and Cultural Boycott of Israel. At: https://bdsmovement.net/pacbi (Accessed on 21 January 2024).

Bradley, Douglas/*Werner*, Craig, 2015: We Gotta Get Out of This Place. The Soundtrack of the Vietnam War. Amherst, University of Massachusetts Press.

Brown, Steven/*Volgsten*, Ulrik, (eds.), 2006: Music and Manipulation: On the Social Uses and Social Control of Music. New York, Berghahn Books.

Bryant, Miranda, 2024: Finnish and Icelandic Artists Call for Israel to be Banned from Eurovision. The Guardian, January 11. At: https://www.theguardian.com/tv-and-radio/2024/jan/11/finnish-and-icelandic-artists-call-for-israel-to-be-banned-from-eurovision (Accessed on 12 April 2024).

Chastagner, Claude, 1999: The Parents' Music Resource Center. From Information to Censorship. In: Popular Music, 18:2, pp. 179–192

Chicago Tribune, 1989: "More War Will Bring Peace" Say Peru's Maoists After 15,000 Die. Chiago Tribune, July 9. At: https://www.chicagotribune.com/1989/07/09/more-war-will-bring-peace-say-perus-maoists-after-15000-die/ (Accessed on 3 April 2024).

Creative Community for Peace, 2024: Open Letter. Eurovision 2024. Creative Community for Peace blog, February 14. At: https://www.creativecommunityforpeace.com/blog/2024/02/14/eurovisionccfp2024/ (Accessed on 15 April 2024).

Elliott, Paul, 1987: Slayer. Blood Money. Sounds, April 18. At: http://www.rocksbackpages.com/Library/Article/slayer-blood-money (Accessed on 13 August 2023).

Eurovision, n.d.: Rules of the Contest. At: https://eurovision.tv/about/rules (Accessed on 13 March 2024).

Ferris, D. X., 2008: Reign in Blood. New York, Bloomsbury.

Global Conflict Tracker, n.d. At: https://www.cfr.org/global-conflict-tracker/ (Accessed on 11 April 2024).

Guesdon, Jean–Michel/*Margotin*, Philippe, 2017: Pink Floyd, All the Songs: The Story Behind Every Track. New York, Black Dog & Leventhal Publishers.

Halperin, David M., 1995: Saint Foucault: Towards a Gay Hagiography. New York, Oxford University Press.

Hintjens, Helen/*Ubaldo*, Rafiki, 2019: Music, Violence, and Peace–Building. In: Peace Review: A Journal of Social Justice, 31:3, pp. 279–288.

iHeartRadio, 2016: Bon Jovi on This House Is Not For Sale Song Meanings. iHeartRadio, November 4. At: https://www.iheartradio.ca/en/music-news/interview-bon-jovi-on-this-house-is-not-for-sale-song-meanings-1.2128388.html (Accessed on 13 December 2023).

International Court of Justice, 2023. Press release, December 29. At: https://www.icj-cij.org/si tes/default/files/case-related/192/192-20231229-pre-01-00-en.pdf (Accessed on 21 January 2024).

ITV News, 2022: Concert for Ukraine Raises Millions for Humanitarian Effort. ITV News, March 30. At: https://www.itv.com/news/2022-03-29/concert-for-ukraine-raises-millions-f or-humanitarian-effort (Accessed on 7 April 2024).

Jones, David Martin/*Smith*, M. L. R., 2023: Blowin' in the Wind? The Musical Response to the War on Terror. In: Studies in Conflict and Terrorism, 46:12, pp. 2454–2477.

Khan, Sami, 2022: "You are Cursed". Ukraine Woman's Confrontation with Russian Soldier goes Viral. International Business Times, February 25. At: https://www.ibtimes.co.in/yo u-are-cursed-ukraine-womans-confrontation-russian-soldier-goes-viral-details-846075 (Accessed on 3 April 2024).

Lahav, Doron, 2024: Israel: From "October Rain" to "Hurricane" – The Main Lyrics Changes Have Been Revealed. ESC Beat, March 10. At: https://escbeat.com/2024/03/10/israel-from -october-rain-to-hurricane-the-main-lyrics-changes-have-been-revealed/ (Accessed on 12 April 2024).

Limone, Noa, 2024: Israel's Perfect Eurovision Entry is Basically a Visionless Vision. Haa-retz, February 27. At: https://www.haaretz.com/opinion/2024-02-27/ty-article-opinion/.pre mium/israels-perfect-eurovision-entry-is-visionless-vision/0000018d-e6c3-dda5-a18d-e7ef 6ae90000?v=1712608511796 (Accessed on 3 April 2024).

Lott, Tim, 1978: The Sex Pistols. Biggsy. Record Mirror, July 15. At: https://rocksbackpages.c om/Library/Article/the-sex-pistols-biggsy (Accessed on 14 March 2024).

Mabbett, Andy, 1995: The Complete Guide to the Music of Pink Floyd. London, Omnibus.

Madarang, Charisma, 2024: Roger Waters Dropped by BMG After Pink Floyd Co–Founder's Israel Comments. Rolling Stone, January 30. At: https://www.rollingstone.com/music/m usic-news/roger-waters-pink-floyd-bmg-israel-comments-1234957036/ (Accessed on 13 February 2024).

Marshman, Sophia, 2005. From the Margins to the Mainstream? Representations of the Holocaust in Popular Culture. In: eSharp, 6:1. At: https://www.gla.ac.uk/research/az/eshar p/esharp/6i/ (Accessed on 19 June 2023).

Musicians for Palestine, 2023. 2023 Letter. At: https://musiciansforpalestine.net/2023-letter/ (Accessed on 3 January 2024).

Navabi, Armin, 2023: "Queers for Palestine" and the Death of Irony. Queer Majority, October 17. At: https://www.queermajority.com/essays-all/queers-for-palestine-and-the-death-of-ir ony (Accessed on 3 April 2024).

Omar, Shahla, 2023: Soundtrack to Genocide. Inside Israel's Military-Pop Complex. The New Arab, December 21. At: https://www.newarab.com/features/soundtrack-genocide-insi de-israels-military-pop-complex (Accessed on 8 January 2024).

Petridis, Alexis, 2022: "This Is a Crazy, Unjust Attack". Pink Floyd Re–form to Support Ukraine. The Guardian, April 7. At: https://www.theguardian.com/music/2022/apr/07/pink -floyd-reform-to-support-ukraine (Accessed on 3 April 2024).

Pluckrose, Helen/*Lindsay*, James, 2020: Cynical Theories. How Activist Scholarship Made Everything About Race, Gender, and Identity—and Why This Harms Everybody. London, Swift Press.

Price, Simon, 1999: Everything. A Book About Manic Street Preachers. London, Virgin.

Queers for Palestine, 2024: Instagram post, March 28. At: https://www.instagram.com/p/C5D oI0EIDdH/?igsh=Mm5oMGp1N2hpaWQy&img_index=1 (Accessed on 13 April 2024).

Rose, Axl, 2022: Twitter/X post, July 16. At: https://twitter.com/axlrose/status/154829274699 7166080 (Accessed on 13 March 2024).

Rose, Axl, 2023: Twitter/X post, February 26. At: https://twitter.com/axlrose/status/14975809 31456061452 (Accessed on 13 April 2024).

Rose, Gillian, 1996: Mourning Becomes the Law. Philosophy and Representation. Cambridge, Cambridge University Press.

Saafan, Farah/*Madi*, Emilie/*Shakhshir*, Bushra, 2024: Arab Musicians' Songs About Gaza Put Spotlight on Palestinian Issues. U.S. News, February 29. At: https://www.usnews.com/new s/world/articles/2024-02-29/arab-musicians-songs-about-gaza-put-spotlight-on-palestinian -issues (Accessed on 3 April 2024).

Savage, Mark, 2022: Pink Floyd Reunite for Ukraine Protest Song. BBC News, April 8. At: https://www.bbc.co.uk/news/entertainment-arts-61037080 (Accessed on 15 April 2024).

Schiff, Einav, 2024: Israel Folds Like a Deck of Cards in Time for Eurovision. Ynet News, April 3. At: https://www.ynetnews.com/article/bynk3gx6a (Accessed on 8 April 2024).

Sky News, 2023: UK Eurovision Act Olly Alexander Criticised for Signing Statement Calling Israel an "Apartheid State" and Accusing it of Genocide. Sky News, December 21. At: https://news.sky.com/story/uk-eurovision-act-olly-alexander-criticised-for-signing-stateme nt-calling-israel-an-apartheid-state-and-accusing-it-of-genocide-13035601 (Accessed on 3 January 2024).

Steinberg, Jessica, 2023: Guns N' Roses Rocks Sold–Out Crowd of 60,000 in Tel Aviv. The Times of Israel, June 6. At: https://www.timesofisrael.com/guns-n-roses-rocks-sold-out-cro wd-of-60000-in-tel-aviv/ (Accessed on 1 April 2024).

Stern, Itay, 2024: After Facing Criticism, Israel Has Revised its Entry for the Eurovision Song Contest. NPR, March 10. At: https://www.npr.org/2024/03/10/1237089104/eurovision-isra el-eden-golan-gaza-october-7 (Accessed on 3 April 2024).

Sultan, Asfa, 2024: "Dead Nazi" to "Sons of Amalek". How Israel is Weaponising Music to Dehumanise Palestinians. Images, April 3. At: https://images.dawn.com/news/1192364 (Accessed on 7 April 2024).

United Nations, 2023: Russia. International Criminal Court Issues Arrest Warrant for Putin. United Nations, March 17. At: https://news.un.org/en/story/2023/03/1134732 (Accessed on 3 December 2024).

United Nations, 2024: The Question of Palestine. United Nations, March 24. At: https:// www.un.org/unispal/document/anatomy-of-a-genocide-report-of-the-special-rapporteur-o n-the-situation-of-human-rights-in-the-palestinian-territory-occupied-since-1967-to-hum an-rights-council-advance-unedited-version-a-hrc-55/#:~:text=This%20report%20finds% 20that%20there,deliberately%20inflicting%20on%20the%20group (Accessed on 3 April 2024).

United Nations, n.d.: War Crimes. At: https://www.un.org/en/genocideprevention/war-crimes. shtml (Accessed on 13 September 2023).

Unpacked for Educators, n.d. At: https://unpacked.education/ (Accessed on 13 April 2024).

Walsh, Dermot P. J., 2000: Bloody Sunday and the Rule of Law in Northern Ireland. London, Palgrave Macmillan.

Waters, Roger, 2022: Letter to Alina. Facebook, March 9. At: https://www.facebook.com/roge rwaters/videos/ukraine/653402945774406/ (Accessed on 13 March 2024).

Waters, Roger, 2023: Roger Waters Full Speech at the UN Security Council (February 8). At: https://www.pressenza.com/2023/02/roger-waters-full-speech-at-the-un-security-council/ (Accessed on 13 January 2024).

Weiss, Shayna, 2021: Arabic Music, Israeli Mainstream Culture, and the US Military. Nice Jewish Girls Podcast. At: https://jewishunpacked.com/shayna-weiss-arabic-music-israeli-m ainstream-culture-and-the-us-military/ (Accessed on 3 March 2024).

Witter, Simon, 1987: To Hell and Back: Slayer. In: New Musical Express, March 21. At: http://www.rocksbackpages.com/Library/Article/to-hell-and-back-slayer (Accessed on 3 September 2023).

Wlodarski, Amy Lynn, 2015: Musical Witness and Holocaust Representation. Cambridge, Cambridge University Press.

Yaakov, Itay, 2024: Does Israel's Eurovision Music Video Hide Oct. 7 Messaging? Ynet News, May 9. At: https://www.ynetnews.com/culture/article/sjqcl8er6 (Accessed on 9 May 2024).

Young, Matt/*Bachman*, Brett, 2023: Taylor Swift Faces Pressure on Both Sides of Israel-Gaza War. The Daily Beast, November 7. At: https://www.thedailybeast.com/taylor-swift-faces -pressure-on-both-sides-of-israel-gaza-war (Accessed on 10 March 2024).

Zaltzman, Lior, 2024: How Israeli Music Changed After October 7. February 16. At: https:// www.kveller.com/how-israeli-music-changed-after-october-7/ (Accessed on 23 March 2024).

Audio Visual Sources

Bashar, Murad, 2024: Bashar Murad. Wild West (Official Music Video). YouTube, February 27. At: https://www.youtube.com/watch?v=VlUEFmVd7ss&t=23s (Accessed on 21 April 2024).

Bon Jovi, 2019: Bon Jovi. We Don't Run, Live from Tel Aviv (July 25, 2019). YouTube, August 27. At: https://www.youtube.com/watch?v=xX4822phj7U (Accessed on 21 April 2024).

BradPaisley, 2023: Brad Paisley. Same Here ft. President Volodymyr Zelenskyy. YouTube, February 24. At: https://www.youtube.com/watch?v=qt3WVHLywto (Accessed on 21 April 2024).

Cohen, Yifat, 2015: Bon Jovi. We Don't Run Live in Israel, Tel Aviv 2015. YouTube, October 5. At: https://www.youtube.com/watch?v=AWgX739JLdc (Accessed on 21 April 2024).

Eurovision Song Contest, 2024: Eden Golan, Hurricane, Israel IL, Official Music Video, Eurovision 2024. YouTube, March 10. At: https://www.youtube.com/watch?v=lJYn09tuP w4 (Accessed on 21 April 2024).

Global Citizen, 2022: Jon Bon Jovi Performs "We Don't Run" for Ukraine and Calls for Refugee Relief, Stand Up for Ukraine. YouTube, April 10. At: https://www.youtube.com /watch?v=xTfbPcEzkgY (Accessed on 21 April 2024).

Israeli Songs with English Subtitles, 2024: Ness X Stilla (Prod. By Stilla). Harbu Darbu, English Subtitles. YouTube, February 15. At: https://www.youtube.com/watch?v=R6yZPQ fREhc (Accessed on 21 April 2024).

Manic Street Preachers, 2014: The Intense Humming of Evil (Remastered). YouTube, December 6. At: https://www.youtube.com/watch?v=6jFXgBWaFt8 (Accessed on 21 April 2024).

Ness Ve Stilla, 2023: נס X דרבו חרבו - סטילה (Prod. By Stilla). YouTube, November 14. At: https://www.youtube.com/watch?v=1rk3n9V-aQs&t=0s (Accessed on 21 April 2024).

Pink Floyd, 2016: In the Flesh. YouTube, January 12. At: https://www.youtube.com/watch?v= GGGO9nPO0Po (Accessed on 21 April 2024).

Pink Floyd, 2022: Pink Floyd. Hey Hey Rise Up (feat. Andriy Khlyvnyuk of Boombox). YouTube, April 7. At: https://www.youtube.com/watch?v=saEpkcVi1d4 (Accessed on 21 April 2024).

Politics Joe, 2022: Volodymyr Zelensky Gives Powerful Speech at the GRAMMYs. YouTube, April 4. At: https://www.youtube.com/watch?v=cyJ6GMoeDTw (Accessed on 21 April 2024).

Sting, 2022: Sting. Russians (Guitar / Cello Version). YouTube, March 25. At: https://www.yo utube.com/watch?v=6w3037nq23o (Accessed on 21 April 2024).

SubliminalOfficia, 2024: סאבלימינל והצל עם רביב כנר - זה עלינו [Subliminal and The Shadow, with Raviv Kanner. It's On Us]. YouTube, January 29. At: https://www.youtube.com/watc h?v=gpoX7w2RayQ&t=171s (Accessed on 21 April 2024).

The Human Exploring Society, 2023: Roger Waters Full Speech at the UN Security Council. YouTube, February 11. At: https://www.youtube.com/watch?v=mduvXzjeZXs (Accessed on 21 April 2024).

U2, 2022: U2. Walk On Ukraine. YouTube, April 8. At: https://www.youtube.com/watch?v=z i8wxpzTvY4 (Accessed on 21 April 2024).

Steve Greenfield

The Rising: *Mangal Pandey* and India's First War of Independence

1. Introduction

The Rising: Mangal Pandey (India, 2005) was directed by Ketan Mehta, produced by Bobby Bedi, with the screenplay written by Farrukh Dhondy and starring Aamir Khan, Rani Mukerji, and Toby Stephens.[1] The casting of Aamir Khan, one of the most eminent Indian actors, gave the film a high profile and ultimately commercial success grossing over $22m.[2] It has classic elements of a Bollywood film with several interludes of songs and dancing between the 'serious' events. *Mangal Pandey* garnered positive reviews on both Rotten Tomatoes and the Internet Movie Data Base.[3] It also attracted a degree of controversy, within India, for elements of the portrayal of Pandey notably being shown to take marijuana and enjoying an 'intimate' relationship with one of the characters, Heera, who is a sex worker. The complaints led to political demands for showings to be cancelled and eventually, a defamation claim was initiated in the Delhi High Court by 'descendants of Pandey'. The essence of the protests was the historical importance of Mangal Pandey and his role in the Sepoy Mutiny of 1857 controversially described as India's First War of Independence. This is highlighted at the end of the film by the narrator:[4]

> "And so began the bloodiest rebellion in human history. The British called it a Sepoy Mutiny. But for the Indians, it was the first war of independence.
> An officer by the name of Captain William Gordon was recorded as having joined the rebel forces and fought against the Company Raj. The rebellion was finally put down after a year, but it destroyed the East India Company. And the British Crown took over the governance of India.

---

1 The casting of Khan in the pivotal role of Mangal Pandey led to some rewriting of the romantic relationships with Pandey 'linked' to Heera rather than Emily. Interview with Farukh Dhondy London November 2023.
2 Khan was once described as: 'an anomaly in the film industry as it exists today—the last of the true global movie stars.' Tufayel Ahmed https://www.newsweek.com/bollywood-icon-aamir-kh an-secret-superstar-worldwide-success-dangal-and-688775 (Accessed on 29 March 2024).
3 At: https://www.rottentomatoes.com/m/the_rising_2005 (Accessed on 5 January 2024); https://www.imdb.com/title/tt0346457/ (Accessed on 5 January 2024).
4 The narrator of the film is Om Puri a well-known actor in his own right who in 2004 received an OBE.

Mangal Pandey in his death became a hero, a legend who inspired a nation to fight for freedom. The dream of freedom ignited by Mangal finally came true 90 years later on 15th August 1947 when India became free."

What is surprising is that little seemed to be known of Pandey before the film with few media portrayals despite the importance of the event. The basis for the Indian criticism of the film was the characterisation and portrayal of Mangal Pandey as the lead figure that undermined his historical significance. The criticism from outside India concentrated on the historical inaccuracies that were introduced, by the writer and director, for dramatic purposes. Cinematic depictions of actual events, that introduce dramatic elements, frequently attract this type of critique as it distorts the 'truth.'[5]

The film contains a mix of both brutality and romance, in many ways, it could be considered a love story as Pandey's love of both his country and then Heera are significant threads to the storyline. There is also a hint of his 'love' for Gordon, an officer, that transcends their formal relationship of Officer/Sepoy into a very close friendship which is viewed with some disgust by many of the other officers. The context to the events is the corrupt and malign operation of the East India Company with its preeminent position in the British colonisation and rule of India. The viciousness of its actions features heavily as does the callousness and indifference of its officers. One exception to the Company's brutality is the figure of Captain William Gordon, played by Toby Stephens, who builds a very close relationship with Pandey, empathises with the ordinary people and falls in love with a widow he rescues from a 'forced' Sati, the sacrificial burning of the widow on the top of her deceased husband's funeral pyre.[6] This event and his subsequent relationship with Jwala contribute to the increasing rift between Gordon and his fellow officers and his status as an untrustworthy outsider develops. Thus, the film explores numerous themes around personal relationships and the idea of 'belonging' in addition to the story of the uprising itself. This chapter focuses on the events in the film that show the Sepoy rebellion and addresses the criticisms drawing upon both historical sources and the Delhi High Court transcript. It starts with the film itself. [7]

---

5 See *Greenfield/Osborn* 1996.
6 *Mani* 1998; *Weinberger-Thomas* 1999.
7 The chapter draws upon both the visual aspects of the film and the relevant dialogue. It is hoped that this material does not disclose too much and deter the reader from viewing what is a creative piece of cinematography based on an excellent script and superb cast. It is highly recommended.

2. Mangal Pandey: The Rising

The film commences with a contrast, starting with a joyous scene by the river Ganges featuring a painted elephant being ridden by a group of singing men. It then switches to the Barrackpur army base, the elephant goes past the entrance to the building guarded by soldiers. The viewer is taken inside where preparations are being made, by the red–coated soldiers, for what is clearly an execution by hanging with the gallows being constructed. The narrator duly informs the audience of the context.

> "1857 A.D The entire Indian subcontinent is ruled by a company,
> the British East India Company.
> The most successful business enterprise in history.
> The Company has its own laws, its own administration,
> its own army.
> It controls the destiny of one fifth of humanity."

Pandey, the prisoner, is seen for the first time as, wearing a white robe, he is led shackled and manacled, to the gallows. His face is framed by the noose. The charges against him are read out:

> "Mangal Pandey, Sepoy, 34th Regiment, Native Infantry at Barrackpore. You have been found guilty of mutiny and conspiracy to overthrow the government of the Honourable East India Company by a duly constituted court martial.
> You have been sentenced to death."

To the dismay of the impatient officer in charge, the execution does not happen as the hangman has refused to carry out the execution and run away. Another soldier is ordered to hang Pandey but refuses on the basis it is against his faith as a Brahmin.[8] It is at this point that the context of Pandey's actions is intimated when asked if he has a last wish. A serene Pandey quietly intones: "You cannot grant my last wish. Yet it will be fulfilled."

Pandey hints at a greater collective cause and the hanging is postponed whilst a new executioner is sought. One of the officers who is later revealed to be Captain Gordon is shown relieved by the abandonment. The film then shows Gordon four years earlier fighting in Afghanistan. Pandey is also on the battlefield and despite being shot and wounded he bravely saves Gordon's life. The audience now understands the origins of the close bond between the two men and why Gordon looked so relieved at the failure to carry out the execution. This scene becomes the source of one of the historical accuracy criticisms explored below. The next scene of an opulent ballroom dance is used to introduce some of the key figures; Lord Canning the Governor General of India, Mr Lockwood an auditor who has arrived from

---

8 *Lalrinawma* 2007.

London and Mr Kent a trader. Lockwood has been sent to investigate corruption within the East India Company.[9] The characters represent the different interests that were present in India during the period; politicians, army officers, and traders as well as the company representatives. The film sets out the role of the Company and questions its behaviour.

Aside from the major issue, the Sepoy rebellion, the film covers other aspects of British rule and the vital role of the East India Company which provides three specific areas worthy of analysis. First the opium trade and the consequent impact on the relationship with the local population. This is dealt with in some detail below as it is a significant contribution to the change in perspective that Mangal Pandey experiences. Second the interactions between the male officers and the local women specifically the nautch girls (female dancers).[10] These relationships, particularly those between Hewson and Heera, anger Pandey and elicits a violent response. Heera is an important figure due to her relationship with Pandey which becomes one of the sources for the legal complaint. Thirdly, an area that overlaps in the film with the second point above, is the portrayal of a Sati. This scene explores a controversial cultural clash between the British and the local population. It is the second such example of this clash, the first being when Emily Kent, Pandey and Gordon come across a slave auction at a vibrant market where "All is for Sale".

Kent's attention is drawn to an auctioneer crying out:

AUCTIONEER: Take her, take her at a throwaway price, buy yourself a slave. Look at this beauty, check out her curves. Slave or servant, wife or whore and then some more.

Kent looks horrified and turns to Gordon.

EMILY KENT: Slavery was abolished in Britain, why does the company allow it here?
NARRATOR: Emily was surprised that though slavery was abolished in Britain the Company allowed it in India. Gordon explained that the Company itself bought these girls for the pleasure of white soldiers. It helped prevent the spread of disease in the army.
(The auctioneer strikes the girl.)
EMILY KENT   I think I've seen enough.
(disgustedly):
AUCTIONEER: Quick or this meat will go to the whites and you'll be left ogling.

The woman (Heera) is then shown at Lol Bibi's place and told that: "this is a pleasure house exclusively for the whites." She does not disclose her name, so they

---

9   *Anushree* 2021.
10   *Wald* 2014.

christen her Heera meaning diamond, Heera is later a source of conflict between Pandey and Hewson.

A further source of conflict between the villagers and the Company is explored when a group of men discuss the situation regarding the case of Nana and the refusal to pay him an inherited allowance. This involved the application of the doctrine of lapse which enabled the Company to annex territory where there was no 'natural heir'.[11] This ran contrary to Hindu customs and laws and so provoked discord among the wealthier classes.

VILLAGER 1:   When traders become rulers then the common man pays the price.
VILLAGER 2:   But now Nana Saheb will make the Company pay.
VILLAGER 3:   Really How?
VILLAGER 4:   His minister, Azimullah, has returned from England with Queen Victoria's letter which clearly states that Nana Saheb is right and the Company is wrong.
VILLAGER 5:   Futile. Nana Saheb has only a letter while the Company has guns.
VILLAGER 6:   But sir, the gun is a treacherous lover there's no telling whom she'll set her sights upon!

Nana Saheb is an important figure in the mutiny and representative of the "princely families who had lost out during Dalhousie's time as Governor–General."[12] It is a short but important scene as it indicates a further grievance that fuelled the rebellion. It connects to the major cause as a horse–drawn cart, led by Company soldiers, breaks in front of the villagers and boxes of cartridges are spilt onto the ground. Quickly stray dogs start to sniff and lick the cartridges. This news filters to the Sepoys who are to be issued with the new rifles and cartridges. The film switches to the parade where an officer demonstrates how the end of the cartridge must be bitten off and the gunpowder and lead poured into the barrel of the rifle. He orders some of the Sepoys to try out their new equipment, but they stand unmoved. He asks the Corporal what the problem is:

CORPORAL: The grease, sir. We cannot put the grease in our mouth.
OFFICER: Then where will you put it, man? Come on be sensible.

General Anson appears and after a quick discussion with the quartermaster, who assures him the supplier has said that animal fat has not been used, he orders Gordon to reassure the Sepoys. Gordon is at first reluctant but follows the order and explains:

---

11 *Choudhary* 2009.
12 *David* 2002, p. 46. Nana Saheb's dispute related to an inheritance from Baji Rao and specifically a huge pension.

GORDON: The Company respects all religions and will never break faith. And I, as an officer of the Company, give you my word that this cartridge is greased with neither the fat of pigs or cows.
Will a loyal Sepoy please step forward and volunteer to fire the gun.

Pandey, trusting his friend, breaks the line, marches forward, takes a cartridge, bites the end, loads the rifle and fires it. As he is doing so the camera pans to fellow Sepoys who look downcast at his actions. After the parade a group of Sepoys confront Pandey telling him he is now an outcast and that he has betrayed them he tells them that "Gordon sahib will never lie to me." One Sepoy asks him: "but what if the cartridge–story turns out to be true?" Pandey, with a fierce stare, ominously replies: "then I'll burn the company down."

Pandey and Gordon are talking together, Gordon is painting a landscape when he sees a Sati about to take place. He mounts his horse and rides at the group who are about to burn the widow with the body of her dead husband. Brandishing his sword, he shouts at them to stop and seizes her from the funeral pyre.

VILLAGER: Sahib, you better leave. These are sacred ceremonies.
GORDON: But Sati has been banned, burning a widow is a crime.
VILLAGER 2: Captain sahib, don't interfere. You're tampering with our ancient customs.
GORDON: And you're tampering with my ancient custom. I don't stand by and watch murder.

The funeral party become more hostile demanding that the widow be returned to them. However, Gordon makes it clear that he will fight to the death and is battling with the villagers when Pandey charges to the rescue. Whilst Pandey routs the villagers Gordon rides away with Jwala and takes her to the safety of his house. This has created a major problem as it is a serious matter of honour for the relatives, Gordon though is determined to protect her, and in doing so demonstrates a strong moral side to his character. The village chieftain arrives at the property to request the return of the woman, but Gordon refuses and threatens him. Gordon's house is later attacked and he also prevents Jwala from taking her own life. This raises the question about the role of the British as a 'civilising' force and how existing customs and practices were accommodated, ignored or confronted.[13] Pandey becomes intrigued by Heera, they have a similar rebellious spirit, and arrange to meet where Heera explains that as a child she was kidnapped and trafficked and a close bond forms between them. As they are falling in love a parallel relationship is forming between Gordon and Jwala – the outcasts finding solace in each other.

An interaction with an untouchable who tells Pandey that because he bit the bullet he is now of the same caste leads to a group of Sepoys visiting Jabeera's factory:

---

13 *Fischer-Tiné/Mann* 2004, *Watt/Mann* 2011.

JABEERA: I won't stay silent any longer, even if it costs me my life. It's true
             about the cartridges. See for yourself, pig fat and cow fat.

The Sepoys inspect the premises and see clear evidence, vats of boiling grease and
animal carcasses, that they have been misled. Jabeera explains that the factory is
owned by an Englishman and that they have used pig and cow fat for grease as it
is cheap, this is all about saving money regardless of the religious implications. All
eyes are on Pandey as this information is relayed to them and it is clear they all
expect him to take the lead. He goes straight to Gordon's house to confront him:

PANDEY: You lied to me! I trusted you and you lied to me.

He explains he has seen the grease personally and Gordon realises the implications.
Pandey explains he is now an outcast, shunned by his community, and of course,
now has nothing to lose. Gordon tries to placate him pleading that the Company has
also lied to him but Pandey is incandescent:

PANDEY: You plunder our land, you abuse our faith and now you want our souls.
            Sahib you've enjoyed a black man's loyalty. Now taste his fury. Mark
            my words, Captain sahib! This cartridge will explode. And it will bring
            to an end the Company Raj.

He returns Gordon's pistol to him with the words; "we are brothers no more." The
point about the Company wanting their souls harks back to his conversation with
Heera where she accused Pandey and the other Sepoys of selling their souls. Pandey
is bereft but finds solace in his comrades who go to him to express their loyalty and
unity. Meanwhile, the Company Officers debate the use of the cartridge and whilst
some, including Gordon, urge caution, Colonel Mitchell is bullish and tells them his
regiment at Behrampore is loyal and will use the cartridge. It is agreed that some of
the Barrackpur regiment will be sent to Behrampore to witness the cartridge being
used and (hopefully) follow suit. However, the plan fails dismally as the Sepoys
refuse to adopt the cartridge. A furious Colonel Mitchel orders that the artillery
be used to fire on the Sepoys if they refuse to obey. The canons are threateningly
moved into position facing the Sepoys as Mitchel begins a count to ten, on the count
of nine Pandey breaks ranks and marches forward to the canon and places his chest
in front of the barrel. This act galvanises the Sepoys who charge *en masse*, then
raid the armoury equipping themselves with weapons. A confrontation ensues with
Mitchel threatening the Sepoys with cannon. Gordon is distressed by the turn of
events telling Mitchell he has no authority to fire. Realising they are outnumbered
Mitchell orders the withdrawal of the canons and a return to barracks.
      The mutinous Sepoys meet to draft a list of demands which make it clear that the
problem goes beyond the infringement of their religious rights. Gordon meets with

Pandey to explain the Company will not back down and tries, unsuccessfully, to get the cartridges withdrawn. At a frosty meeting with the senior officers, his view is dismissed.

NARRATOR: Gordon once again urged that the cartridges be discontinued. But the officials paid no heed to him. Instead, they cast aspersions on his loyalty, and said he could share his bed with a native, but not his loyalty.

The Officers conscious of the lack of troops at their disposal to quell the rebellion send for Queen Victoria's regiment that was based in Rangoon. To stall for time and enable the troops to arrive they order an enquiry. It is clear at this point that battle lines are being drawn and this has spiralled out of control beyond the question of the cartridges. This is made clear when representatives of the Sepoys including Pandey meet with emissaries of Nana Saheb who want to fight against a common enemy – the Company. Historic differences are to be set aside and they are to unite under the symbolic banner of Bahadur Shah, linked to the Red Fort in Delhi. The die is cast and the different factions united to defeat the East India Company, 300,000 trained Sepoys against 40,000 British soldiers, and they agree the date of May 31st for the uprising. This moment of unity is celebrated in the film with the festival of Holi.[14]

Heera learns, from Hewson, that the Rangoon regiment is due to arrive on April 1st and attack the Sepoys and execute the leaders of the rebellion. She pleads with him to take her and leave but Pandey says he cannot run away, he is fully committed to the cause. The rebels decide to bring their attack forward to the 30th March but this information is unwittingly leaked. This knowledge allows the Company commanders to alter their planning and disrupt the revolutionaries. The British ships, with the Rangoon regiment, are spotted sailing to port which leads Pandey to summon the rebels by blowing a bugle at the parade ground.

PANDEY: Come on! The time has come! Time to fight, time to be free!

Pandey realises they have no time to wait; "It's now or never". Pandey with an impassioned speech, rouses the Sepoys some of whom had expressed reluctance to engage the British troops until the rest of the rebel force arrived.

PANDEY: Don't you see, the moment we have all been waiting for is here! It's time to honour your pledge, it's time to do or die. Pick up your guns and fight. Fight for your freedom. For once fight for yourselves.

This convinces the group and Pandey shoots Captain Hewson in the shoulder. Gordon confronts Pandey and the two friends fight furiously whilst the officers

---

14 *Crooke* 1914.

are attacked. Pandey has the opportunity to kill Gordon but instead of dealing a fatal blow with his Talwar knocks him out saving him for the third time. The hopelessly outnumbered Sepoys face the might of the British army and they are told to "surrender or die." Pandey is unrepentant:

PANDEY: All of India is looking at us. If we surrender now the rebellion dies before it is born. We can't let that happen. I won't let that happen.

Pandey realises that even though they cannot win this particular battle there is a longer–term fight; "We will win, even if it takes a hundred years." Some of his comrades implore him to surrender saying that the rebellion needs him to which he replies, "the rebellion needs blood. Let it be mine." There are clear parallels to be drawn here with the 1916 Easter Rising against the English in Ireland with the sacrifice of the rebels which is set out in WB Yeats' poem, The Rose Tree. The emphasis is on self–sacrifice to spark greater awareness amongst the population placing the collective above the individual. The crucial lines refer to using the blood of the revolutionaries to water the withered 'The Rose Tree' which is the symbol for Irish nationalism.[15]

Pandey is left alone on the parade ground and fires shots at the English troops, a lone figure taking on the might of the British army who want to take him alive. Pandey though is determined to be martyred and tries to shoot himself, but only suffers injuries, Gordon rushes to help him and Pandey is taken to hospital. The insistence on keeping Pandey alive is to stop him from becoming a martyr to the cause of independence. News of Pandey's actions spread and unified the disparate opposition. Gordon visits Pandey in hospital and tells him that if he offers a public

---

15 *The Rose Tree*
'O words are lightly spoken,'
Said Pearse to Connolly,
'Maybe a breath of politic words
Has withered our Rose Tree;
Or maybe but a wind that blows
Across the bitter sea.'
'It needs to be but watered,'
James Connolly replied,
'To make the green come out again
And spread on every side,
And shake the blossom from the bud
To be the garden's pride.'

'But where can we draw water,'
Said Pearse to Connolly,
'When all the wells are parched away?
O plain as plain can be
There's nothing but our own red blood
Can make a right Rose Tree.'
At: https://research.ucc.ie/celt/document/E910001-061 (Accessed on 26 June 2024).

apology his life will be spared. Pandey tells him: "I am not sorry for my actions and I am not scared to die." Gordon is distraught and blames himself for the events as he promised Pandey the bullets did not contain animal fat. Pandey makes it clear that the real issue is freedom:

PANDEY: Gordon sahib, our fight is no longer against grease on a cartridge, it is for our dignity, our freedom our right to hold our head as high as the next man.

The message of the film is clear, events have been set in chain and this is about independence and freedom not a dispute over religious sensibilities. Pandey tells Gordon "India is rising, nothing and nobody can stop it not even my life". Pandey's court–martial is a formality and he appears disinterested though Gordon does his best to defend him when he gives evidence. Feeling he is being ignored an incensed Gordon shouts out at a surprised court–martial:

GORDON: But mark my words if you hang this man, Mangal Pandey, there will be rebellion, bloody rebellion that will sweep through this land like wildfire. A rebellion that will lead to the end of this Company Raj.

Gordon cuts a lonely figure alienated from his fellow officers and unable to help his friend. The final scenes are dominated by the unrepentant and impressive Pandey walking manacled to the gallows watched by both sides of the conflict. His last word before being hanged is 'attack' and the unarmed crowd charge.

3. The Historical Criticisms

One of the issues the film explores is the relationship between the East India Company and the Sepoys. Before the mutiny, there is seemingly unquestioned loyalty notably when innocent villagers are massacred. Their 'crime' has been to supply opium breaching the Company's monopoly.[16] The opium trade is referred to at several points in the film and the Sepoys are a vital part of the effort to retain control over the market. The narrator, at a Company social event, outlines the way the business operates:

> "One of the Company's biggest trades was that of opium. It forced Indian farmers to grow it, bought it from them at a pittance and sold it in China at a profit. When the Chinese Emperor resisted the Company waged a war against him. To fight and die, Indian Sepoys were there after all. And they called it the Free Market."

---

16   *Richards* 2002a and 2002b; *Deming* 2011; *Turner* 1876; *Richards* 1981.

The appearance of the naïve but feisty, Emily Kent is a vehicle to explain how the Company behaves. She picks up a vase containing a beautiful bunch of red poppies and asks why the crop is so large occupying many acres and innocently asks: "are they part of some religious ritual?" The officers look embarrassed and shamefaced but Gordon who has just been mocked by her father over his schooling and religion seizes his opportunity:

GORDON: The poppy, Miss Kent is the sole source of opium. The Honourable East India Company forces Indian farmers to grow them.
EMILY KENT: Opium?
GORDON: Indeed. Most of it is bought up by the Company at prices fixed by them. And then shipped to China to help turn an entire nation into opium addicts.
EMILY KENT: But why?
GORDON: It's the only thing we can sell the Chinese in return for the tea and silks that we Europeans are addicted to.
HEWSON: I think Gordon, the ladies ought to be spared this lecture.

Gordon undaunted carries on.

GORDON: But the Chinese Emperor resists, he no longer wants to trade in opium. So, the Company decides to wage a war against him. And in this war, it wants Indian Sepoys to fight and die.
The circle is complete. And we call it the free market.
KENT: Sir. You abuse my hospitality.
GORDON: If I have spoken out of turn sir, I apologise. After all, I'm just a common soldier. It's a subject you'd know more about than me!

The opium trade is a source of conflict between the Company and China but also with the local population and crucially within the Company itself. The audience learns that an auditor, Mr Lockwood, has been sent from London to investigate: "all the monkey business going on in the Company." Lockwood investigates and his findings lead him to take troops to search the premises of a trader, Sorabjee. The search reveals a huge amount of hidden opium which is seized as the trader has been privately buying and selling contrary to the Company's monopoly position. Sorabjee explains that there are 'private arrangements' in place with Company Officials effectively being bribed to permit Sorabjee to continue to trade. Lockwood refuses the bribe offered, described by Sorabjee as a small gift. The value of the illicit trade is indicated by the fact that the 'gift' offered starts at £300, in gold, but is immediately increased to £3000. Lockwood is incredulous but refuses. Instead, he finds out who has been supplying the merchant and takes a group of armed soldiers to confront the villagers.

In a combative and brutal scene, the gathered villagers are told they have broken the law by growing and selling opium, without Company permission, and accordingly are subject to punishment. The extremity of the sentence, confiscation of their land and property, causes terrible distress and they plead for mercy. A fight ensues as the villagers resist by throwing dung at the Sepoys. The Magistrate orders the Sepoys to fire on the men who are now standing without resistance begging for their lives. Gordon shouts that he can deal with it without resorting to violence, but the Magistrate insists and the Sepoys, including Pandey, shoot the unarmed villagers. Pandey is shown firing his rifle with a remorseful expression realising the enormity of what he and the others are undertaking. Prior to the massacre, a shout from the villagers rings out: "don't shoot. We are brothers." The Sepoys then raze the village to the ground and Pandey appears anguished. With a backdrop of burning huts, he sits with Gordon both reflecting on what they have just done.

GORDON: We're soldiers. It's our job to fight, to kill.
PANDEY: To kill an unknown enemy is easy. But to kill people who are your own.
GORDON: You were obeying orders Mangal. That's our duty. That is the price of the salt we eat.
PANDEY: Sometimes I wonder if there are more important things in life than salt.

The shared look between them, without words, indicates that this is a turning point for both as the realisation of the barbarity of the Company and their role in its cruelty hits home. Pandey's comprehension of his situation later leads him into an aggressive altercation with Hewson as Pandey seeks to protect Heera from the officer's advances.

It is this incident that was the source of one of the criticisms of the film. Saul David, author of *The Indian Mutiny*, noted: "the East India Company did trade in opium but I have no knowledge of a massacre like this and I do not believe it happened." He described this scene and another involving the selling of sex workers, as "vilification of the British just for the sake of it."[17] Company dishonesty involving the opium trade is explored in a scene where Lockwood confronts Kent with his findings into corruption:[18]

LOCKWOOD: In the course of my investigations into the Company I have discovered that you have been compromising senior officers, falsifying accounts, in fact, sir, you have been cheating the Company.
KENT: I have done nothing that others have not done before me.
LOCKWOOD: I know that you have been smuggling opium into China on your own behalf, Mr Kent.
KENT: You have evidence?

---

17   *Hastings/Jones* 2005.
18   *Anushree* 2021; *Gilding* 2022; *Robins* 2012.

Kent is very assured that nothing will happen even when Sorabjee comes out to explain the nature of the transactions and implicate the trader. He makes it clear that powerful political forces were behind the East India Company who would prevent any action from being taken.

KENT: If you lay a hand on me the reverberations will reach the House of Lords.

Kent refers to the political support for the East India Company but there is no doubt that physical force, through the army, was a key part of the Company's strategy to maintain control over India and protect and promote its trade, described as an "exclusive right to violence."[19] The creation and application of the army created a range of economic political and social issues as the Company sought political sovereignty and these are explored in the film. The brutality was integral to colonisation: "violence, it must be emphasised, was an essential component of the British presence in India. It was violence that served as the ultimate imprimatur of colonialism."[20] The savagery took several different forms:

> "It was an era of brutal floggings and of Indian women being forced to become mistresses of white men; of recalcitrant elements being blown from cannons so that their bodies were effaced and the onlookers covered with blood and fragments of flesh. British rule thus visibly manifested itself by marking the body of the Indian."[21]

The film portrays this side of Company rule in several ways. Hewson brutally beats a waiter for spilling a drink on Emily Kent and appears to relish the force until he is stopped by Pandey. Hewson and three fellow officers also savagely attack Pandey and in a reversal of roles it is Gordon who intervenes to save Pandey. There is the collective punishment meted out to the unarmed villagers who are callously murdered and of course eventually Pandey's (unseen) execution which is a response to the uprising. Overall the criticism is related to the detail rather than the holistic picture that has been created.

4. The Legal Claims

A further area of controversy, surrounding the film, was it becoming subject to legal action with a case in the Delhi High Court.[22] The judgement by Judge A.K. Sikri is wide–ranging and draws upon diverse sources from the Bible through Psychology to

---

19 *Alavi* 1995.
20 *Mukherjee* 1990, p. 93.
21 Ibid, p. 94.
22 Sh. Raghu Nath Pandey and Anr. vs Sh. Bobby Bedi and Ors. 2006 Latest Caselaw 319 Del., p. 1236.

Dan Brown's novel *The Da Vinci Code*.[23] The claim was brought by the descendants of Mangal Pandey against *inter alia* the Producer Bobby Bedi, the Director and the Screen Writers. The defendants argued that the plaintiffs were not related to Pandey and accordingly had no *locus standi*.[24] The fundamental nature of the complaint was the way Pandey was portrayed and notably his relationship with Heera who was shown as a prostitute:

> "...they feel pained and anguished at the introduction of some of the characters and scenes in the film associating Mangal Pandey with them. According to the plaintiffs, defendants have, by doing this, distorted the history of freedom struggle for independence of India and also defamed and disreputed Mangal Pandey and the entire Pandey family as well as their generations."[25]

Contemporaneously the family indicated they were grateful that the film glorified "the great freedom fighter." Given the popularity of Aamir Khan, seeking to ban the film was likely to generate critical publicity and of course, draw further attention to the scenes the plaintiffs found offensive. A potential example of the *Streisand Effect*, whereby the Plaintiff's lawsuit for privacy objecting to the publication of a photograph of her home led to a blaze of publicity and multiple viewings of the previously little viewed picture.[26] The Pandey descendants alleged the controversial parts were defamatory of their relative and that the defendants were motivated by personal financial gains. The scenes, it was alleged, were designed to increase the commercial success of the film thus ignoring any duty they had to preserve the integrity of Mangal Pandey and "his coming generations and the place he belonged to and even the entire nation. They, therefore, feel cheated and are unhappy."[27] The remedy sought was to edit the film and remove the offending scenes before the film could be publicly exhibited.[28]

The judge pointed out that Mangal Pandey despite his significant role in the struggle for independence was, previously, a little–known figure:

> "Mangal Pandey, though the first martyr of freedom struggle of India of 1857, but lesser–known earlier, is a household name today. It was a name known to the students of history earlier. Even history students, except those who studied the freedom struggle of India in depth, may not have known in detail about his deeds except that there was a

---

23 Brown 2009.
24 Sh. Raghu Nath Pandey and Anr. vs Sh. Bobby Bedi and Ors. 2006. p. 1239. The case was dealt with on the basis that the plaintiffs had sufficient locus standi at p. 1262. On the principle of *locus standi* see *Gupta* 1984.
25 Ibid., p. 1237.
26 At: https://www.yahoo.com/entertainment/streisand-effect-barbra-streisand-invasion-of-pri vacy-lawsuit-new-memoir-130024264.html (Accessed on 24 June 2024), Barbara Streisand vs. Kenneth Adelman et. al., Superior Court of California, County of Los Angeles, Case No. SC077257.
27 Sh. Raghu Nath Pandey and Anr. vs Sh. Bobby Bedi and Ors. 2006, p. 1237.
28 Ibid., p. 1239.

character Mangal Pandey who was in the British Army and revolted against the Britishers in the 1857 Mutiny. Today heroic deeds of Mangal Pandey are known to every person–be it a student of history or not; be it a highly educated person or illiterate; be it an old or a young; be it a college going student or a child studying in primary school."[29]

The judge pointed out that it was the film that created recognition and a new understanding and appreciation of Pandey and especially the role he played in the struggle for Independence.

"It is because of the movie titled *Mangal Pandey — The Rising* produced and released in India and abroad in the month of August 2005. The impact of Bollywood films — even when they are commercial films — is well known among Indian public. The impact becomes greater and deeper when the movie cast is the icon. Glamourisation and widespread advertising adds to this impact. Much before the movie *Mangal Pandey – The Rising* was released, media hype about this movie was created when it was being shot. That is the reason that on its release it created ripples. Whether it became a Box Office hit, i.e. commercially successful venture or not, is immaterial. The fact remains that it was much talked about, particularly the character of Mangal Pandey who is depicted as the great freedom fighter and on whose life the film has been produced as a historical movie to present to the young generation his personal and patriotic life."[30]

This demonstrates the power of film, and the stars of Bollywood, to add to and create 'new' knowledge and recognition about significant historical figures and events. It is even more pronounced when the film has a superstar in the lead role which in turn generates greater publicity and interest. The question is raised of the need for accuracy or 'truth' when a film is based on real life. But these are not documentaries, but dramatic films designed to entertain, and they are first and foremost commercial ventures. The Plaintiffs' argument contained two elements. First, the objectionable scenes that depicted him as a drug taker and associating with a prostitute, with whom he falls in love, 'tarnishes' his reputation. Secondly, Pandey was a known bachelor so showing his love affair with Heera 'distorted history'. In addition to the point about *locus standi* the defendants also argued that no action lies for defamation when the party allegedly defamed is deceased on the basis it is a personal right.[31] This is noted in the historic maxim *Actio personalis moritur cum persona*.[32] Thirdly not all the defendants named were capable of providing the relief sought. Fourthly there was a typical disclaimer at the start of the film which is also referred to. In the judgment:

"This story is based on actual events. In certain cases, incidents, characters and timelines have been changed or fictionalized for dramatic purposes. Certain characters may be composites or entirely fictitious. Some names and locations have been changed. The

29 Ibid., p. 1236.
30 Ibid., p. 1236.
31 *Herzog* 2017.
32 *Power* 1900.

scenes depicted may be a hybrid of fact and fiction which fairly represent the source for the film, believed to be true by the filmmakers."[33]

This type of information for the audience is designed to make it clear that historical accuracy is not warranted and that some dramatic licence has been employed.[34] Thus some characters may be completely fictitious, or a hybrid mix of two or more individuals. The plaintiffs sought to argue that the disclaimer was not just ineffective but potentially misleading in that the opening line refers to 'actual events' that could lead the audience to believe that *everything* (my emphasis) in the film was based on reality. Furthermore, they claimed that as the disclaimer was only in English its impact was limited.

In response to the plaintiff's claim that the defendants were only interested in commercial exploitation their previous considerable artistic achievements were pointed out.[35] They also stressed the creativity involved in the production.[36] Furthermore, they claimed the film was a celebration not an unfair critique of his life and activity:

> "Thus, far from denigrating Mangal Pandey the film is a recognition of his role as the first spark of freedom struggle and thus glorifies and extols his sacrifices and courage and tells his story in the backdrop of the 1857 Revolt. The intent and effect of the film has been to generate interest, respect, and admiration among Indians for Mangal Pandey."[37]

The judge acknowledged the power of film to influence and educate and with this film the provision of an insight into the life of a significant figure who had escaped detailed attention and analysis. It undoubtedly left a clear impression for the audience of Pandey as a great heroic figure which made it difficult, for the plaintiffs, to argue that this film cast aspersions on his character and legacy. Furthermore, the film needed to be considered as a 'whole' and not based on a few 'controversial' scenes

---

33 Sh. Raghu Nath Pandey and Anr. vs Sh. Bobby Bedi and Ors 2006, p. 1249-1250.

34 *Stubbs* 2013.

35 "Defendants claim that they are responsible citizens who have excelled in each of their fields and have earned immense respect and admiration not only among [the] Indian public but also film lovers around the world. Defendant No.1 is a reputed film producer who has produced award-winning and critically acclaimed films including 'Bandit Queen', 'Maqbool', 'Fire', 'Sathia' etc. He has pioneered the introduction of international industry standards and professional business practices into Indian movie making and has been successful in bridging the gap between Offbeat and Main Screen cinema by making films that appeal to the sensibilities of the audiences." Sh. Raghu Nath Pandey and Anr. ss Sh. Bobby Bedi and Ors. 2006, p. 1239.

36 "Producer has brought together and synergised the creative and artistic talents of some of the best and the most popular actors, musicians, artists, writers, technicians and craftsmen in the country for making of the film. Together they have put in their creative energies and imaginations to bring to life and portray as a human being in flesh and blood, the heroic figure of Mangal Pandey." Ibid., p. 1240.

37 Ibid., p. 1240.

that lacked context.[38] The defendants argued that they had undertaken significant research to establish as much factual evidence as possible. They established the following:

"i)   In 1857, the British East India Company ruled a large part of the Indian subcontinent.
ii)   The British East India Company had a large army of Indian Sepoys.
iii)   In 1857, greased cartridges were introduced in the army with new Enfield rifles.
iv)   There was grave concern and resentment about this cartridge amongst the Hindu and Muslim Sepoys because it was believed that the cartridges were greased with cow and pig fat and the Sepoys refused to bite these cartridges.
v)   At Berhampore, Col. Mitchell tried to force the Sepoys to bite the cartridges with threat of using the cannon. There was a mini mutiny and the Sepoys captured the Bell of arms.
vi)   At Berhampore, on 29th March 1857, Mangal Pandey rebelled, shot two British officers and when faced with a large force, shot himself.
vii) On the 4th of April 1857, he was subjected to court martial and sentenced to death.
viii) On the 7th of April 1857, they failed to hang him because no hangman was available.
ix)   On the 8th of April 1857, there was a public hanging of Mangal Pandey."[39]

The defendants used these 'established facts' to provide the core features of the film and used other events to establish Pandey's patriotism and commitment to the cause of independence. Part of this was his relationship with Heera who caused him to reflect and reconsider his position as a Sepoy as she taunted him about selling his 'soul' to the British. That the Sepoy fought on behalf of the British and were involved in suppressing the local population was an important element of Pandey's radicalisation. The complaint about Pandey being shown to consume 'bhang' (cannabis) was dismissed given it was not viewed at the time as being controversial. There was also a suggestion that Pandey was known to indulge in the practice. The right of the filmmakers to practice free speech in terms of the content was also raised and the judge, discussing previous case law, noted the established framework and restrictions imposed by law and the policing role of the courts. It was not a significant issue in this case.

According to the judge, there was one outstanding point to be resolved or as it was nicely put "one aspect which still lingers on in the mind" that related to the known fact that Pandey had never married. His romantic relationship with Heera was, therefore, a fiction created for purely dramatic purposes. The Sindoor scene, with Heera in the prison, at the close of the film, *could* be interpreted by members of the audience as Pandey committing to marriage. The filmmakers were quite entitled

---

38 Ibid.
39 Ibid.

to create this additional piece of drama, but the judge thought that the public ought to be informed specifically about the Heera character to clarify Pandey's bachelor status. Accordingly, an announcement should be made at the end of the film in both English and Hindi:

"The character of Heera is fictionalised. There was no such Heera in the life of Mangal Pandey. Mangal Pandey died a bachelor."[40]

It is not apparent that this announcement was ever displayed even though it was the subject of a judicial direction, and appears to be something of a sop to the plaintiffs. The case was concluded and as there was "no merit in the grievance of the plaintiffs" thus the defendants were free to show the film.

5. Conclusion

On a more superficial level, the film is a very well–produced and enjoyable viewing experience with both dramatic and romantic elements and incorporating typical Bollywood features. At a deeper level, the film explores significant historical events and uses them as context for the other parts of the story, the different characters, and the involvement between them. It offers a critical account of the workings of the East India Company and its interaction with the local population. The concept of this Limited Company effectively acting as a state power in this historical context is explored and perhaps offers a surprising insight into this aspect of colonisation. The illicit opium trade is portrayed, as is corruption and the use of sex workers by the officers. There is an undercurrent of violence and brutality both individually where for example Hewson beats a waiter and collectively when the villagers are massacred. At the same time, elements of the local population are shown to engage in drug use, participate in the slave trade and support *Sati*. Sepoys are involved in the massacre of the villagers and there are tensions between the different castes.

On an individual level, it is a story of outsiders and their relationship with both the main group and understanding themselves and the position they have found themselves in. Five significant characters do not fit into the established order and part of the story revolves around their personal struggles. Gordon is singled out by his background, his catholic religion and his close relationship with both Pandey and Jwala. Gordon refuses to accept the Sati and risks his life to save Jwala. He confronts the villagers and provides her with safety also at great personal risk. Gordon is prepared to wrestle with Pandey and is very close friends and also realises that he cannot have a relationship with Emily Kent as he does not fit in. Yet, to a degree, Emily Kent is also rebellious, she starts off by dressing as a 'nautch girl'

---

40   Ibid, p. 1261.

much to her father's disgust. She finds the buying and selling of Heera abhorrent and is surprised by the revelations about the opium trade. Jwala is also an outsider refusing to accept her fate as a widow and commences a relationship with Gordon that is frowned upon by both sides. Heera also has a rebellious streak from the outset as she clashes with the slave trader. She is independent and tells Pandey that the girls "sell our bodies but you sell your souls." Before his execution, Heera visits Pandey in the condemned cell and brings *Sindoor* that he applies to her hairline, a symbol of marriage demonstrating their love and reconciliation.

Pandey is also an outsider but undoubtedly portrayed as a heroic figure able to inspire and rouse his comrades to fight the oppression of the East India Company and British rule. Whilst religion is shown as the spark that ignites the rebellion the film also explores some of the other underlying causes so offers a more nuanced picture than might be seen at first glance.

A further dimension of the film is that it feeds into the myth and legend of Mangal Pandey creating a heroic figure in true Bollywood tradition. Concentrating on the divergence from historical accounts and the 'dramatic licence' employed ignores the overall picture that the film presents. The legal case demonstrates the subjectivity of film with the 'relatives' interpreting events and the role of Heera in a more negative way whilst the defendants and the judge adopted a more rounded holistic perspective. If historians cannot agree on whether the *uprising* or *rebellion* or *mutiny* amounted to the First War of Independence for India, the role of Mangal Pandey and the events that took place, then it seems rather harsh to criticise filmmakers whose ultimate task is to produce a film that entertains.

Bibliography

Ahmed, Tufayel, 2017: Bollywood Icon Aamir Khan on 'Secret Superstar,' Worldwide Success of 'Dangal,' and Empowering Women. At: https://www.newsweek.com/bollywood-icon-a amir-khan-secret-superstar-worldwide-success-dangal-and-688775 (Accessed on 19 June 2024)

Alavi, Seema, 1995: The Sepoys and the Company. Tradition and Transition in Northern India, 1770-1830. Oxford, Oxford University Press.

Anushree, Anubha, 2021: The East India Company and the Regulation of Corruption in Early-Nineteenth-Century India. In: *Kroeze,* Ronald/*Dalmau*, Pol/*Monier,* Frédéric (eds.), Corruption, Empire and Colonialism in the Modern Era: A Global Perspective, Basingstoke, Palgrave Macmillan. pp. 79–103.

Brown, Dan, 2009: The Da Vinci Code. London, Corgi Books.

Byrne, Suzy, 2023: What is 'the Streisand effect'? Barbra Streisand Addresses Infamous Invasion of Privacy Lawsuit in New Memoir. At: https://www.yahoo.com/entertainment/st reisand-effect-barbra-streisand-invasion-of-privacy-lawsuit-new-memoir-130024264.html? fr=sycsrp_catchall (Accessed on 19 June 2024).

Choudhary, Amod, 2009: Doctrine of Lapse – A Frayed Link for Expansion of the British Empire in India. In: Journal of Law and Business, 16 pp. 41–56.

Crooke, William, 1914: The Holi: A Vernal Festival of the Hindus. In: Folklore, 25:1, pp. 55–83.

David, Saul, 2002: The Indian Mutiny. London, Penguin Books.

Deming, Sarah, 2011: The Economic Importance of Indian Opium and Trade with China on Britain's Economy, 1843–1890. In: Economics Working Papers, 25.

Fischer–Tiné, Harald/*Mann*, Michael (eds.) 2004: Colonialism as Civilizing Mission. Cultural Ideology in British India. London, Anthem Press.

Gilding, Ben, 2002: 'A New Tide of Corruption': Economical Reform and the Regulation of the East India Company, 1765–84. In: *Cawood*, Ian/*Crook*, Tom (eds.): The Many Lives of Corruption. Manchester, Manchester University Press. pp. 75–95.

Greenfield, Steve/*Osborn*, Guy, 1996: Pulped Fiction – Cinematic Parables of (In) Justice. In: University of San Francisco Law Review, 30, pp. 1181–1198.

Gupta, R. S, 1984: Widening the Rules of Locus Standi. In: Journal of the Indian Law Institute, 26:4, pp. 424–444.

Hastings, Chris/*Jones*, Beth, 2015: Lottery–funded Film under Fire for Anti–British Bias. Telegraph, London 13/08/2005. At: https://www.history.org.uk/secondary/module/1140/tea ch-online/1168/33-why-might-an-interpretations-focused-enquiry-q#:~:text=Saul%20Davi d%2C%20the%20author%20of,%22It%20is%20nonsense (Accessed on 29 March 2024).

Herzog, Don, 2017: Defaming the dead. New Haven, Yale University Press.

Internet Movie Database (n.d.): Mangal Pandey. At: https://www.imdb.com/title/tt0346457/ (Accessed on 5 January 2024).

Jamwal, Balbir Singh, 2015: Importance of Cultural Festivals and Visits. In: Shabd Braha International Research Journal of Indian Languages. At: https://shabdbraham.com/ShabdB/ archive/v4i1/sbd-v4-i1-sn4.pdf (Accessed on 19 June 2024).

Lalrinawma, V. S., 2007: Major Faith Traditions of India. Delhi, ISPCK.

Mani, Lata, 1998: Contentious Traditions. The Debate on Sati in Colonial India. Berkeley and Los Angeles, University of California Press.

Mukherjee, Rudrangshu, 1990: Satan Let Loose Upon Earth: The Kanpur Massacres in India in the Revolt of 1857. In: Past and Present, 128:1, pp. 92–116.

Power, John J., 1900: Actio Personalis Cum Persona Moritur. In: The Canadian Law Times, 19, pp. 215–233.

Richards, John F., 1981: The Indian Empire and Peasant Production of Opium in the Nineteenth Century. In: Modern Asian Studies, 15:1, pp. 59–82.

Richards, John F., 2002a: The Opium Industry in British India. In: The Indian Economic & Social History Review, 39:2–3, pp. 149–180.

Richards, John F., 2002b: Opium and the British Indian Empire: The Royal Commission of 1895. In: Modern Asian Studies, 36:2, pp. 375–420.

Robins, Nick, 2012: The Corporation that Changed the World: How the East India Company Shaped the Modern Multinational. London, Pluto Press.

Rotten Tomatoes, 2005: The Rising: Ballad of Mangal Pandey, https://www.Rottentomatoes.c om/m/the_rising_2005 (Accessed on 5 January 2024).

Stubbs, Jonathan, 2013: Historical Film. A Critical Introduction. London, Bloomsbury.

Turner, Frederick Storrs, 1876: British Opium Policy and its Results to India and China. London, Low, Marston, Searle, & Rivington.

Wald, Erica, 2014: Vice in the Barracks: Medicine, the Military and the Making of Colonial India, 1780–1868. Basingstoke, Palgrave Macmillan.

Watt, Carey Anthony/*Mann*, Michael (eds.) 2011: Civilizing Missions in Colonial and Postcolonial South Asia: From Improvement to Development. London, Anthem Press.

Weinberger–Thomas, Catherine, 1999: Ashes of Immortality. Widow–Burning in India. Chicago, University of Chicago Press.

Cases

Barbara Streisand vs. Kenneth Adelman et. al. Superior Court of California, County of Los Angeles, Case No. SC077257.

Sh. Raghu Nath Pandey and Anr. vs Sh. Bobby Bedi and Ors. 2006 Latest Caselaw 319 Del.

Authors

Nathan Abrams BA (Hons), MA, PhD is Professor in Film at Bangor University and lead director for the Centre for Film, Television and Screen Studies. He co-convenes the British Jewish Contemporary Cultures network. Professor Abrams lectures, writes and broadcast widely on British and American popular culture, history film and intellectual culture. He co-founded "Jewish Film and New Media: An International Journal". His most recent books include "Kubrick: Odyssey" (with Robert Kolker; Faber and Faber/Pegasus, 2024); "Alien Legacies: The Evolution of the Franchise" (edited with Greg Frame; Oxford University Press, 2023); and "Eyes Wide Shut: Behind Stanley Kubrick's Masterpiece" (edited with Georgina Orgill; Liverpool University Press, 2023).

Michael Asimow is Dean's Executive Professor of Law, Santa Clara Law School, and Professor of Law Emeritus, UCLA School of Law. He previously was a long–term visitor at Stanford Law School. His JD is from Berkeley Law School. Michael specializes in administrative law and is co–author of a three–volume treatise on California Administrative Law and of a casebook, "State and Federal Administrative Law." He has also written several articles about comparative administrative law. Michael also teaches and writes in the area of law and popular culture, including a teaching book co–authored with Jessica Silbey "Law and Popular Culture – A Course Book." He is also co–author with Paul Bergman of "Real to Reel: Truth and Trickery in Courtroom Movies" (a video guide to the courtroom movie genre).

Ann Ching BA MBA LLM JD is Clinical Professor of Law, Sandra Day O'Connor College of Law, Arizona State University. She served as an Army lawyer (2001–2012) and achieved the rank of Major. Following her Army career, Professor Ching was an Assistant Professor of Law at Pepperdine University (2013–2015) and Ethics Counsel for the State Bar of Arizona (2016–2019). In 2023, Professor Ching became a fellow with the National Institute of Military Justice. In that capacity, she has served as an observer of the military commissions at Guantánamo Bay, Cuba. Professor Ching teaches and writes in the areas of appellate advocacy, legal ethics, international humanitarian law, and military justice.

John Cunningham BMus MA PhD is Reader in Music at Bangor University. A member of the editorial committees of the Purcell Society and of Musica Britannica, John Cunningham's research covers a broad spectrum of topics and periods, with a main interlinking theme of music as cultural history. He has published on a range of topics, especially looking at secular music in Britain and Ireland, c.1600–1900, including a monograph on William Lawes (2010 Boydell and Brewer). He is also interested in modern popular music, especially its interconnections with visual culture through the music video and other media.

Steve Greenfield PhD. LLB. MSc (Econ), Professor of Sports Law and Practice: University of Westminster Law School, and Extraordinary Professor: North West University South Africa Faculty of Education. He has written and taught for over 30 years in different areas of Cinematic Justice alongside other research areas of Sports Governance and Education. Steve Greenfield co–wrote with Peter Robson and Guy Osborn "Film and the Law" (Cavendish 2001) and the later version "Film and the Law" (2010 Hart Publishing). He has also contributed chapters to edited collections covering Tobia Beecher the jailed lawyer in the TV Series Oz and the Executioner Albert Pierrepoint from the film Pierrepoint. Work in 2024 includes developing a human rights framework for law films.

Michael Lipiner is a PhD Candidate in film studies at Bangor University in Wales. He created the ongoing film studies program at Bayside High School in conjunction with St. John's University in New York City. His publications are on the topic of American cinema.

Stefan Machura, Dr. rer. soc., Dr. rer. pol. habil., is Professor of Criminology and Criminal Justice at Bangor University. He has studied sociology and political science at the Ruhr–Universität Bochum (Germany), where he got his PhD and later taught sociology of law and political science. In his second dissertation (*Habilitation*, Universität der Bundeswehr München in 2000) he researched the cooperation of lay and professional judges at criminal courts. Publications include "Law and Film" (co–edited with Peter Robson, 2001, Blackwell), "Recht im Film" (co–edited with Stefan Ulbrich, 2002, Nomos) and "Krieg im Film" (co–edited with Rüdiger Voigt, 2005, Lit).

Iker Nabaskues Martínez de Eulate PhD is Adjunct Professor for Legal Theory at the Faculty of Law of the Basque Country University in Leioa, Biskaia. Before, he worked in Social Services of Public Administration for a decade. Since 2010 he specialized in research on Law, Literature and Cinema. His publications include "Globalización y Nueva Política Local" (2003) describing the impact of Globalization; and he published on local public policies, "Robert Louis Stevenson: ética, narrativa y justicia" (2012); on the sense of justice shown in Stevenson´s novels and authored over 20 articles or book chapters on issues of Law and Popular Culture.

Peter Robson, Professor emeritus, had worked at the Faculty of Law, Strathclyde University, Glasgow, for 50 years. He has published on landlord and tenant law (his book "Residential Tenancies: Private & Social Renting in Scotland", 2019, is in its fourth edition), housing law and social security law, law's interaction with architecture (in his co–authored book "Spaces of Justice: The Architecture of the Scottish Court" (with Johnny Rodger). The portrayal of the law in film and popular culture forms a major area of his work. With Stefan Machura, he co–edited "Law and Film" (2001), with Steve Greenfield and Guy Osborn, he co–authored "Film and the Law" (2010), and there are more books to his name.

Ferdinando Spina Ph.D. is Associate Professor of Sociology of Law at the Department of Human and Social Sciences of the University of Salento (Italy). From 2009 to 2011 he was a research fellow at the Department of Social Sciences and Communication of the same University. He has been visiting Ph.D. candidate at the University of Trier (Germany), visiting scholar at the International Institute for the Sociology of Law, Oñati (Spain), and visiting researcher at the Faculty of Arts and Design/School of Humanities, Coventry University (U.K.). Professor Spina is a member of the Executive Board of the Research Committee on Sociology of Law of the Italian Sociological Association.

Bereits erschienen in der Reihe STAATSVERSTÄNDNISSE

Arnold Brechts Staatsverständnis in Praxis und Theorie
Deutscher Verwaltungsjurist – amerikanischer Staatswissenschaftler –
transnationaler Politikberater
Von Prof. Dr. Michael Ruck. 2024, Bd. 181

Zur Entstehung des Staates
Staat und Souveränität im politischen Denken der Frühen Neuzeit
Von Prof. Dr. Peter Schröder, 2024, Bd. 180

Joseph Schumpeter und der Staat
Von Prof. Dr. Richard Sturn, 2024, Bd. 179

Der Staat in der Krise
Von Dr. Joris Steg, 2024, Bd. 178

Otto Hintzes Staatssoziologie
Historische Prozesse, theoretische Perspektiven
Von Prof. Dr. Andreas Anter und Prof. em. Dr. Hinnerk Bruhns, 2024, Bd. 177

Georges Sorel
Auf der Suche nach einer Politik der Erhabenheit
Von Assoc.-Prof. Dr. Norbert Campagna, 2024, Bd. 176

Der Sozialstaat in Deutschland
Von Prof. Dr. Gerhard Bäcker, Prof. Dr. Jürgen Boeckh und Prof. Dr. Ernst-Ulrich Huster,
2024, Bd. 175

Die Neuvermessung der Säkularität
Zum Selbstverständnis des Staates im Angesicht islamischen Rechts
hrsg. von Dr. Rike Sinder, M.A., 2023, Bd. 174

Staat und Revolution bei Georg Lukács
hrsg. von Dr. Rüdiger Dannemann, Gregor Schäfer, Ph.D., M.A. und
Prof. Dr. Hans-Ernst Schiller, 2023, Bd. 173

Staat und Kriegsmaschine
Das Staatsverständnis der Schizo-Analyse von Gilles Deleuze und Félix Guattari
hrsg. von Prof. Dr. Hans-Martin Schönherr-Mann, 2023, Bd. 172

Der Staat der Netzwerkgesellschaft
Karl-Heinz Ladeurs Verständnis von Staat und Gesellschaft
hrsg. von Prof. Dr. Dr. Ino Augsberg, 2023, Bd. 171

Postkoloniale Staatsverständnisse
hrsg. von Martin Oppelt, Christina Pauls und Nicki K. Weber, 2022, Bd. 170

Oliver Cromwell und das Commonwealth
Staatsverständnisse zwischen Revolution und hergebrachter Ordnung
hrsg. von Prof. Dr. Ulrich Niggemann, 2022, Bd. 169

Dystopie und Staat
hrsg. von Dr. Peter Seyferth, 2023, Bd. 168

Zugang zum Machthaber
hrsg. von Prof. Dr. Wolfram Pyta und Prof. em. Dr. Rüdiger Voigt, 2022, Bd. 167

Denkwege des Politischen
Beiträge zum Staatsverständnis Martin Heideggers
hrsg. von Dr. Jan Kerkmann, 2022, Bd. 166

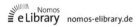

Nomos eLibrary nomos-elibrary.de

Bestellen Sie im Buchhandel oder
versandkostenfrei online unter nomos-shop.de
Bestell-Hotline +49 7221 2104-37
E-Mail bestellung@nomos.de | **Fax** +49 7221 2104-43
Alle Preise inkl. Mehrwertsteuer